EXIT PATH

HOW TO WIN THE
STARTUP END GAME

TOURAJ PARANG

Mc
Graw
Hill

New York   Chicago   San Francisco   Athens   London   Madrid
Mexico City   Milan   New Delhi   Singapore   Sydney   Toronto

1 2 3 4 5 6 7 8 9   LCR   27 26 25 24 23 22

ISBN: 978-1-264-70332-6
MHID: 1-264-70332-5

e-ISBN: 978-1-264-70581-8
e-MHID: 1-264-70581-6

Library of Congress Cataloging-in-Publication Data

TK

McGraw Hill books are available at special quantity discounts to use as premiums and sales promotions or for use in corporate training programs. To contact a representative, please visit the Contact Us pages at www.mhprofessional.com.

McGraw Hill is committed to making our products accessible to all learners. To learn more about the available support and accommodations we offer, please contact us at accessibility@mheducation.com. We also participate in the Access Text Network (www.accesstext.org), and ATN members may submit requests through ATN.

To Shabnam, Sophia, and Cece,

my champions on every path

Contents

PART III
Playing the Long Game

PART IV
Mastering the Short Game

Introduction

will never forget the panic I felt in January of 2009, when amidst a historic global financial crisis I had to find a way to sell our startup, Jaxtr, before running out of cash six months later. We were not at all prepared for this turn of events. In the prior three years, we had raised nearly $20 million from top-tier Silicon Valley investors in successive oversubscribed rounds. Jaxtr had won numerous awards and quickly risen to prominence with over 10 million registered users. Everything seemed to confirm that we were well on our path to achieve our mission, which was to end the era of global telecom monopolies by bringing free calling and texting over the internet to all mobile phones. In that way, Jaxtr was the interim step between Skype (which at the time was primarily used from desktop and laptop computers) and today's free mobile calling and messaging apps such as WhatsApp and Telegram.

Buzzed by all the positive press coverage, awards, glowing user feedback (such as an email from one of our users in Texas who thanked us for making it possible for him to connect with his grandmother in India for the first time), and investor interest, we never seriously or systematically pursued a sale process. But that became our only hope for survival at the start of 2009.

To be fair, having to sell our startup shouldn't have been a complete surprise. The storm clouds had gradually been gathering around us for at least six months. On September 15, 2008, Lehman Brothers filed for Chapter 11 bankruptcy protection, an event that marked the largest bankruptcy filing in US history and is credited with setting off the global chain reaction that crystallized into what we now refer to as the Great Recession. It also just so happened that the lead investor of our latest fundraising round was the venture arm of that same financial services firm. Shortly after, as a prudent response to the general market conditions, we laid off a third of our employees and then struggled through a difficult CEO transition. To top it all off, our otherwise-supportive venture capital investors gave us the courtesy warning around Thanksgiving that it was unlikely they would make any additional investments in Jaxtr due to the uncertain economic conditions. The writing was not just all over the wall, it was being etched on the surface of our rose-tinted glasses.

We were hardly unique in receiving that kind of holiday greeting card that year. This was the harsh reality for many portfolio companies as investors' attention and funds became increasingly focused on those investments that were perceived to have the highest chance of reaching profitability. After all, no one seemed to have a clue how long the financial crisis would last, and expert predictions ranged from 1 to 10 years or more.

Prior to the recession, our focus was on optimizing for *user growth* and *market share* as opposed to *monetization*, so we didn't really have a clear path to financial sustainability and understandably didn't make the cut for our investors. Sequoia Capital put out its sobering presentation "R.I.P. Good Times" and advised all its portfolio companies to cut costs and pivot to profitability.[1] It felt as though a portal had opened and we had been sucked into a parallel universe, where all VCs suddenly spoke a different language.

At first, the news of our investors' lack of appetite to put more cash into Jaxtr felt like a personal disappointment, but it didn't seem like an existential threat. After all, in the previous year we had the good fortune to raise several million dollars in venture debt to bridge us to our next round of financing if we ever needed it. This allowed us to (naively) think we had enough runway to ride out what we thought would be the worst of the storm through Thanksgiving and Christmas. But when our lead investors informed us in January that they expected us to return the venture debt to our lenders, true panic took a firm grip. It didn't take a financial genius to realize that without dipping into that debt, we had at best only six months of cash left before our lights and servers would be turned off by PG&E.

Taking a page from Entrepreneurship 101, we tried to use the sense of urgency as a motivational call-to-arms for the whole company and channel the negative news into a positive outcome. Our new mantra became the proclamation by Rahm Emanuel after Barack Obama's 2008 electoral victory: "a crisis is a terrible opportunity to waste." And this wasn't just motivational mumbo jumbo. As an optimist, I was convinced deep in my heart that we could innovate our way out of this problem, too. All we needed to do was shift our focus from growth toward improving our freemium conversion rates and find creative ways to reduce our burn rate. How hard could that be?

It was all-hands-on-deck, and at first, everyone felt a new burst of energy as we pushed out new releases at a faster pace than ever. We accelerated our release cycles, and within a few weeks, we even managed to launch a new product that we considered a revolutionary step forward for global communications: one that promised to bring free worldwide calling to every mobile phone, even without an internet connection (back in 2008, less than 25 percent of the US population had smartphones with broadband connectivity).[2] But product innovation is less serendipity and more iteration where through a painstaking process of A/B tests, you gradually tune the product for the right user experience and metrics. In particular, we needed time to run tests and experiments to optimize the monetization funnel. Meanwhile, the clock seemed stubbornly determined to tick at a faster pace every day.

Weeks quickly gave way to months. Despite the team's extraordinary efforts, we could not achieve that magical user experience that would convert sufficient numbers of our free users to paying users, which would at least have helped us cover our costs. The increasing stress of the ever-louder ticking clock and the pressure to innovate started to stifle our creativity and sap any remaining energy we had. Bugs were finding their way into the code when we could least afford them (including hide-under-the-covers embarrassing ones like when our app started routing calls to the wrong destinations all over the world). The cracks in team culture became more visible with each passing day as well. On one not-so-happy occasion, I found myself shouting at two of our developers for taking excessive Ping-Pong breaks—to my and their horror. That Ping-Pong table became such a painful reminder of a seemingly long-gone era that soon thereafter I folded it and shoved it into a walk-in closet that we had converted into our server room, another historic relic in its own right. And when our most critical engineer who had architected the bulk of our platform infrastructure handed in his resignation, we knew we had to face the inevitable: either we would find a way to sell the company quickly or see the efforts of the past four years disappear with our last *TechCrunch* coverage (if we were even lucky enough to get that esteemed eulogy).

Against that backdrop and with just six months of cash left in the bank, we kicked off 2009 with a strategy meeting—or perhaps more accurately described, a panicked huddle—around finding an exit option. Given our extremely constrained runway at that time, all we could do was to come up with a list of potential acquirers and assign who would reach out to each company. We didn't have good contacts at most of them, so we frantically took to LinkedIn to find sources of warm introductions to these potential saviors. It took us a while to navigate the two or three degrees of separation to land those warm introductions, and while we waited, we kept burning our precious cash.

As one would expect, we received hardly any replies. And when we did get one, it was more or less a "Thank you and good luck" sympathy note from one entrepreneur staring deeply into the abyss to another. The only interested party ended up being a startup with whom we had been exploring a partnership in India, which agreed to purchase our assets. Although we didn't technically end up shutting down Jaxtr that summer, the outcome from a founder, employee, or investor perspective was the same: Jaxtr, as we knew it and hoped it would become, ceased to exist.

For me, the silver lining to all of this was the hard lessons learned, although I am still haunted by all the "should haves" and "could haves." Fortunately, I found the opportunity to leverage those learnings when I joined my next startup, Webs, a then-popular website building platform. I made it my priority to devise the exit strategy for that startup even though the founding team had no immediate intention of selling Webs, having just reached cash flow breakeven. But I was determined not to repeat the biggest mistake we had made at Jaxtr.

The process of creating and executing that exit strategy set the course for a complete strategic transformation over the subsequent two years, involving a repositioning of our offering from a generic website creation tool to one aimed at small businesses across web, mobile, and social platforms. At the conclusion of that transformation, we successfully sold Webs to Vistaprint, one of the top acquirers on our wish list. Vistaprint's leadership appreciated the disruptive threat of online presence to their core business of selling business cards and needed a robust suite of digital presence solutions. Being prepared, thoughtful, and deliberate about our exit path and the kind of acquirers we wanted to attract allowed us to be in charge of our destiny, pick the right strategic trajectory, and seize on opportunities in the right order.

I have since been advising entrepreneurs to create an exit strategy well before they're contemplating an exit, regardless of the stage of their startup. I have seen my advice validated not only when those startups manage to create meaningful strategic partnerships and exit options, but also when I found myself on the other side of the table for seven years as a corporate development executive at GoDaddy, where I led numerous strategic partnerships and acquisitions. Being on the acquirer side made it clear for me why it is so critical for startup entrepreneurs to plan for strategic relationships years in advance: savvy acquirers lay the foundation years in advance and keep a close eye on the landscape, developing relationships and creating their own wish list of strategic partners and targets. Landing on top of that wish list is outcome defining for most startups.

This book captures these and other critical lessons I have learned as someone who has been in the trenches and on *all* sides of strategic transactions in Silicon Valley since 1999, with direct involvement in hundreds of mergers and acquisitions (M&A) transactions, strategic partnerships, and investments as a corporate lawyer, serial entrepreneur at four startups that have been acquired, venture capital investor and strategic advisor to numerous startups that have had successful exits, and as mentioned above, an acquirer myself.

For too long M&A has been an esoteric topic for tax, accounting, finance, and legal practitioners with hardly any accessible practical guidebooks for the high-tech entrepreneur. This book is intended to fill that gap and inspire you to create and execute an exit strategy that will help you confidently grow your startup in the years ahead while providing you with strategic direction and actionable steps. The right exit strategy will enable you to both maximize your startup's upside potential and minimize the risk of catastrophic failure should things take a turn for the worse. Put differently, your exit path can be both your success path *and* your survival path.

A BLUEPRINT FOR SUCCESS AND SURVIVAL

Entrepreneurs are in the business of creation: we are constantly generating new ideas and working tirelessly to bring them to life. But the odds of success and survival are seriously stacked against us. Increasingly, our startups are caught between two existential threats: On one side, we face the competitive threat of dominant incumbents such as Google, Amazon, Microsoft, and Apple, which continue to grow their arsenal of cash reserves and can enter any new field at a moment's notice. On the other side, we struggle with the competition for market share and resources that the ever-growing cohort of new startups pose, as it has never been easier to start or get funding for a new venture.

Although all entrepreneurs believe they have a good chance of overcoming these challenges, the reality is that the most likely fate for any new business, including venture-backed startups, is to go out of business. And most of those that do manage to beat the odds are the ones that are acquired. It is an open secret among Silicon Valley investors and experienced entrepreneurs that acquisitions are the most likely path to success for startups.

Since the first recorded acquisition in 1708 which consolidated the power of the British East India Company,[3] the pace of M&A activity has been increasing worldwide, punctuated by periodic episodes of excited hyperactivity or "merger mania," often catalyzed by some major economic or regulatory transformation. We seem to have entered another such period, with industry-altering deals being announced almost weekly. By 2021, we had enjoyed six consecutive years of the highest number of M&A deals worldwide, averaging nearly 50,000 deals per year.[4] Between 2013 and 2020, acquirers had spent $10 trillion on domestic transactions,[5] nearly half of the US annual GDP in 2020. And 2021 proved to be another record setting year, with global deal value surpassing $5 trillion.[6] Factors powering the recent dealmaking boom include increasing cash reserves of public corporations and private equity firms, the low interest rate environment reducing the cost of capital for acquirers, as well as historically high public stock market valuations that provide an additional source of transaction funding for strategic acquirers. Even IPOs are now increasingly preceded by an acquisition thanks to the emergence of special purpose acquisition companies (SPACs) formed by private equity firms, venture funds, and experienced operators.

M&A has been the default exit strategy for both startup entrepreneurs and their investors since the dot-com era. And there is no indication that the future will be different. According to the last three years of Silicon Valley Bank's Startup Outlook Reports, the majority of US startups consider being acquired to be their "realistic long-term goal" as opposed to an IPO or remaining private.[7] While IPOs are also successful exit events, they are the outliers. In 2020, there were nearly 30 times more acquisitions than IPOs (1,600 IPOs[8] vs 45,000 acquisitions[9]). And many companies during their IPO process pursue the "dual track" of both an IPO and an M&A, with a distinct preference for the latter due to its certainty of outcome and faster path to liquidity for stakeholders. Even if they don't do the sale, a solid acquisition prospect leads to a boost in the IPO valuation, resulting in a better outcome for the company, employees, and existing shareholders in the IPO.

As is the case with any other part of startup development—whether it's achieving product market fit, competitive differentiation, or scale—advance planning and deliberate execution are key to a successful outcome. The entrepreneurial community appreciates the fact that overnight successes are the outcome of years of thoughtful strategic planning and execution. Which makes it all the more peculiar that exit strategy creation and execution doesn't rank high on the list of priorities for most entrepreneurs or their investors until there is a desperate need to sell their startup or to react to inbound interest from a potential acquirer.

This lack of preparation catches most entrepreneurs off guard and destroys the value they've worked so hard to build, causing them to reject or accept an acquisition offer prematurely. Of course, sometimes things turn out for the best when entrepreneurs hold firm and decide to stay the course instead of pursuing a sale, as was the case with Google, Netflix, Facebook, and Dropbox, each of which spurned acquirers early in their life cycles. The once-popular web portal Excite's proposed acquisition of Google for $750,000 in the late nineties fell apart because Google cofounder Larry Page insisted that after the acquisition Excite should fully replace its search engine with Google's, as recalled by the CEO of Excite at the time.[10] Netflix similarly spurned an acquisition offer by Amazon only two months after it had launched in 1998,[11] and Dropbox founders did the same when Steve Jobs expressed an interest in buying the company in its early days.[12] These were not easy decisions, of course. Mark Zuckerberg recalls that the decision to reject Yahoo's $1 billion offer to acquire Facebook in July 2006 (a mere 2.5 years after launching the social network) was "really stressful" and one of the "hardest parts" of the history of Facebook as it resulted in him losing all of his management team members who favored the sale.[13]

But those are the outliers. Far more common are the hasty, irreversible mistakes that lead to missed opportunities and shattered dreams, not just when startups run out of funds and effectively shut down as was the case with my first startup, but even when there is a sale, as many would consider to be the case with Flickr's decision to sell to Yahoo for reportedly $25 million in 2005. That is because without a well-formulated and well-thought-through exit strategy, you will be dangerously unprepared to either create or properly take advantage of strategic opportunities. And you will certainly not be able to handle sudden changes in market conditions posing an existential threat to your business. In which case, what ends up unfolding for most entrepreneurs who find themselves in that unfortunate chaotic situation, as I did, is either a Greek tragedy or a romantic comedy. In that reactive, frenzied state, some entrepreneurs approach the potential sale of their startup as an epic battle: they set up a "war room," engage an army of advisors, and strategize around "forcing functions" to increase their leverage, only to find out that their fate had been sealed long before and no amount of posturing will accelerate a sale or gain them better terms. Other entrepreneurs are more "romantic" about their prospects. They spruce up their profile and create a charming pitch deck, ask for introductions to potential suitors, and wait for Cupid's arrow to do its magic. They, too, find out that courtship takes a lot more time than they have and cannot close on a deal before they have to close down their startup permanently. Both groups, in the throes of desperation, often resort to otherwise uncharacteristic tactics: they exaggerate their strengths, hide or de-emphasize their weaknesses, and sometimes even completely distort the truth, which will ultimately backfire and ruin the fledgling relationships they were trying to build. In the process, they commit what many competitive tennis or chess players refer to as "unforced errors": mistakes that are entirely due to the player's own blunder, rather than their opponent's skill or effort.[14]

And as in tennis or chess, it's possible to minimize unforced errors with advance planning and deliberate practice. When it comes to the ultimate fate of your startup, you can either *act* strategically and with purpose or *react* in panic and fear. And you have to make that choice today. As seasoned dealmakers like to say, *good exits happen when companies are bought, not sold.* By devising and implementing a thoughtful exit strategy, you can join the ranks of companies that are *bought.* But that's if, and only if, you act soon enough. Having an exit strategy should not be an afterthought; it should become part of the DNA of every startup as it is core to a successful outcome and survival for that startup.

So why is it that so few startups actually take the time to create and execute on an exit strategy? This is particularly puzzling since entrepreneurs are almost always in planning mode, be it for their next product release, next round of financing, next set of tests, next round of recruiting, or any other activity; there is always some kind of action plan. I am convinced that much of this is due to deep-rooted misunderstandings about exit planning that have grown to block the communication channels between entrepreneurs, investors, and others involved in supporting our startups. These misunderstandings and their underlying causes need to be exposed and addressed before anyone can engage in a productive discussion on exit planning. There is a *signaling problem* associated with exit discussions that in many circles has made the whole topic a taboo that we need to fully acknowledge and circumvent. I have devoted the first part of this book, "A New Perspective on Exit Planning," to providing you with the data and arguments you will need to overcome this taboo and other misconceptions around exit planning so you can open up the requisite communication channels.

Building on that foundation, in Part II, "Creating Your Exit Strategy," you will learn how to create an effective and actionable plan aligned with your startup's values, mission, and aspirations. The process starts with gathering your team for a "strategy offsite" that enables you and your team to step back from the day-to-day and gaze critically inward (into your motivations) as well as outward (into your industry, competitive landscape, and potential acquirer motivations). You will locate your startup's place in the wider ecosystem as the initial step toward becoming an active participant in it. The output of this exercise provides you and your team with the orientation and framework by which to assess and prioritize how you will build and nurture strategic relationships for your startup.

In Part III, "Playing the Long Game," I will provide you with detailed guidance on how to develop the needed strategic relationships, champions, exit team, and leverage to maximize your startup's chances for success and survival. As the name implies, this process can unfold over a relatively long period of time, which makes advance preparation even more necessary.

Last but not least, in Part IV, "Mastering the Short Game," I will demystify the process of selling your startup and provide you with the insider perspective on how to obtain and negotiate acquisition offers. You will want to revisit this part of the book when you are actively thinking about selling your startup.

As you may have already surmised, this book is not just about learning how to successfully sell your startup. It is about tapping into the power of strategic relationships to unlock outcome-defining options for your startup. It is about learning how to think, act, and negotiate strategically. It is about ensuring that you don't lose the war while you battle the endless daily emergencies of startup life. And most of all, it is about showing you the tremendous amount of agency you and your team have in determining your ultimate fate in the startup game.

PART I

A New Perspective on Exit Planning

CHAPTER 1

THE EXIT TABOO

If you change the way you look at things,
the things you look at change.
—Wayne Dyer[1]

Soon after I started socializing the core idea of this book with other founders, entrepreneurs, and investors in Silicon Valley, I noticed that there was a general reluctance to seriously engage in the subject, in the same way I imagine there would be in discussing the necessity of creating a will with a teenager. Although everyone agreed with the general premise that a strategic sale would be the best possible outcome for their startups, I felt strong resistance to engaging any deeper and actually discussing the specifics around an exit strategy for any startup that was not desperately looking to sell. Many would tactfully change the subject. It seemed that I had stumbled upon a taboo in the otherwise irreverent tech startup community. And as it is with most taboos, this one is also born out of a combination of miscommunication and ill-informed assumptions.

We could leave this taboo alone were it not of vital importance for you to have internal allies and leadership alignment whenever you engage in any strategic initiative, especially one that would determine the fate of your startup. To devise an effective exit strategy, you need the ability to openly communicate and discuss it with your cofounders, key leadership members, board members, and major investors at the very least. And not only their initial input is of vital importance, but so is their continued support throughout the years.

Thus, we need to address and overcome this taboo and any other misunderstanding that could inadvertently block your communication channels with these critical stakeholders.

Fortunately, this is quite feasible. But it requires a thoughtful approach. An approach that starts with empathy and a deep understanding of what gives rise to this taboo among entrepreneurs and investors, who are viewing the prospect of a potential future exit through very different lenses. Let's address each of them separately, starting with entrepreneurs.

Among entrepreneurs, I have found those who are reluctant to seriously enter into exit planning discussions generally fall into one of the following two camps:

- **Missionaries.** Missionaries consider a sale to be a betrayal of the independent spirit and selfless idealism that is at the core of starting a new venture. These entrepreneurs see themselves as rebels whose mission is almost defined by a resistance to the temptations of the Siren call of near-term financial gains. Missionaries view with opprobrium those who actively pursue a sale of their startups instead of fighting to the bitter end, labeling them as sellouts, hypocrites, and mercenaries.
- **Pragmatists.** For pragmatists, the topic of exit strategy is not worth near-term consideration from a practical point of view. While pragmatists admit that an acquisition is the likely outcome for their startups, it is always sufficiently far away in the future not to be a priority today because if you build a successful startup, then it should have many exit options anyway.

These two camps are perhaps best thought of as the two ends of a continuous spectrum. There are also those who have one foot in each camp, believing that there is both something morally objectionable as well as impractical about planning to sell one's startup before one is imminently looking to sell. While each camp initially appears to make some valid, principled arguments, they arise from cognitive biases that lead to the wrong conclusion. In fact, once those biases have been accounted for, both missionary and pragmatist positions would and should support exit planning.

MISSIONARY FALLACY (OPTIMISM BIAS)

Missionaries seem to ignore the reality of dismal startup survival rates, in light of which a successful sale to a strategic partner becomes one of the most likely viable means of continuing to execute on a startup's true mission and aspirations. Even for the most ambitious entrepreneurs, the facts are quite sobering. In the United States, only one-third of small businesses survive beyond 10 years.[2] And the odds are worse for venture-backed startups, where one study found 75 percent of startups that raise more than $1 million didn't even manage to return the money invested in them.[3]

In a survey I conducted of founders of early-stage startups in the fall of 2021, the overwhelming majority (over 90 percent) agreed that less than 25 percent of all startups will succeed, in line with what startup statistics indicate. But after this, things got interesting. When I asked the same founders what they considered to be their own likelihood of success, they considered it to be much closer to certainty, which indicates that our entrepreneurial optimism simply blinds us to our own reality. And that is troubling. In fact, as I was examining the results of this survey, I was painfully reminded of my parents' decision to purchase a failing coffee shop on a side street of downtown Palo Alto several years ago. They were well aware that the last several owners of that coffee shop had all gone out of business due to lack of a steady customer base, and several years later, my aging parents also realized that they could not make that business sustain itself either. Sadly, their optimism ultimately cost them their health and savings.

Of course, the societal upside of this entrepreneurial optimism is that every quarter we see over 70,000 new startups form in the United States,[4] undeterred by the dire statistics. But the same optimism gets in the way of each individual startup's ability to achieve its mission. Running a startup toward a goal with unrealistic expectations about the probability of achieving that goal is as dangerous as driving at full speed toward an obstacle on the road assuming that it will suddenly move out of your way when you reach it. In both cases, survival, let alone success, is only possible once we have a realistic forecast and assessment of our chances. Because then we can make plans and course correct with a view of *reality as it is*, not as we wish for it to be.

Entrepreneurs who are serious about achieving their mission need to consider ways to achieve that mission in light of the reality that it is unlikely their startup will be able to remain an independent entity in perpetuity. Selling that startup to a strategic acquirer aligned with the startup's mission is one of the best ways to achieve that mission.

PRAGMATIST FALLACY (PRESENT BIAS)

While the majority of entrepreneurs consider an acquisition to be the most likely fate of their startups, their actions paint a very different picture. In my survey of founders, I also found that over 70 percent had spent little to no time on creating an exit strategy, and around 60 percent considered themselves quite unprepared to respond to an acquisition interest. This unfortunate discrepancy is quite consistent with what psychologists have labeled our "present bias," which is our tendency to overvalue payoffs that are closer to the present time while heavily discounting the future.[5] Classic examples of this bias are some of our eating, drinking, or financial decisions that sacrifice our long-term health and well-being for immediate gratification.

As we all know too well, we can't improve what we don't pay attention to. Because a strategic exit is the single most outcome-defining event in a startup's life cycle, ignoring one's exit strategy today simply results in a suboptimal outcome in the future. While that certainly doesn't mean exit strategy should become any startup's sole focus, it does mean that it is impractical and even irresponsible for entrepreneurs not to give exit strategy creation and execution some amount of time and attention.

While entrepreneurs *over*estimate their ability to predict market needs and customer behavior, they gravely *under*estimate their agency in shaping the future strategic fate of their startups. Successful strategic relationships and transactions don't happen by accident. As you will learn in this book, there is much each and every entrepreneur can do *today* to pave a viable exit path for their startup. And the opposite is also true: lack of planning today will most certainly hurt their prospects in the future, resulting in a sale at the wrong time, to the wrong party, and/or on poor terms, and that's for the lucky few who are able to sell at all before having to turn the lights off permanently. Therefore, building a viable exit path is not just a practical, but also an *existential* imperative for all entrepreneurs, regardless of the stage of their startup.

THE FAULT IN OUR SIGNALS

I have observed that many investors, from angel investors to venture capitalists, become visibly irritated by any mention of "exit strategies" during pitch sessions, board meetings, or even in casual conversations, even though they are fully aware that their own financial success is inextricably linked to a successful sale of that startup. These investors yield tremendous influence over the priorities of the startups they are involved with and thus can effectively shut down exit planning conversations with a simple frown or yawn. But having worn the investor hat on many occasions, I fully appreciate their predicament.

The best way to understand investors' negative emotional reaction is as a *signaling problem*. Investors, by their nature, are always attracted to entrepreneurs who aspire to build scaled businesses and have the courage to take massive risks. Their mental model of a great entrepreneur is aptly captured by a familiar refrain by Reid Hoffman (serial entrepreneur, founder of LinkedIn, and beloved investor and mentor to many of Silicon Valley's greatest entrepreneurs), who often says, "Starting a company is like throwing yourself off the cliff and assembling an airplane on the way down."[6] Investors expect entrepreneurs to be fearless, audacious, and ambitious. Venture capitalists seek out entrepreneurs who not only have their skin in the game, but also whose fierce passion and dedication inspires teams to make outsized sacrifices to tackle what others believe to be impossible. Investors are drawn to entrepreneurs who not only have the courage, but also the unwavering commitment, to stay the course during times of extreme hardship. Thus, they immediately shy away from entrepreneurs who show signs of a get-rich-quick or mercenary mindset, because they are worried those entrepreneurs will not be able to persevere and innovate their way out of inevitable storms in their path, giving up both too soon and too easily. This is why discussions with investors about exit strategy can quickly go off the rails.

Whenever you approach the topic of exit strategy with investors, you will inadvertently set off many alarm bells in their mind. They may be asking themselves, "Why are we talking about a potential sale when there are so many other obstacles to overcome first?" "Is the ultimate goal of this entrepreneur a quick sale or building a lasting, profitable company?" or "How will I keep this entrepreneur at the helm of the ship when the storm clouds gather?" And before you know it, you will have lost those investors in a reverie filled with their worst nightmares and ghosts of failed portfolio companies past.

Given how quickly your intentions can become misinterpreted, it is essential to address and alleviate investor concerns before even talking about your exit strategy. The good news is that you already have the ultimate alignment of interest with your investors: just like you, your investors want your startup to succeed. Selling your startup at the right time, to the right strategic

8

buyer, on the best possible terms is what venture investors consider *success* anyway. Your task becomes convincing them that formulating and executing on an exit strategy will help you best achieve that shared goal.

What I have found effective in such conversations is to clearly relay, reiterate, and reinforce that your primary motivation remains building a successful startup and executing its mission to the best of your abilities. Whenever you don't provide intent, others fill in the blank for you, and often not in the best possible way. If you don't make your true intentions crystal clear, investors' minds easily gravitate toward the most negative conclusions. So, take the time and set the stage, making it clear to your audience that you remain as committed as ever to building a successful startup and executing on your mission.

Once you have put your investors' minds at ease, you are ready to discuss why you believe you need an exit strategy, i.e., a Plan B, that would provide strategic optionality and alternatives for your startup. Help your investors recognize that to create viable long-term strategic options, you need to plan ahead, gather data, and test your hypotheses, just as you do when you are in search of a product-market fit or explore a go-to-market strategy. Devising an exit strategy comes with the added benefits of providing your startup with better strategic direction and unlocking potential strategic partnerships ahead of your competition. But the biggest benefit is the most counterintuitive one: having an exit strategy will help you and your team build a stronger and more valuable startup, one that will have much less need to be acquired.

THE UPSIDE OF OPTIONALITY

Many assume that since the business of innovation involves risk, increasing risk should boost innovation. This leads some investors to fear that having an exit path would make it too tempting for an entrepreneur to rush to a quick sale rather than work through the hardships and reach for the stars. They worry that the safety net provided by an option to sell their startup would undermine entrepreneurs' motivations and incentives.

But those fears are misplaced.

While I have found no evidence in support of the claim that risk mitigation hurts innovation, there is mounting evidence about the harmful side effects of excessive risk and the toll it has taken on the mental health of entrepreneurs.[7] High-risk situations cause stress, anxiety, and burnout, which not only wreak havoc on the entrepreneurs' health, but also undermine their mental abilities and performance. Anyone who has spent time at a startup knows that innovation is not forged in overburdened entrepreneurial brains; instead, innovation is a result of repetitive, iterative, and creative experimentation. Thomas Edison pointed this out over a century ago: Genius is 1 percent inspiration and 99 percent perspiration. Adding stress to the mix makes success even harder to achieve.

Now this is where having a viable exit path drastically transforms the experience for an entrepreneur, tapping into an often-overlooked aspect of human psychology. An exit path provides the entrepreneur with optionality. Besides the fact that exit options will automatically boost your startups' leverage and valuation (as discussed in detail in Chapter 11), they make running your startup much less stressful. This is a phenomenon psychologists refer to as the "panic button effect": believing one has the option to escape a stressful situation will reduce the amount of stress actually experienced in that situation.[8] In the classic experiments, a set of participants were exposed to stress-inducing noises while trying to solve certain quizzes. Some of those participants were provided with the option to press a button to stop the noise, which they were told would also stop the experiment. Even among participants who never pressed this "panic button," the stress-induced aftereffects of the experiment were much less compared with participants lacking the option. Participants with the panic button option derived considerable comfort just from the awareness of its presence. Your exit path can very much serve as that stress-reducing panic button. Regardless of whether or not you desire to sell your startup, knowing you have a viable path to do so will take a significant amount of stress off your chest in the day-to-day operations, giving you the confidence, peace of mind, and mental space to innovate, experiment, and think strategically.

It should come as no surprise, then, that smart risk mitigation seems to be a distinguishing characteristic of successful entrepreneurs. In his book *Originals*, organizational psychologist and Wharton professor Adam Grant recounts stories of many successful entrepreneurs, including Bill Gates, Pierre Omidyar, Sara Blakely, and the founders of Warby Parker, who all went to great lengths to hedge their risks as much as they could before committing full-time to their respective startups.[9] Most entrepreneurs work on their ideas as a side hustle and gradually build conviction in the idea before they commit. And while running their startups, they usually only take measured, calculated risks instead of betting the company on every whim. But not all risk mitigation strategies are helpful or efficient. To hedge their risks, some entrepreneurs pursue multiple product lines or business models that can seriously hurt their startup's chance of success. For instance, one of the biggest regrets of Aaron Levie, Box's founder and CEO, is that early on he wasted a year and a half trying to hedge his business model between a consumer product and an enterprise product. Instead, he believes that had he focused on one big idea and committed to it, Box would be a much bigger company today.[10] As far as attaining strategic options goes, devising and putting in motion an exit strategy would have a far higher return on effort invested than running multiple versions of your startup in parallel.

While entrepreneurship necessarily involves some amount of risk-taking, entrepreneurial passion and commitment neither springs from, nor grows stronger with, excessive risk. Instead, what I have found motivates entrepreneurs above everything else is their conviction that they are involved in the creation of something that will have a lasting impact. Which is exactly what a viable exit path enables.

CHAPTER 2

EXIT PATH AS YOUR SURVIVAL PATH

In order to succeed, you must first survive.
—Warren Buffett[1]

YouTube, Instagram, Pixar, and many other innovative endeavors owe their continued existence today to the fact that they were acquired. An acquisition is the most likely path for a startup's long-term survival since an IPO, the only other option, is out of reach for the overwhelming majority of startups. Most startups perish because they run out of money before they can reach financial viability. Even after a startup attains the coveted product-market fit, it still needs to figure out how to scale its operations, how to acquire customers profitably, how to fight competition, and the myriad of other challenges the market has in store. The right acquirer would have already overcome most of those challenges and would have the resources to give the startup its best fighting chance, as was the case when Google acquired YouTube, Facebook acquired Instagram, and Disney acquired Pixar.

The fact that the majority of startups fail is sadly a failure of *preparation* rather than a necessity of *innovation*. For each of those failed startups, chances are there would have been one or more willing and able strategic acquirers who could have helped it survive in some form. But that would have required those startups to have properly found, courted, and nurtured those strategic relationships.

Think of an exit strategy as a parachute that every entrepreneur-who-jumps-off-a-cliff-to-build-an-airplane, to follow Reid Hoffman's metaphor, would be able to access. A lifesaving tool in their toolkit of entrepreneurship. One may never have to deploy that parachute, but it would be insane not to wear one.

As entrepreneurs, we all want to see our startups survive and thrive. To be clear, the kind of "survival" that is at stake here is not the technical existence of a legal entity, a website, domain name, or even the brand or a specific product. Instead, true *survival* of a startup is the continuation of something much deeper, more intimate, and of vital importance to the core of what we understand to be a startup's ultimate mission. That survival is what gives meaning to the whole endeavor and the pain and suffering that we endure along the entrepreneurial journey. For many entrepreneurs, a startup becomes an extension of their own self and their deeply held values; it becomes as much a part of their personal legacy as some perceive their children to be. Thus it is not a surprise that millions of entrepreneurs see and refer to their business as their "baby." Just a simple Google search for an exact match on the phrase "my business is my baby" in August of 2021 yielded over 14,200,000 results!

Given how personally and emotionally demanding it is to start and run a business, it is understandable that over the years such a strong parent-child-like bond forms between entrepreneurs and their businesses. In that light, an acquirer can be seen as a new parent for this "baby," with the task of helping it get to the next level.

A sale to an acquirer is often the only means by which your startup can continue to survive and even thrive, albeit under a different roof and with somewhat different leadership. Whether that *survival* constitutes survival of those deeply held values and other things that you fundamentally care about is for the most part a function of how much advance planning and preparation you and your team have put into devising and executing your exit strategy prior to the sale.

As with most worthwhile endeavors in life or in business, you reap what you sow. Successful acquisitions are typically the result of years of careful planning and deliberate execution. And when executed well, acquisitions can serve as a continuation or even rejuvenation of your mission. For instance, consider Amazon's acquisition in June 2020 of Zoox, a startup that had raised a billion dollars in funding to build an autonomous vehicle from the ground up. In the announcement of the transaction, Amazon mentions that "We're acquiring Zoox to help bring their vision of autonomous ride-hailing to reality."[2] In other words, one of the largest and most valuable companies in the world, whose annual revenue of more than $300 billion surpasses the GDP of 180 countries, is putting its full faith and credit behind this initiative at a time when the company was struggling to raise funding from investors as reported by the *Wall Street Journal*.[3] Similarly, the sale of your startup could be just another milestone along the path to achieving your ultimate mission.

The central point of this book is that there are proactive steps you can take *starting today* to increase the chances of survival for your startup even when that means selling your startup to an acquirer. Even though you cannot fully control everything, you will discover that there is still a lot that is within your control. And the sooner you act, the more influence you will be able to exert over the outcome. After all, the future is nothing other than a series of short terms. You can, and with the help of this book, you will create better strategic relationships and options for your startup. And it starts with creating an exit strategy and the will and discipline to implement it over time.

CHAPTER 3

THE M&A FAILURE MYTH

For most folks, no news is good news;
for the press, good news is not news.
—Gloria Borger[1]

You may consider it either naive or overly optimistic to claim that an acquisition could result in a positive outcome for your startup and its mission. After all, you may ask, don't most acquisitions fail?

As it happens, the popular perception of acquisition failure has less to do with facts and more to do with news reporting and how our brains tend to hold on to negative information. Yes, there are plenty of stories of mergers gone wrong. For instance, in 2015 Microsoft laid off 15,000 employees and wrote off almost all of the $7.9 billion it paid to acquire Nokia's handset business just the previous year. And a year before that, Google lost $10 billion for the handset business it had acquired from Motorola. Both are astounding amounts unless you compare them against the ill-fated AOL–Time Warner merger ($164 billion in size) at the height of the dot-com bubble. And not all stories of M&A failures have been just about financial loss. Many of us are still upset about the slew of acquisitions by Yahoo of some of the most promising internet properties in the early 2000s such as GeoCities, Flickr, or

Tumblr, which then lost their momentum and viral growth, only to be superseded by the newer platforms such as Wix, Facebook, and Medium.[2]

But despite all those headline-grabbing losses, the pace of M&A activity is at an all-time high. So how do we explain that? Are acquirers and entrepreneurs just insane and doing the same thing repeatedly expecting a different result? Or are there lots of successful deals out there that no one hears about?

To solve this puzzle, we should start with the definition of "success", which is highly subjective. First, "success" for an acquirer can have quite a different meaning as compared with the target's point of view. And "success" can also have quite different meanings for various stakeholders within each of the acquirer and the target entities. For instance, to founders and angel investors in a startup that exits at same valuation as its Series B round of financing valuation, the transaction may be considered a true "success," whereas to Series B and later investors who do not get any return for their investment it would be a "failure." For employees who get to join the acquirer with comparable or better compensation packages and titles, such acquisition may be considered a "success," whereas for those employees whose positions are rationalized (a term of art for cost savings realized through headcount elimination), the acquisition may seem like a dismal "failure." Users of a beloved application that gets shut down or neglected because of an acquisition, again, would likely view the transaction as a heartbreaking "failure."

When studies set out to determine the success or failure of M&A transactions, they usually focus on the acquirer perspective and try to assess whether the transaction was a net gain or net loss to the enterprise value of the acquirer within a defined time frame. The reason for the focus on the acquirer is due to the inherent difficulties of tracking the success metrics for the target and its stakeholders after an acquisition.[3] And anything other than financial metrics is also quite challenging to track. Hence, the narrow focus of these studies is on whether the shareholders of the acquirer received a direct financial gain as a result of the transaction. But even if you were to just consider that narrow metric, how can you separate out the impact of the acquisition from the impact of all the other things that influence the trajectory of a business, including the composition of its team, its leadership, culture, mission, resources, products, location, focus, competitive strategy, intellectual property, and the like? And what is the relevant time frame anyway to assess the impact of an acquisition? A day, a week, a month, a year, or multiple years? Those factors and others make it practically impossible to develop a realistic objective assessment of the impact of an acquisition on the acquirer's shareholder value. That is not something one can accurately measure, just as you cannot accurately measure how differently things would have turned out for someone if they had attended a different college or high school or lived in a different city. There are just way too many variables to account for.

Of course, as mentioned above, there have been deals that have failed to deliver on their promise on a large scale. Unfortunately, those are usually the ones that most of us have heard about thanks to the media's love affair with breaking and regurgitating disaster stories. But for every one of those, there are many more transactions that have actually gone right. And I am not just referring to the big success stories like the acquisitions of Next, PayPal, YouTube, Instagram, or Zappos. Nor deals like Disney's series of acquisitions of Pixar (2006), Marvel (2009), and Lucasfilm (2012) that paved the path for Disney to become a streaming content powerhouse nearly a decade later. Instead, I am referring to the majority of 50,000 or more acquisitions a year that take place without any attention-grabbing press headlines.

The media's spotlight on acquisition disaster stories combined with our brain's primal impulse to hang on to negative information far more readily than positive information, what is now commonly referred to as "negativity bias,"[4] has caused some of us to treat the myth of acquisition failures as fact. And then others casually refer to this "fact" in their articles or reporting, which further perpetuates and ingrains the negative narrative, bringing us to the state of affairs today and the popular misconception around acquisition failures.

But you should take as the best proxy for measuring the likelihood of success or failure of M&A transactions to be their popularity and the rate at which they occur, giving the transacting parties the benefit of doubt that they are actually as smart and as data-driven as the rest of us, with perfectly valid reasons for entering into those transactions. Acquisitions don't just happen based on a whim. As you read more about the M&A process in following chapters, you will learn that most take years to plan and accomplish. Much detailed analysis and planning goes into the process with many people and approval levels involved. In fact, for most acquirers, inertia pours heavy buckets of ice water over any fevered dealmaker. Expectations from the outcome of a transaction would have to be very high and the deal champion would have to convert many doubters to get the deal across the finish line. And contrary to the negative narrative, dealmakers continue to do deals at an increased rate. According to Deloitte's annual survey of 1,000 M&A practitioners in the fall of 2018 and 2019, a majority of corporate executives consider more than half of their acquisitions to have been successful, generating the expected value or return on investment.[5] How is that for a narrative violation! Don't let the unfounded myth of M&A failures bias your judgment and get in the way of creating a game-changing outcome for your startup.

PART II

Creating Your Exit Strategy

CHAPTER 4

RATIONALE AND TIMING

Plans are worthless, but planning is everything.
—Dwight D. Eisenhower

Selling your startup is unlike any other business transaction you have been involved with. Preparing for the sale of your startup as yet another business negotiation is like preparing for a NASCAR race by practicing at your local go-kart track: in both cases, there will be blood—*your* blood. The difference in what is needed to prepare for either is not merely a *difference of size*, but also a *difference in kind*. The increased size of the vehicles and racetracks in NASCAR necessitate an entirely different set of driving skills and years of physical and mental conditioning to survive, let alone succeed. Similarly, although it is certainly helpful to be a skilled negotiator when you are in acquisition talks with potential suitors, a decent outcome requires months, even years, of advance strategizing and careful preparation.

Just as "location, location, location" is the age-old advice for success in real estate investing, "preparation, preparation, preparation" is the well-kept secret of savvy dealmakers. At its most fundamental level, a successful exit only happens if you manage to tie the knot with *the right acquirer, at the right time*, and *with maximum negotiation leverage*. Unless you are supernaturally lucky, you actually need to create a plan and work on it to orchestrate the perfect confluence of these events. They won't spontaneously come together in a chance encounter with the perfect acquirer. While many human marriages result from serendipity, corporate marriages don't; they require careful advance planning. Without a plan, how would you even know who is that *right acquirer*, when is the *right time* to sell, and what are the *right terms*? While your starting plan will most likely not get everything right, the framework and general direction resulting from the planning *process* itself is the key to success.

Exit planning starts you on a journey to discover your goals, aspirations, and hypotheses and to assess your startup's current position in relation to those. Most important, it forces you to define what *success* would mean for you and your stakeholders. To know who could potentially be *the right acquirer* for you, you need to define your criteria for evaluating acquirers and then assess who could actually meet them. To have any idea as to when is the *right time* to sell, you will need to become clear on the goals for your startup, your timing to achieve them, and where along that trajectory you think you would both be willing to sell and have a strong negotiation position. All of this soul-searching and market research activity needs time and iteration to yield meaningful results.

No matter how nascent or established your startup is, your exit planning should start today. To understand why, let's step back and distill an acquisition down to its core essential components:

1. A willing buyer
2. A willing seller
3. A set of terms everyone agrees with

Each of these three ingredients needs time to manifest. A buyer's willingness to do a deal needs to be cultivated over time. Similarly, you and your critical stakeholders also need to be far along on the journey to clearly see how an acquisition fits within the arc of the narrative for your startup. And finally, neither you nor your acquirer would settle for a set of terms that are not aligned to each side's ultimate corporate goals and objectives. It takes time to uncover what yours and your desired acquirers' ultimate objectives are and how you can best align them.

Regardless of the size of the transaction, for you as the selling entrepreneur and your startup, an acquisition will be a transformational and life-changing experience. Your exit may very well change the career or life trajectory for your employees, could delight or frustrate millions of customers, might shift the competitive dynamics of an industry, or perhaps much more. To ensure that the end result meets your expectations as much as possible, you need to have done your homework. Just as having a business plan is a great way to prepare and create the blueprint for the business activities of your startup, an exit strategy is a great way to prepare and create the blueprint for the strategic activities of your startup. In fact, a business plan without an exit strategy is only half complete as it leaves unanswered many important strategic questions about the ultimate fate of your startup—the "who," "why," "when," and "how" of an eventual exit.

The exit strategy creation process laid out in the following three chapters follows these basic steps in sequence:

Step 1: Gather. You and the team need to align on a realistic picture of your place in the market, and grounded in that reality, brainstorm on your go-forward strategy.

Step 2: Document. There is no plan unless it is written down. You will need to memorialize the results of your research and brainstorming sessions in an accessible format. This will become your exit strategy.

Step 3: Iterate. Just because you write it down, of course, doesn't mean you can't revise it. A good exit strategy, just like a good business strategy, needs to be constantly revisited and revised in light of observed, real-world data.

If these "basic" steps seem to entail a lot of work, that is because they do. I call them basic in a similar vein that *walking* is basic. Learning how to put one foot in front of another while maintaining our balance took the good part of the first year or more of our lives. Devising an exit strategy will demand diligence, patience, and attention. It will take some of the valuable resources of your startup, especially time and focus. Therefore, it is critical to recognize that without the right process and diligent follow-through, it would be a waste of time.

If you are wondering whether such somewhat elaborate process for creating an exit strategy is worth the effort, you are in good company. I used to have many reservations about structured strategy activities myself. But over the years and many trials and errors, I have come to realize that following a formal and thoughtful process actually makes a tremendous difference in the outcome. In a study conducted by management consulting firm McKinsey, researchers found that 79 percent of executives whose companies had a formal strategic planning process were satisfied with their approach in contrast with only 49 percent satisfaction for the companies that didn't have such formal processes.[1] The *right process* will take you a long way toward arriving at the *right outcome*.

In the following chapters I will lay out a structured process for you to create an exit strategy, drawing on expert research along with my personal experience working with various teams over many years to formulate and implement strategic plans, including exit strategies.

CHAPTER 5

STEP 1: GATHER

The best way to have good ideas is to have lots
of ideas and throw away the bad ones.
—Linus Pauling[1]

While some insights about your exit strategy could suddenly appear while you are on a run or seated in deep meditation, you will need to put in the sweat equity to get to an actionable strategy. Just as it is with your overall business strategy, or even marketing or product strategy, your exit strategy should be the output of extensive real-time deliberations with your leadership team. At a minimum, you need one productive meeting with them to kick off the process, get all the ideas on the table, and make sure you and your team are aligned on the path forward. I call this meeting your "strategy offsite" for reasons that should soon become clear.

Do not expect to simply put a meeting on your leadership team's calendar and come away with fruitful results. Proper advance preparation is a prerequisite. In an effective strategy offsite, participants don't waste valuable time arguing about what the meeting objectives ought to be or rehashing known data. Nor do they leave the meeting feeling that no real decisions were made or genuine insights gained. Instead, participants in a productive offsite are fully engaged, aligned, and collaboratively generating creative insights. In terms of return on effort, it is very hard to beat the impact of a well-prepared offsite, while the opposite is also true: an ill-prepared offsite is not worth anyone's time.

INGREDIENTS OF AN EFFECTIVE OFFSITE MEETING

To prepare for your strategy offsite efficiently, focus on the following six common elements of well-run sessions. I have listed them here in the order of the advance preparation time each requires prior to the date of the offsite, with the first one demanding your most immediate attention:

1. **Core values.** Alignment around mission, vision, and principles
2. **Participants.** Involvement of critical participants
3. **Agenda.** Clarity of the offsite's agenda and specific topics discussed
4. **Data.** Access to the relevant background information
5. **Setting.** Meeting at a conducive location
6. **Mindset.** Adopting the appropriate mindset

Let's review each in more detail so you can better appreciate the role these elements play in the outcome of your offsite and properly address them in your preparations.

Core Values

Your startup's core values consist of its foundational mission, vision, and principles. "Know thyself" were the words inscribed on the Temple of Apollo at Delphi, where the best-known oracle of ancient Greece imparted sage guidance and made prophetic predictions.[2] You can't decide what destiny or destination to choose without a clear understanding of your own desires and preferences. During a keynote speech at a conference in Palo Alto in 2018, Aaron Levie, Box's reflective founder and CEO, said that if he could go back in time, the first thing he would do would be to identify and implement his startup's values early on so that the entire team could be guided by them because "your values are literally the core operating system of your company."[3]

In any strategic activity, your core values serve as the ultimate criteria for evaluating and prioritizing your goals and objectives. Now, by "core values" I am not referring to a tagline or set of buzzwords to be hung on a wall or put on a website. Instead, I am referring to those deeply held beliefs that encapsulate the founding mission and principles of your startup and provide purpose and meaning for all your activities. As such, having a clear articulation, understanding, and alignment around your core values is crucial for any strategy exercise, as you will use these values as the ultimate compass to evaluate alternate outcomes and possible paths to get there.

If you have not yet had a chance to clearly formulate your core values, now is the time to do so. Document them and ensure there is general alignment on them in your leadership team well before the team heads out for the offsite.

Participants

Just like most other creative and innovative undertakings by your team, exit strategy creation is a collaborative exercise. As such, you cannot have an effective offsite without the right participants at the table, actively brainstorming with you about the possibilities and collaborating on the decision criteria for the best path forward.

While it is important that as much of your leadership team as possible be involved, there is a limit to how many participants you can effectively assemble in the room before productivity and engagement suffers. In my experience, once you exceed 10 people, you have gotten dangerously close to the too-many-participants threshold. Keep this constraint in mind as you assemble a representative group.

A strategy is best executed by those who participate in creating it. Each member of your senior leadership team (such as the heads of operations, finance, legal, engineering, business development, product, and marketing) will have a role in executing your exit strategy in the years to come, just as they do in executing the business strategy. Their active participation is critical, so make sure they are able attend.

As you consider the list of attendees, pay close attention to the diversity of perspectives in the room. The benefits of diversity in workplace have been well documented. A series of McKinsey studies from 2014 to 2018 found that gender and ethnic diversity are clearly correlated with profitability among over 1,000 companies globally.[4] A study of 600 business decisions made by 200 teams over two years found that inclusive teams make better, faster, and more effective decisions.[5] Benefits of diversity include its ability to increase empathy and creativity for all involved. Also, diversity helps "keep your team members' biases in check and make them question their assumptions,"[6] paving the way for a fact-based, data-driven approach to decision-making. One of the main goals of your offsite is to explore strategic options for your startup and how various ecosystem players may view you. You need to think in new ways, evaluate alternatives, and check your existing blind spots. The more creativity, empathy, and sound judgment the team brings to that exercise, the more effective the result will be. The last thing you want is to gather around a table with a group of like-minded colleagues who can finish each other's sentences.

Agenda

Any meeting without a proper agenda will quickly become unproductive. An agenda provides the context and framework from which to collect and then interpret the information gathered for the offsite. In fact, sharing the offsite's agenda as you distribute the background information and material for prereading enables your team members to efficiently process and mentally prepare for the gathering.

While your particular situation will demand specific adjustments, you can use the sample agenda below as a starting point. I recommend that you start the offsite with context setting and data sharing to establish the common ground among the participants before moving on to more collaborative exercises.

Sample Offsite Agenda
- Review of meeting's objectives, timeline, and ground rules
- Company updates
  - Overall mission, vision, and strategy
  - Product, financial, and customer updates
  - Business performance review and key metrics
  - Current product road map and initiatives
  - Financial projections
- Industry updates
  - Market evolution and observed trends
  - Competitor news
  - Alliances (noteworthy partnerships, M&A, and investment activities)
- Strategy sessions (these sessions will be described in detail later in this chapter)
  - Warmup exercise
  - Session 1: Defining success
  - Session 2: Selecting strategic partners
- Recap

Data

While your core values will bring clarity to the ultimate destination the team will want to navigate toward, it is equally important to determine your starting location by having an accurate *description* of the current state of your startup. All participants need to become intimately familiar with the current state of affairs of your startup as well as the environment in which it operates before they can intelligently analyze and opine on the possible paths ahead.

Ideally, you should divvy up the task of data collection and market research among the attendees four to six weeks before the offsite, with the goal of disseminating that information to the participants at least one week before the meeting. This allows everyone to have a chance to digest the content and be prepared to draw upon it during the offsite. In today's data-rich environment, it is very easy to overwhelm yourself and your team with stats, market data, analyst reports, and the like. Everyone will need to exercise judgment about what is signal versus noise for the purposes of your strategy offsite. Clarifying the meeting objectives and sharing the agenda in advance can help. Make sure to clarify for everyone what material is intended as background that needs to be read in preparation for the meeting, versus material that will be presented and discussed during the offsite, as there will simply not be enough time to review it all together in real time.

Setting

As we all know, there is a time and place for everything. This is particularly true when it comes to strategy meetings. Think of the setting as another participant, one that will have a direct impact on how much every other participant contributes to the meeting. The right setting will go a long way toward bringing about the conditions for full concentration, engagement, motivation, and creativity for all involved.

When I led a strategy offsite for Webs soon after I joined that startup in 2009, I asked our leadership team to spend a full day at a beautiful hotel in Chesapeake Bay, an hour drive away from our headquarters in Silver Spring, Maryland. This meant that we also had to splurge on spending two nights at that hotel. Fortunately, the founders decided to take a chance and go along with my proposal even though there was no prior budget for such an outing. The hotel's conference room had a panoramic view of the majestic bay, where we gathered around comfortably and had food brought in to maximize our time together. We tried to anticipate every aspect of the day and plan it to fit our agenda, including the timing and kind of food and drinks served, equipment in the room (we needed a projector to share our research as well as an easel to write down ideas and action items), and areas for taking breaks. The meeting went as planned, and the team came away with a renewed energy and clear objectives for where we wanted to take our company over the next few years. Looking back with the team many years later, we fondly acknowledge that the Chesapeake Bay offsite was a pivotal moment for our startup and a catalyst for a successful acquisition two years later. What might have seemed like a luxury or extravagance at the time proved to be one of the best decisions we ever made as a leadership team.

I always recommend that important strategic meetings be done in person. Despite the tremendous advances in videoconferencing technology, there is still no substitute for gathering in person. Collaboration, discussion, and interactions all become significantly more effective when everyone can observe one another's body language and interact with each other. Furthermore, it is much easier for participants to get distracted or tune out a discussion if they are not physically present in the same room with others.

All elements of the setting for your strategy offsite, including location, view, start and end time, food and drinks served, comfort of the chairs, lighting, availability of a projector, collaboration tools, ground rules about using phones or checking emails, and the like will impact whether you and your team will have the right level of psychological and physiological support conducive to a productive gathering. Your objective is to create an environment where distractions are minimized, inspiration is maximized, and every creative thought of the participants is captured efficiently.

Therefore, you need to spend some time thinking carefully about creating a safe, inspiring, and relaxing atmosphere for the participants. Here are some of my key learnings in this regard:

1. Meet at a location other than your office. You want to break old habits.
2. Choose natural lighting and panoramic views when possible. I have found nature to be the best catalyst for relaxation and inspiration.

3. Ensure that during the meetings, participants are well rested and well fed.
4. Minimize caffeine and sugar consumption, opting for healthier options. The food should sustain the participants without creating constant cravings or energy spikes.
5. Make sure any required equipment, such as computers, projectors, or monitors, is present and in working condition, and have a backup plan in case of equipment failure.
6. Have a whiteboard and/or easel available with ample writing implements and sticky notes.

Mindset

One of the major benefits of advance strategy planning is that you get to deliberate without the stress of daily workplace issues, an impending crisis, or an imminent transaction. That lack of psychological pressure should give everyone the ability to take a step back, reflect on the overall picture, and be creative and purposeful in their deliberations. But a lack of crisis should not mean a lack of focus or urgency. Sometimes, in the absence of time pressure, team members may indulge in excessive blue-sky hypothesizing, where the discussion could easily go off the rails and lose its focus. You need an approach that enables you and your team to arrive at actionable insights and conclusions without stifling creativity—an approach that balances the participants' imagination and out-of-the-box thinking with their rational and analytic thinking, referred to as "divergent" and "convergent" thinking respectively in psychology.

Because creative professionals have grappled most with this challenge, they found a way to overcome it using a technique called "design thinking" which harnesses the powers of divergent and convergent thinking. Design thinking is now applied to many other domains, including business strategy, popularized by a *Harvard Business Review* article by Tim Brown, then–CEO and president of global design consulting firm IDEO, the powerhouse at the forefront of many iconic product designs such as Apple's innovations.[7] The design thinking process involves multiple phases, starting with a problem statement, followed by idea generation, prototyping, and iteration.

For the past 10 years, I have studied and experimented with applying the learnings from the design thinking methodology to running strategy meetings, and I have arrived at an approach that is quite effective and efficient in generating actionable results. My approach is a variant of what many refer to as brainstorming. I recommend that your offsite's agenda include at the very least the following two brainstorming sessions: (1) *defining success*, and (2) *selecting strategic partners*. Those brainstorming sessions will be the most critical and outcome-determining sessions of your offsite.

As you prepare for the offsite, it is important to learn the basic principles of brainstorming, which I describe in further detail below, and if possible, practice holding at least one brainstorming session with your leadership team before the offsite. As Dr. Tina Seelig, award-winning Stanford professor and author on creativity, innovation, and entrepreneurship puts it,

> *Brainstorming is NOT a tool, like a hammer or can opener. It is a skill like chess, baseball, or playing the piano. All of these endeavors have rules as well as strategies for success. And, it's impossible to become a master without effective training and practice.*[8]

And there should be no shortage of opportunities to practice a team brainstorming session prior to your offsite since daily life at a startup constantly demands creative problem solving.

Armed with the proper advance preparation, all attendees should arrive at the offsite with clarity of purpose and the grounding to tackle the most mission-critical questions for your startup. As suggested in the sample agenda above, you should start the offsite with general information sharing and level-setting topics, such as reviewing your company's performance and the state of the market, industry, and competitive environment. Think of the review sessions as the appetizers with the main course being your brainstorming sessions. With that in mind, make sure to set aside ample time for brainstorming sessions. Let's look at brainstorming in more detail now.

BRAINSTORMING

"Brainstorming" as an idea-generation process has its roots in the mid-twentieth century and is the work of a man often referred to as the real Don Draper, advertising executive Alex Osborn.[9] Although Osborn's intended audience was creative professionals in marketing and advertising fields, his basic principles and techniques have since been applied to any situation that could benefit from a group's creative input. Brainstorming is a fundamental step in the design thinking process, namely, its ideation phase. And as design thinking has found increasing application in business settings, so has brainstorming.

In a well-run brainstorming session, a carefully formulated question is posed to a group, whose members are then given the opportunity to freely come up with as many potential answers as possible. The guidelines of brainstorming are deceptively simple: withhold judgment and opt for quantity over quality so that each participant's imagination is provided the maximum free rein to generate ideas. That enables the most imaginative ideas to have a chance to be brought into the light rather than suppressed by a conscious or subconscious fear of judgment or ridicule.

Yet, the typical brainstorming session will leave many entrepreneurs unsatisfied. In the business world, especially the startup world, we have a strong bias toward action. We firmly believe that effective execution demands that we prioritize ruthlessly and say no to many great ideas. In fact, many entrepreneurs feel they are drowning in the sheer amount of ideas they have. What they seem to need more than anything else is clarity on which idea to tackle next rather than have even more ideas piled on them. Furthermore, some may ask, why is brainstorming in a group setting better than focused ideation on one's own? After all, isn't there a risk that group dynamics can take over and significantly impact the quality of the ideas generated? As a result of such concerns there are those (including business school professors and innovation executives) who have recently expressed skepticism about the real benefits of group brainstorming, some going as far as calling it a "waste of time."[10]

But those critics are throwing out the brainstorming baby with its bathwater. I agree that we can't apply the same tools used for coming up with a new advertising campaign to coming up with a new business strategy. Context, constraints, and even personalities involved are quite different. But the right solution consists of modifying and refining the brainstorming process to fit these realities rather than give up on it completely. Creating a business strategy requires an approach that enables the participants to *efficiently* generate a set of *actionable* ideas, and to do so in a manner conducive to generating *alignment* and *ownership* around those ideas.

My preferred approach to group brainstorming can achieve all of these objectives—efficiency, actionability, alignment, and ownership—with flying colors. This approach takes only an hour and consists of the following four parts:

Part 1: Definition. Define and clarify the objective of the exercise (about 5 minutes)

Part 2: Ideation. Generate as many ideas as possible (about 20 minutes)

Part 3: Framing. Map the ideas against varying criteria (about 20 minutes)

Part 4: Ranking. Rank the ideas by participant votes (about 15 minutes)

Let's go over each part in more detail so you can incorporate and apply them to any strategy session you lead or participate in, including the two I suggested to include (as a minimum) in your agenda.

Part 1: Definition

The right question leads to the right answer, whereas poorly defined questions lead everyone astray. Therefore, at the start of each session, make sure that all participants have a clear understanding of the objective of the meeting and the question they are tackling, paying particular attention to (a) whose perspective(s) they should take into consideration (e.g., employees, shareholders, customers, partners, regulators, competitors), (b) constraints on the universe of possible answers (e.g., time, funding, resources, regulatory environment), and (c) clarity of definitions, avoiding ambiguous words and unpacking loaded concepts as much as possible. For instance, I once led a brainstorming session for a startup on ways to improve the team's morale given a recent spike in complaints regarding burnout. We could have started by asking, "What can we do to improve morale and reduce burnout?" Undoubtedly, that would have resulted in quite a broad spectrum of answers, including recommendations on various team building exercises around the world, extravagant holiday parties, improvements in compensation structure, promotion practices, and so on. But instead, we took a few minutes to step back and specify the clear objective of the exercise. After a couple of minutes of deliberation, we decided to ask the following question instead: "What can the senior leadership do over the next three months to reduce risk of burnout among employees, without any additional funding or headcount other than what has already been budgeted for?" With that clarifying and specific question, we quickly arrived at many actionable ideas, such as starting a new Slack channel for posts about vacation and outside-of-work activities to reinforce the importance of a balanced lifestyle, starting a training program for managers to enable them to better detect early signs of burnout, investigating resources provided by the company's health plan, and the like. This would not have been possible without clarity around the initial question.

Part 2: Ideation

The ideation exercise is what the uninitiated typically consider to be the entirety of "brainstorming." But as you know by now, it is a part of a larger process. During this part, each and every participant should be given the opportunity to come up with as many answers to the question at hand as possible. To give each participant maximum freedom of thought, my recommended approach is to have all participants jot down their ideas on sticky notes silently. This way, you minimize the risk of distraction and influence by others. Using sticky notes naturally forces the answers to be concise. And by giving the people in the room more time than may initially seem sufficient, you allow participants to reach beyond what comes to mind initially and dig into the more creative recesses of their brain. Typically, the best ideas surface only after the obvious ones have been cleared out of their way.

Part 3: Framing

During this part, you will provide participants with various frameworks against which to map all of the ideas generated so far. While in the ideation exercise you tapped into the divergent, free-flowing, and imaginative thinking of the group, you are now directing them toward greater focus, analysis, and convergent thinking. One simple way to achieve this is to draw on the whiteboard one or more coordinates representing various evaluation criteria and have participants place their sticky notes accordingly on those coordinates. For example, if you are brainstorming about what product you should launch next, you could have one set of coordinates represent *effort* versus *impact*, another set represent *current capabilities* versus *product adjacency*, and yet another represent *execution risk* versus *upside potential*. You will, as a group, decide which of these sets of criteria to use or whether another permutation may be better suited to your ultimate objective. Of course, you would be even more efficient during this exercise if you have gathered some input on these criteria before the meeting so that most of the allocated time is spent on mapping and discussing the ideas generated rather than debating the criteria. Furthermore, gathering some input before the meeting will also allow participants to get their respective teams involved and thereby incorporate an even wider diversity of voices into the meeting. Remember that the main point here is to enable the participants to gain an understanding of how various ideas stack up against different criteria.

Part 4: Ranking

Finally, with the benefit of having just mapped various ideas onto different frameworks, it is time for the participants to decide which ideas should be prioritized. Providing each participant a given number of points that they can allocate among the group's ideas is one way to accomplish this. You could, for instance, give each participant 10 points that they could either put all on just one idea or distribute among up to 10 ideas. Tallying all the points will provide the group with a clear picture of how they collectively rank the ideas, all things considered.

WRAPPING UP

At the conclusion of your offsite, remember to set aside enough time for a proper review and summary, which could take 30 minutes to an hour. You want to make sure that you have captured the highlights and action items from the offsite. Pay particular attention that you end the gathering on a positive note so that the participants leave with renewed purpose and energy for the strategic opportunities ahead.

While a productive offsite is a wonderful achievement, do not be satisfied with just that. Of course, you should recognize and celebrate that success, but also channel that positive energy to build excitement for executing the next steps. The offsite is not an end in itself but just the kickoff for what is to unfold over the course of your startup's life. So don't give yourself the passing grade yet. How you and the team execute on the tasks ahead will determine whether the offsite was worth the collective time, money, and effort.

As you and your team deliberate about the actionable next steps, at a minimum include the following among the tasks ahead:

1. **Create an exit plan.** Draft a document that captures the most important aspects of your exit strategy (the next chapter is dedicated to this).

2. **Create a communication plan.** This is a list of individuals to be informed about the output and insights of the offsite (e.g., board members, key shareholders, employees, advisors) and the method of communication (e.g., board meeting, email, one-on-one sessions).

3. **Further research.** Assign team members to seek answers to questions that came up during the offsite, and share the results with the attendees.

Each action item needs to be assigned to at least one individual, with a clear timeline and deliverable. As the father of modern management Peter Drucker has warned generations of executives, "No decision has been made unless carrying it out in specific steps has become someone's work assignment and responsibility. Until then, there are only good intentions."[11] Meetings and plans are powerful generators of good intentions. Your duty as a leader is to make sure you transform those *good intentions* into specific action items.

For the purposes of creating your exit strategy, the most important action item following the offsite is to create the first draft of an exit plan. The ideal exit plan takes as input the discussions and insights generated in the offsite and frames them in a format that clearly communicates the contours of the exit strategy for your startup. The next chapter shows you exactly how to do that.

CHAPTER 6

STEP 2: DOCUMENT

If it is not written down, it does not exist.
—Philippe Kruchten[1]

Often, important insights and action items from productive meetings don't get implemented, not because there was a lack of alignment or enthusiasm, but because no one bothered to write them down. Most meetings, in my personal experience, are quite *productive*, but whether or not they are *effective* is a function of how organized we were in capturing the notes of the meeting.

By the end of your exit strategy offsite, you and team will have arrived at a general shared understanding of what an exit could (and should) look like. Now you need to memorialize that understanding as the first draft of your exit plan. By this time, you are likely drowning in a sea of information, including many pages of notes, slide decks, and supplementary data that were referenced during the offsite and/or circulated for prereading. Synthesizing all of that information into a coherent, readily digestible format is of critical importance and should be your next step.

Just as it is the case with creating a business plan, your goal with an exit plan is to communicate a complex set of concepts and strategies in an intuitive and simple format without losing the important stuff. What you need to accomplish is akin to saving a high-resolution picture in a much lower-resolution format that takes less space but still looks decent. The intended audience for this lower-resolution exit plan is not only the participating team members who will need to have a quick and handy common reference frame in the months and years ahead, but also other team members and stakeholders who did not attend the meeting, such as current or future board members and key employees, as well as advisors, who will need to be brought along and up to speed in your thinking around the exit strategy.

THE EXIT STRATEGY CANVAS

In order to capture and share the critical information regarding your exit plan in an organized and easy-to-reference format, I recommend an approach like the one used by the increasingly popular Business Model Canvas (BMC). The BMC is a lean startup template the building blocks of which were first proposed by Alexander Osterwalder in 2005[2] and beautifully illustrated in the crowd-sourced *Business Model Generation* handbook, published in 2010.[3] It is a one-page visual document intended to establish a "shared language for describing, visualizing, assessing, and changing business models."[4] It depicts in a simple, yet highly informative visual layout the nine essential building blocks of a business model: customer segments, value propositions, channels, customer relationships, revenue streams, key resources, key activities, key partnerships, and cost structure. The BMC "canvas" was originally intended to be printed out on a large page (or diagrammed on a whiteboard), so that a team can collaborate on filling it out. Increasingly, however, I have seen the BMC utilized less as a collaboration tool and more as a communication framework for new initiatives, be it a new product launch within a larger company or a new startup idea within an incubator.

Which brings us to what I call the Exit Strategy Canvas (ESC) as a template for your exit plan. The main goal of the ESC is to document the essential building blocks of your exit strategy and create a shared language for communicating and iterating on your exit plan. Similar to the BMC, I recommend that you lay out the ESC on one page only, an artificial but nonetheless extremely useful constraint to force everyone to focus on what is absolutely critical and essential.

I recommend that you include the following essential building blocks in your ESC (each of which I will discuss in further detail in the remainder of this chapter):

1. **Success definition.** What would a successful exit look like?
2. **Core hypotheses.** What do you have to believe to be true for a successful exit to happen?
3. **Strategic opportunities.** What are key areas for value creation through partnerships?
4. **Key acquirers.** Who are the potential acquirers, and what are the selection criteria?
5. **Risks and challenges.** What can jeopardize a successful sale to an acquirer?
6. **Key mitigants.** What can you do to improve your chances of a successful sale?

Before you start the documentation process, take a step back and consider the way these building blocks are interrelated. First, as the ordering above may have led you to notice, they build on one another. Your *definition of success* comes first, as it frames the entire conversation. How you define success then enables you to identify your *core hypotheses* and underlying assumptions, tap areas where *strategic opportunities* exist, and illuminate the criteria by which you select potential *key acquirers*. Your list of assumptions, opportunities, and acquirers will in turn lead to a set of *risks and challenges* on your exit path, which will have their respective set of *key mitigants* you will need to implement to achieve a successful outcome.

Success Definition

How you and your team define a successful exit for your startup is the most important insight to be captured from the offsite. That is because the entire exit strategy is worthless unless it is crystal clear to all involved what specific outcome an exit is intended to achieve. Once everyone understands the destination, then they can support the journey. This approach of "working backward" from a goal is similar to the one famously used by Amazon product development teams where they create an internal press release before starting a new product initiative. This internal document is intended to tease out and highlight at the start what is truly compelling about an initiative.

Similarly, you will want to capture what you and team members consider to be the compelling outcome of an acquisition for your startup and its stakeholders. Yes, the size of the acquisition and price tag will be a factor here. But, as your brainstorming session on this topic will undoubtedly have revealed, there are many other factors that come into play, such as how an acquisition can help your startup achieve its true mission or the impact it would have on employees and/or customers. Despite the fact that most press headlines mentioning acquisitions tend to focus on the valuation, for most entrepreneurs achieving a certain exit valuation is just one among a handful of other very important objectives that a successful exit would make possible.

As discussed in Chapter 2, for many entrepreneurs, a successful exit is one that ensures the survival of their startup, with which they have formed a strong and deeply intimate personal connection over time. And this *survival* is all about the continuation of what lies at the heart of a startup's core values and what the founding team considers to be a part of their personal legacy. For mission-led entrepreneurs, a successful exit is one that takes their startup to the next level. That "next level" may consist of taking its products from a regional offering to the national or global level, creating new distribution channels, or enabling new features that can make it appealing to wholly new customer segments. The next level may also be about growth opportunities for the team or ways to ensure the longevity of current product for existing customers.

So, to work backward, think about the hypothetical press release of your successful exit. What will it say about who gains to benefit and how? Why would this transaction be considered a success? There are likely as many definitions of success for an exit as there are startups out there today. As you consider breathing life into your dream scenario, make sure your definition of success answers the following:

1. How would an exit best manifest the values of your startup?
2. How could an exit best promote the mission of your startup?
3. What would be the ideal time frame for an exit transaction?

Core Hypotheses

Continuing to work backward from the ultimate goal of a successful exit, the next task is to make explicit what you would have to believe to be true for that outcome to manifest. Explicitly stating your assumptions helps you and other team members to discuss and gain clarity about what are the necessary conditions for success, and use them to gauge your future progress.

So, it is necessary to put in writing (even if it may be painfully obvious to you) what will need to be true in order to achieve each of your objectives for success. There are some hypotheses that are common for all exit scenarios, such as *finding a suitable acquirer*, *surviving until the exit*, and *consummating a transaction based on mutually agreeable terms*. But other hypotheses will be highly specific to your definition of success. For example, if a successful exit for you would entail providing growth opportunities for your employees, then at the time of the acquisition you have to believe that *your employees have sufficient skills and expertise of value to an acquirer*. Thus, stating the hypothesis allows you and your team to reflect on whether this holds true for the current state of affairs, and if not, what you can do to make that a reality going forward.

As another example, consider that if a successful exit for you entails taking your product offering from a national to an international scale, then at the time of the acquisition you have to believe that *your product can be localized and made suitable for international audiences by the acquirer.* Making this hypothesis explicit sheds light on the need for your current offering to have both the technical localization capabilities as well as user experience attributes to be of use for international customers by the time of an exit.

It should be noted that your core hypotheses are not necessarily limited to outcomes that you can control. For instance, if continuing on your current mission post acquisition is part of your definition of a successful exit, then one of your core hypotheses should be that *you are acquired by a company who believes in your startup's mission.*

To adopt a more quantitative approach, especially if your definition of success has a valuation threshold, you need to investigate and make explicit what it would take to justify your valuation goal based on either other comparable transactions or public market valuation benchmarks. Your desired valuation will likely necessitate achieving a certain set of financial (e.g., revenues, margin, profitability profile, or unit economics) or user (e.g., customer size, growth rate) metrics. A specific valuation goal makes it much more efficient for you to screen and filter acquisition opportunities as they arise. One entrepreneur who recently sold his startup confided that he had a specific valuation threshold for his exit in mind (namely, 10x his prior exit valuation) and that once an acquirer put that number on the table, it was hard not to seriously pursue that exit path.

Strategic Opportunities

Opportunities create attraction between business partners. They are the reason new partnerships form and existing partnerships keep going. Remove opportunities from business discussions and you will see the conversation and relationship fade rapidly.

As acquisitions are the strongest form of a business partnership, strategic opportunities play a central role in every aspect of your exit strategy. In its simplest form, strategic opportunities are the key areas for value creation with your acquirer. They are the areas of complementarity between your strengths and those of the acquirer. As such, to identify areas of strategic opportunity you have to start with a good sense of the strengths and weaknesses of your startup. Then, you need to consider the strengths and weaknesses of potential acquirers and how your strengths can fill in the missing piece for their weaknesses and vice versa. This is what is referred to as "synergy" when companies talk about value creation in a merger.

Your task here is to build on what was discussed in the offsite and identify areas where a synergy with a strategic partner could exist. For instance, if you have a prohibitively high cost of customer acquisition that prevents you from profitably growing and acquiring new customers at scale, you would have a strategic opportunity to partner with a company that has already figured out a way to acquire those customers at scale profitably but is looking for additional products to sell to those customers. This was, for instance, core to many acquisitions I spearheaded at GoDaddy, where our strong brand recognition provided us with millions of new customers per year at a relatively low cost of acquisition. Think of companies in your ecosystem for whom you could fill a strategic need, such as adding revenue, adding profits, staving off a competitive threat, accelerating time to market for a product or service, or improving their market share.

As you enter into discussions with potential strategic partners, you will want to validate and revise your assumptions around areas of synergy and strategic opportunities and be on the lookout to uncover new areas to add to your list.

Key Acquirers

This is your wish list of potential acquirers, preferably prioritized in accordance with a set of criteria discussed at your offsite and brainstorming sessions. It will also serve as the list of potential strategic partners whom you will be building a business relationship with over the course of the coming months and years. Be as aspirational as possible. You are not looking for who could be an acquirer of your startup today; instead, you are looking for whom you would be thrilled to join forces with long-term.

Of course, it is neither necessary nor practical for you to list each and every individual company that could be a potential strategic fit for you. For most cases, you could simply state the category or type of company. For instance, for a startup serving small businesses, you could refer to "domain registrars," "website creation platforms," "e-commerce tool providers" as potential acquirers rather than listing every single individual company that is within those categories since there are hundreds.

I recommend that if your list is prioritized, you make explicit the criteria used to make the prioritization. Such criteria, for example, could include *strategic fit, customer fit, culture fit, financial means*, or other attributes of a potential acquirer you deem critical. Keep in mind that at this stage you and team are mostly relying on intuitions and educated guesses, so precision is not the objective. Rather, your goal is to provide directional guidance as to what are critically important criteria for assessing strategic partners and what the universe of those potential partners looks like.

Risks and Challenges

As we all know, hope is not a strategy. No strategy should be blind to risks and challenges that are in its path. So far, the components of the ESC discussed above were primarily focused on orienting you and your team to where you want to go, but we haven't discussed the landscape to be navigated on the journey there. Is it flat, uphill, or downhill? Would it be a straight or winding path? Will we need to have chains or other special wheels to traverse it? Will there be refueling stations along the way? When considering your exit path, there are in general three types of risks that most businesses have to contend with: execution risk, market risk, and competitive risk.

Execution Risk

Execution risk is a reflection of your core competencies, external relationships, reputation, and capitalization structure, all of which can make or break a successful exit. Weakness in your core competencies (such as an inability to manage the M&A process effectively, leadership gaps, lack of a scalable business model, insufficient ownership of IP, poor customer satisfaction or retention metrics, or deficiencies in your technology) can stop many acquirers in their tracks. That is why building a strong business is table stakes for a successful exit. Furthermore, without strong external relationships and a decent reputation, you may not even be able to get beyond an initial introductory interaction with the acquirers on your wish list. And an often-overlooked risk factor in selling one's startup is its capitalization structure: you increase your exit risk as you raise more money at higher valuations as well as when you grant voting rights to financial and strategic investors, as it reduces the founding team's control and increases the possibility for others to block a transaction. This is not to say that you should never raise money; instead, it's important that you understand the implication of those increasingly lofty valuations which at some point may render you "too expensive" for many acquirers. That is why, as I will discuss in detail in Part IV of this book, considering a sale before raising a new round of funding could be a smart decision for many entrepreneurs.

Market Risk

As those of us who have tried to sell a company during a market crash know, market risk is always around the corner, and changes in macroeconomic conditions can very much impact the appetite of potential acquirers without forewarning. Because market risk is always present, the more desperate you are to sell, the higher the impact of market risk will be on your startup, so it is ideal not to time a potential exit around a time when you think you will be running out of cash.

Competitive Risk

No matter how unique your startup's offering is, there is always competition in the market. And thus there exists the competitive risk that your ideal potential acquirers snatch up your competitor instead. The smaller the number of your ideal potential acquirers and the larger the number of your competition, the more competitive risk you face. Chances are that your competitors are working to build bridges and create strong relationships with the acquirers on your wish list as well. They may enter into exclusive relationships with them, or try to amplify the negatives about your business in the market to their advantage. They may also be working hard to close off (for instance, by exclusive deals or acquisitions) certain critical supply or distribution channels available to you to stifle your growth prospects and make you seem less appealing to potential buyers. Be sure to identify and list your largest competitive threats as an important strategic reminder for your organization.

Key Mitigants

In the final building block of ESC, for each risk and challenge you identify, call out a clear and specific set of mitigants. You may or may not currently have all the mitigants under control, but identifying what they are is the first step toward reaching alignment with your team on the necessity to work on them.

Mitigating *execution risks* and *competitive risks* will generally involve building the requisite capabilities and creating strong relationships with your potential acquirers. I will address these topics in detail in the next part of the book. The best way to mitigate against *market risks*, in my opinion, is to increase your operating runway so that you can live through short-term market fluctuations. And there are many paths to that destination, including reducing your burn rate, raising additional funding, and putting aside some "rainy day" funds for 18 to 24 months of runway, or stepping up your relationship building activities with strategic partners so that you have several viable potential acquirers when an exit is desirable.

Remember that the ESC is a tool intended to efficiently capture and communicate your exit plan. As you create your ESC, feel free to customize it to your own needs, modifying what is captured in each block or adding new blocks that you may find to be particularly well-suited for your startup's unique set of values, challenges, and opportunities.

CHAPTER 7

STEP 3: ITERATE

Reality never stands still very long.
—Peter Drucker[1]

The first draft of your exit plan serves as a blueprint for the journey ahead, marking your starting position, the final destination, and the contours of the terrain in between. But these are reflections of your collective thoughts at a given moment in time, corresponding to a set of knowns and unknowns, which start changing the moment you put the plan into writing. As such, your exit plan (and any other plan, for that matter) is a *dynamic* or *living* document that is subject to evolution and change as events unfold.

In light of the rapid changes inside and outside of your startup, you must stay vigilant in observing the changing conditions, testing your hypotheses, and reassessing your stated assumptions regularly. Once you have enough evidence that an assumption or hypothesis is no longer valid, then it is time to revise the plan. The same principle even applies to your definition of success. As your organizational mission and values evolve, they will have a direct impact on what you would consider to be a successful exit. Invite your leadership team to periodically review your exit strategy. The sooner you can course correct if needed, the better. Achievement of your goals is significantly impacted by the direction you choose:

the less time you take on detours, the higher your chances of arriving at your desired destination.

Often, the changes are small tweaks and mere refinements to what you already have. For instance, you may have to eliminate some potential acquirers or add others. Or you may identify a new risk factor or challenge. Even though each change may be small, the continued reflective improvement of the strategy over time makes it stronger and more actionable as it aligns closer with market realities and your evolving values. Sometimes the evidence you and your team obtain may necessitate a wholesale pivot of the strategy, in which case you would be well-advised to repeat the offsite exercise and the brainstorming sessions.

I also recommend having some tools to gauge your progress. To minimize the overhead, you should consider periodically (quarterly, or at least annually) distributing the ESC with a red/yellow/green traffic light assessment for each of its building blocks, with the three colors indicating your level of confidence in each set of assumptions. Invite your leadership to comment on your assessment and continue to reengage with the framework so that it stays top of mind.

There is a subtle yet powerful benefit to keeping the exit strategy continually top of mind. I have found that it makes a lot more "lucky coincidences" possible, such as the time I ran into a former executive of one of the top potential acquirers for one of my startups at a dinner party. This phenomenon, sometimes referred to as synchronicity or serendipity, has less to do with some mysterious cosmic force than it does with a core aspect of human psychology. As I am sure you have experienced, when you think about something (say, chess), you may suddenly notice that throughout the day the same word or related concepts have a way of coming up (for instance, you may notice Netflix's recommendation of *The Queen's Gambit* or hear a friend talk about having always wanted to learn how to play chess). The underlying psychological explanation for this seemingly nonrandom set of coincidences is that our perception of reality is highly selective, filtered by what we are looking for (sometimes referred to as *Suchbild*, German for a "search image").[2] Our attention is selective, and for good reason, as otherwise we would notice so many of the details in our everyday life that we couldn't function. Because of this, once we are primed for a specific question, task, word, or image, then our attention starts picking up that specific signal among all the other sensory data it receives.

Bringing this back to the world of M&A, your exit plan can perform that priming function for the attention of your team. As long as there are periodic reminders about it, you will start picking up on news, connections, opportunities, and threats relating to your potential exit without having to actively look for them. Ideally, any relevant new information, relationship, or insight should be captured, communicated, and incorporated into a revised plan as appropriate. This will perpetuate a virtuous cycle through which your exit plan keeps up with the evolving realities of the market and your startup's needs while continuing to stay in the awareness of your team, priming their attention to pick up the right signals as they continue along your startup's journey. Actively engaging in the exercises and activities of the next part of this book will further contribute to keeping your exit strategy in your team's conscious attention.

PART III

Playing the Long Game

CHAPTER 8

FOCUS ON MOMENTUM

Vision without action is a daydream.
—Japanese proverb[1]

D o you know what large, successful acquisitions such as Facebook's purchase of Instagram and WhatsApp, Google's purchase of YouTube, or Microsoft's purchase of LinkedIn all have in common? They are all *overnight successes years in the making*. The following chapters are focused on deconstructing the "years in the making" aspect—the *long game* that entrepreneurs play to get to that overnight success. The long game in M&A involves taking your exit strategy and implementing it deliberately and patiently, with a purposeful mindset and orientation.

The conventional approach to implementing a strategy is that you systematically proceed from the planning phase to the execution phase, starting by setting priorities, assigning roles and responsibilities, and then following them up with periodic check-ins against the stated goals in the plan. These steps are certainly important because they take your plan from a mere statement of "good intentions," per Peter Drucker,[2] to carrying it out in the real world. But if you try to implement your exit strategy that way, you will have forgotten all about it within a couple of quarters.

When it comes to long-term, multiyear strategy execution, you need a process that will breathe life into the implementation of your strategy and sustain its relevance over time. It's already challenging enough to make progress against monthly, quarterly, and annual plans with all the daily fire drills. Thus, even when your core team comes out of the exit strategy offsite highly inspired, pumped up, and motivated to get stuff done right away, it is not trivial to sustain that energy and motivation for months and years ahead. I have yet to meet a fellow mortal who has been able to stick to a New Year's resolution (be it a new exercise routine, diet, or reading list) for more than a few months. By the time summer comes around, most New Year's resolutions have already taken their vacation.

To effectively implement a long-term plan, we need to approach its execution differently than shorter-term objectives like attaining certain product, marketing, or hiring goals. My recommended approach to long-term strategy execution is to focus on *building momentum*. Lacking momentum behind your strategy execution is like being on a highway without fuel in your tank: you may be on the quickest path to your destination, but sooner or later you find yourself stalled on the road while others zoom past you. Momentum is the fuel that keeps your long-term strategy moving forward. And without it, strategic activities become another set of dreaded chores.

One of the key features and benefits of momentum is that it builds slowly and gradually gains strength without requiring an all-out up-front effort. Focusing on momentum makes things actionable by allowing you to take smaller steps initially. As momentum builds, your job as the leader becomes more *steering* and less *pushing*. And once there is sufficient momentum behind any initiative, the strength of the initiative becomes as formidable as unstoppable ocean waves that have gained strength for many miles out at sea. Moreover, as you gain momentum, you enter a virtuously sustainable feedback loop: each step becomes a cause for celebration, which, once acknowledged, in turn motivates everyone and fuels additional action to feed the momentum.

What I find particularly appealing about focusing on momentum is that it orients your organization toward immediate action instead of the attainment of an intangible, lofty long-term goal. Recall that the purpose of creating your exit strategy was not to go out and sell the company right away, but to create a viable exit option that improves the chances of success and survival for your startup. Now that the planning phase is behind you, the mandate for you and your team is to use that plan as a guide to build momentum around creating viable exit options in the future. Your measure of success becomes whether each week you are a step closer to that ultimate goal compared to the previous week.

And the best way to gauge your progress is by incremental steps you take to strengthen your (a) *relationship* with potential acquirers, (b) *capabilities* to act on opportunities, and (c) *leverage*, which have been the core ingredients of all successful transactions I have been involved with. You need to cultivate a strong *relationship* with your ideal acquirers so that you are on their radar and perceived as one of their top targets when the timing is mutually right. You need to improve your execution *capabilities* by building an exit team that can skillfully navigate the courtship and handle the acquisition negotiations. And you need to boost your negotiation *leverage* to obtain the best possible terms should you decide to pursue a sale.

Attaining these goals will take years of purposeful and persistent effort to create the necessary business connections, cultivate those relationships, and build new organizational muscles. To do it well, your execution will need to become part of the DNA of your startup and part of the daily habits and rituals of your team.

In the following chapters, I will expand on each of these three long-term execution focus areas (relationships, execution capabilities, and leverage) and provide you with practical guidelines on how to build massive momentum in each area in small steps over time. Taking action, no matter how small, is the key to making progress. Just like you can't learn how to ride a bicycle from an instruction manual, knowing that something is important is quite different from making it part of your daily practice.

At my first startup, I failed to translate my intellectual appreciation for the importance of these areas into a sustainable action plan; instead, I prioritized putting out one near-term fire after another for several years, which ultimately resulted in the fire sale of that startup at the worst possible time in our recent economic history (as covered in more detail in the Introduction). My hope is that you can avoid such hard lessons and find out, as I subsequently did, that by focusing on gradual improvement in these areas, you will not only attain a better eventual outcome, but also find your entrepreneurial journey more enjoyable and rewarding.

CHAPTER 9

BUILD RELATIONSHIPS

Your network is your net worth.
—Porter Gale[1]

The most life-changing discovery I have made as an entrepreneur is the realization that meaningful business transactions only happen when the parties actually know and like each other. That is because companies don't do deals, people do. This seemingly trivial detail somehow was never taught or discussed in any of my undergraduate economics courses at Stanford or business and contract law courses at Yale Law School. Prior to this realization, I rather naively believed that business deals were made when the parties evaluated the pros and cons of the business relationship and then made a purely objective, rational decision to proceed when the pros outweighed the cons. The cold and compelling logic of the cost-benefit calculus was all that I thought did, and should, matter.

But once it actually became part of my day job as an entrepreneur to build business relationships, I started noticing how much personal relationships influenced the business outcomes. As anthropologists had long before figured out, human beings are social animals, regardless of job title or location. We gravitate toward our friends and tend to avoid dealing with strangers. To be clear, by this I am not referring to forms of nepotism or any kind of personal favoritism in business dealings. Instead, what I have found is that genuine personal connections bring about trust, confidence, and credibility, which are the attractants and the glue in a healthy business relationship. Conversely, we tend to have a much higher degree of skepticism and risk aversion when interacting with those we don't really know.

Think about how most of us react to emails in our inbox: imagine you get the same exact email requesting a meeting to discuss a new business opportunity from someone you know and trust versus someone you have never heard of. Which one do you take more seriously? Similarly, potential deals with strangers become delayed or deprioritized, while those with known parties get on the faster track to review and approval. This social bias becomes more pronounced as the size of the transaction and stakes become larger, since higher stakes amplify the need for trust, confidence, and credibility between the parties.

Appreciating the role of our social bias is particularly important in the M&A world as acquisitions tend to be among the highest-stakes business transactions that anyone enters into. Even for Doug McMillon, the president and CEO of Walmart (the largest company by revenue in the world), acquisition decisions are among the most "truly difficult" decisions he has to make, regardless of the size of the target.[2] Reflecting on the gravity of his responsibilities as an acquirer in Walmart's acquisitions of Jet.com, Bonobos, and Flipkart in an interview with Tim Ferriss, Doug admitted that he and his team "fret over" how to make those transactions a success, and that M&A is an area where he has "a lot of self-doubt."

A decision to acquire a company results from extensive evaluation and involvement from multiple stakeholders on the acquirer side, even if the size of the transaction is relatively small compared to the size of the acquirer. At a minimum, you will have a leader from a business unit sponsoring the transaction, who will need to obtain the requisite buy-in and participation cross functionally, including technology/engineering, security, accounting, finance, legal, HR, and PR teams. And in most cases, the bulk of the heavy lifting for the acquirer really starts once the deal has been signed and the cash has been wired: months or even years go into ensuring that an acquired company and team is integrated effectively into the acquirer and the business case for doing the transaction gets properly implemented.

Given the highly sensitive and costly nature of acquisitions, the teams involved in advocating for an acquisition understandably set a high bar for the level of conviction needed in the integrity, transparency, and competence of the target teams they evaluate. An acquisition seldom happens without the parties having had an extensive period of courtship that builds familiarity and trust between them. In the overwhelming majority of acquisitions that I have been involved with on the buyer or seller side, the acquirers have had at least one year of prior familiarity with the target leadership before signing the merger agreement. Sometimes this familiarity comes from a strong partnership or previous working relationships, as evidenced for instance by how much Google and Cisco love buying startups founded by former employees.[3] At other times, such familiarity arises from a regular cadence of communication between the parties.

A classic example of this phenomenon is how Adobe and Behance grew fond of one another. When Adobe acquired Behance in December 2012, they had already been working with each other as partners for four years.[4] Similarly, reflecting on the acquisition of Menlo Ventures' portfolio company, Scout RFP by Workday for $540 million, partner Houman Haghighi shared that the acquisition was "a great example of how important it is for founders to get to know corporates and work towards partnerships and customer engagements that lead to 'AHA! moments.' Corporates like to get to know their targets at various milestones as they go through their thought process of buy vs. built vs. partner."[5] And most other acquisitions are no exception.

Building meaningful business relationships is not hard, but they take consistent effort to establish and nurture. Just as you cannot artificially accelerate a personal friendship and cram four years of goodwill into a lunch meeting, you cannot manufacture a business relationship overnight. Both need time to take root and flourish. One study found that it takes at least 50 hours with someone to create a casual friendship and almost twice as much to attain the official "friendship" status.[6] Of course, the takeaway here is not that you should spend 50 to 100 hours with each decision maker at a potential acquirer, but that you should plan on earmarking a significant amount of your time as an entrepreneur on building and nurturing genuine business relationships within your ecosystem.

I know the last thing you want is yet another item on your ever-growing to-do list. But this is what it takes if you are serious about a successful exit and a meaningful contingency plan for the survival of your startup. To help you get started on this path, I recommend the following four-step approach to building relationships:

Step 1: Adopt the networker mindset.

Step 2: Grow your network of contacts.

Step 3: Harvest your contacts to create alliances.

Step 4: Cultivate champions among your allies.

STEP 1: ADOPT THE NETWORKER MINDSET

Often how we perceive an act influences our desire to engage in it. Fashion and cultural trends, such as our current relative societal dislike of smoking versus love of wine drinking (both arguably equally harmful to our health), are good examples of how our below-the-radar perception influences our daily actions. I was always averse to "business networking" until I became aware not only of its tremendous benefits, but also its compatibility with my worldview and aspirations. I couldn't bring myself to engage in any meaningful act of networking until I changed my mindset and embraced relationship building as part of my identity. Once you adopt a mindset that truly appreciates both the intrinsic benefits and the utility of building genuine human connections, what I refer to here as the "networker mindset," you will be able to tap into the tremendous potential that your network of personal and business relationships has in store for you.

As numerous studies have shown, our network of relationships determines the extent of our success, health, and happiness in life.[7] For most of us, this should not be a surprise as our most connected friends tend to also be the ones thriving in life. Personally, the biggest part of any success I have had in life and business I attribute to my network of friends and acquaintances. Throughout my working life, my network of contacts has helped me get the right mentorship, unlock important business relationships, raise money for my startups, and join incredible teams. Despite my academic credentials, except for my first job out of law school, every position I have held for the past 20 years has come about through an introduction by someone who knew me. The only part of any success that I can really take credit for is the active creation and nurturing of those connections over time. And even for that, much credit goes to a wonderful set of role models I have had the fortune to know and learn from, including my partner in life who has an incredible ability to stay in touch with friends and relatives no matter what time zone they may be in.

A New Perspective

As I suspect is the case for many, I am not what you would consider a natural-born networker. I am a bona fide introvert. Social interactions, even phone conversations, physically deplete my energy. Also, as mentioned above, I used to have an adverse reaction to the whole concept of "business networking." Since only deep, meaningful relationships matter, my logic was, I should focus on deepening the friendships I have instead of chasing after the ones I don't. The whole enterprise of "business networking" reeked of insincere opportunism. So, I deliberately limited my social activities to only a handful of "authentic" friends and didn't take a proactive role in pursuing new relationships or connections.

I needed a serious attitude adjustment when I started working as an associate at a venture capital firm in the early 2000s. In order to do my job, which consisted of sourcing new investment opportunities and conducting diligence on various potential new investments, I had to reach out far beyond my existing, very limited personal contacts and actually meet new people. Once I started to peek beyond my immediate direct connections, I was pleasantly surprised by how beneficial networking could be: each new contact had the potential to unlock opportunities and accelerate my learning about new domains. After a couple of years, I felt more serendipity and lucky coincidences in my life, from meeting the perfect potential cofounders, employees, investors, and advisors for the startups I had invested in to finding the right expertise to help with diligence on new businesses we were evaluating.

Although I began to appreciate the utility of networking, I still viewed it through a transactional, self-centered lens; as a means to an end, and not as an end in itself. My real conversion came gradually over the course of the subsequent few years as I got to know and work with a number of remarkable individuals such as the highly sought-after early-stage investor Pejman Nozad, whose genuinely selfless ability to build strong human connections not only has changed my life, but those of many others. As I began to internalize the networker mindset, I grew more and more attuned to the realization that many of the most influential and impactful investors and entrepreneurs in the world also tend to exhibit that mindset and are some of the friendliest and most approachable human beings one would have the pleasure to meet.

In his insightful bestseller *Give and Take*,[8] organizational psychologist and Wharton professor Adam Grant provides a compelling argument for how being a "giver," someone who genuinely helps others without a quid-pro-quo expectation, is the optimal path toward long-term success in business. Those who are "givers" (as opposed to "takers" and those who expect "reciprocity" in interactions), he argues, build goodwill into their network and create a support ecosystem that will help and elevate them for a lifetime. And I agree. But there is a catch-22 here. By definition, you cannot be a true *giver* if you are only behaving as a giver in order to gain some benefit in the future; that would put you in the *reciprocity* camp. To be a genuine giver, you would have to do so out of a purer, other-regarding intention without expectation of a personal gain.

What I have observed in my interactions with numerous givers such as Pejman Nozad is that the giver behavior is a by-product of what is even more important and primary for these individuals. And that is their deep appreciation and care for human connections, their openness to new friendships, or in short, their networker mindset. These individuals seek out relationships without any transactional expectation: to them, being a giver is just a part of their personality, a mindset that helps them nurture and strengthen those relationships, rather than a calculated strategy.

However, being a giver is not enough in and of itself to get you closer to your goals and aspirations. You need to have a sufficiently large network of contacts before that network can work its magic. As disappointing as it may sound, the likelihood that any one individual can meaningfully change the trajectory of your life is low. But the potential power of any network grows exponentially with the number of nodes in it (a mathematical reality commonly known as Metcalfe's Law). So, a giver who can count his or her contacts on two hands would not benefit nearly as much from that network compared with someone with a few more connections.

What a casual observer might call "luck" in business actually comes about as the by-product of one's contacts and friendships. This is because the range of opportunities we are exposed to in life is largely shaped by our human connections. Investor, entrepreneur, and author Ben Casnocha eloquently summarized this truth when he noted "Opportunities do not float like clouds in the sky. They're attached to people."[9] As such, networking is at the heart of building any viable startup, which for its founders becomes the nexus of their personal relationships, determining whom they bring onboard as their key employees, advisors, and investors as well as the range of business opportunities that their startups have a real shot at pursuing, including strategic relationships with potential acquirers.

So, adopt the networker mindset today and set out to grow your network. Whoever claims that entrepreneurship is a lonely game is not going about it the right way.

STEP 2: GROW YOUR NETWORK OF CONTACTS

While networking doesn't come easy to most of us, it is nonetheless a skill that can easily be learned. The more you practice, the sooner it will become a habit.

Growing your network demands a fair amount of courage and persistence. But most important, it requires that you remember to prioritize relationship building in all daily interactions. Evaluate how you show up in discussions with customers, vendors, suppliers, and partners and adjust your approach as necessary to create a human connection in addition to a business relationship. Every time you interact with someone, ask yourself whether you are doing your part to strengthen your personal connection. Are you learning about the people you are interacting with? Have you provided them with a glimpse of who you are as an individual beyond your title and role at your startup? It is one thing for people to know me as an investor or executive at a certain company, but it is a completely a different thing for them to learn that I am a father of two young daughters, that I live in the Bay Area close to Stanford University campus because I fell in love with this place as an undergrad, or that I think some of the most underrated philosophers of our time are comedians Jerry Seinfeld, Ricky Gervais, and Steve Martin. Those details create real human connections that are more likely to transcend beyond, and be remembered after, the details of any business transaction.

Challenge yourself to seize on every opportunity to make a genuine personal connection. Follow this guidance especially when you sense you are heading toward a conflict with someone as an effective tool to de-escalate the situation. Long before our world became so hyperconnected and networked, I remember my father's advice that *while you can't have too many friends, one enemy is one too many.*

I found it easiest to start practicing my networking skills by trying to establish a more personal connection to people I routinely come in contact with, such as the cashier or barista at the local coffee shop. Connecting and building relationships is not complicated, although the sheer volume of existing books, talks, seminars, and podcasts on this topic can leave many with the impression that networking is a much more complex undertaking than it really is. If you are still skeptical, give it a shot anyway and you may be surprised to find that you are much better at it than you give yourself credit for. At the very least, take comfort in the fact that as a member of our species, hundreds of thousands of years of evolution have prepared you quite well for this.

Once you get some practice creating new personal connections, you will be ready to start business networking. You get the best results here with a systematic approach and by setting specific goals and milestones that you can hold yourself accountable to. At this stage, your primary objective is to increase the sheer number of your business connections. Once you have a sufficiently large network, you can harvest it for specific purposes, such as getting introduced to potential strategic partners or acquirers, which I will further describe below. But for now, focus on expanding the number of your business contacts. Think of your network as a set of concentric circles, with the innermost circle being your immediate family and friends, and the farther away you get from the center, the weaker the connections become, with complete strangers with whom you have no common bond being in the area outside of these circles. What you want to accomplish is to grow the size of each of these concentric circles by bringing people from the periphery into at least one of the inner circles.

Activate Your Hidden Network

Most of us have a powerful social network, but it is hidden in plain sight. We don't realize the vast network of relationships we are a part of—family, friends, neighborhood, alumni network, affinity groups (including sports, hobbies, and interest groups), and so on. Reach out to those contacts, starting with the strongest connections in the center of your network, and check in with them. Increase your visibility to your network by becoming more proactive in your outreach and providing your contacts with updates on what you are doing and whom you are trying to meet (e.g., engineers, designers, or people in a certain industry or profession). When done judiciously and tastefully, social media posts, blogs, and even email campaigns can be effective in establishing a regular rhythm and elevate your visibility and profile within your network.

Broaden Your Network

As you start attracting new connections, go broad before you go deep. Cast a wide net initially and focus on establishing as many connections as possible rather than focusing too early on a specific group. Remember that you can't always predict who can be of help to you or ultimately connect you with the perfect strategic business partner or potential acquirer, so be an equal-opportunity networker. Stay open to building new connections and don't filter out connection requests or meeting invites too quickly. If you suspect someone is genuinely interested in establishing a connection with you, return the favor. Continue practicing your relationship-building skills by reaching out and pursuing connections with as broad an audience as possible.

If you are an introvert like me, you may want to take smaller steps initially and develop your networking momentum gradually. Start by setting some modest weekly goals, such as attending at least one conference, meetup, or networking event per week (virtually or in person). The Covid-19 pandemic accelerated the creation of virtual communities, including Clubhouse rooms, Slack channels, or Discord servers related to specific topics or affinity groups, so take advantage and participate in those communities and contribute to discussions where you can. Once you meet new contacts (either in person or online), follow up with them to reinforce the connection and build on that nascent relationship. You may consider sending a follow-up email to highlight your takeaways from the meeting and reiterate the reason for your interest in staying in touch. For me, those emails serve as a searchable database of whom I have met on different topics and the perfect context for reconnecting in the future. If you don't have time to send a detailed message, at least reach out to your new contacts with a LinkedIn connection request and add a personal note referring to how you met that person. You can be easily forgotten otherwise. Note that your outreach does not only help you get a step closer to potential acquirers, it can also be extremely beneficial to your business as every new contact can lead you to new customers, investors, advisors, employees, or business partners.

Get to know your startup's industry and the ecosystem in which it operates and attend conferences and events related to it as well. One of the secrets of savvy entrepreneurs is that they remain socially active, using every opportunity to evangelize their cause, gather information, refine their approach, and make new connections. These interactions will help deepen your perspective of your own industry. For my first startup, Jaxtr, that is how I learned the nuances of the telecommunications industry: I went to as many venture capital and telecom events as I could and set up meetings at local coffee shops with founders and investors, most of those early days spending more time outside the office than inside it.

Sometimes you don't even have to attend a physical or virtual event to get some networking benefit from it. On many occasions as recently as this year, whenever I have been unable to attend an event, I have instead sent a note to a particular presenter or participant that I missed the opportunity to meet, explaining the situation and expressing how much I would appreciate the chance to connect with them in the future. I have typically received positive responses to this kind of outreach, with many of those connections evolving into business and personal friendships over time.

Don't let your initial reluctance or anxiety about networking hold you back from participating in industry events. Be excited for this enviable opportunity to meet some of the greatest minds of our time (or any time), at a critical inflection point in history. The bonds you create in this community can literally change the course of history. I have found that reminding myself of this incredible privilege is an antidote to lethargy or fear of rejection.

Gamify It

I know based on personal experience that networking can be psychologically intimidating, and you may find yourself standing in a corner nursing a drink while everyone else seems to easily huddle around excited conversations that you can't find an appropriate way to break into. One trick I have found helpful for summoning up the courage to approach complete strangers is to gamify things for myself and create a personal challenge. For example, early on in my career as a VC, a wise senior colleague used to challenge me to see who would collect the most business cards by the end of the night. That was enough motivation for me to walk up to total strangers, introduce myself, and strike up a conversation, at the end of which I would excitedly hand them my business card (fully expecting they would return the favor and thereby add one point to my score). I was surprised at my own ability to work a room and "trick" unsuspecting bystanders into giving me their business cards. And that gamification turned what could have been a boring evening into a fun and productive night of networking.

Use what motivates you to push beyond your comfort zone in social settings. When I started at Webs in the late 2000s, I realized that one of our biggest problems was our relatively low profile in Silicon Valley, most likely due to the fact that Webs was based out of Silver Spring, Maryland, and backed by East Coast venture funds. We were hardly covered by the press and were nowhere on the radar of any top-tier Silicon Valley investors or potential acquirers despite the fact that we were a fast-growing internet startup with over 30 million websites built on our platform. To change things, I set myself a quarterly quota for the number of Silicon Valley leaders I would personally tell our story to. To meet that quota, I consistently signed up for events I thought influencers and leaders of our industry would participate in–including the twenty-fifth anniversary celebration of .com in Spring of 2010 at San Francisco City Hall, hosted by Verisign.

This exclusive gala was going to be one of the highest-profile technology events of the year, emceed by actor and comedian Dana Carvey (of *Wayne's World* fame). I knew I had to attend this event, which would not only set me way ahead on my self-imposed quota, but also give me the chance to see one of the comedic idols of my youth perform live. But there were no tickets available, and of course, no one from Webs was invited to attend given that few people at Verisign had even heard of us. I knew that my only chance was to lean on my network. Fortunately, a friend happened to be a respected product manager at Verisign, and to my delight, she was able to work her magic and obtain a ticket for me. As it happens, a chance encounter at that event set in motion a series of events that completely changed many people's lives.

During dinner at that gala, by mere coincidence I took a seat next to Steven Aldrich, former VP of strategy and innovation, small business division at Intuit, the company high on our list of ideal potential strategic acquirers. Even more critically to us, while at Intuit Steven oversaw the acquisition of Webs' largest competitor, website creation platform Homestead. The Webs founding team and I could not have dreamed of a better mentor or advisor, and the fact that I was sitting next to him and his wife laughing at Dana Carvey was absolutely surreal. I made sure to keep in touch with Steven after the event and was overjoyed when he accepted my invitation to join our advisory board a few months later. Steven was instrumental in helping us refine our M&A strategy and provided us with a warm introduction to his former colleagues at Intuit, who were among the parties we entered into acquisition conversations with. With the benefit of Steven's guidance throughout the process we were able to close on the sale of Webs to Vistaprint in 2011 for $117 million after having raised only $11 million in venture capital, a financial outcome that transformed the lives of many of the members of the Webs family. And for me, that course of events also led to my being recruited to GoDaddy as a corporate development executive a few years thereafter by Steven himself, who had joined GoDaddy's leadership team on the heels of the acquisition of his own startup, Outright, by GoDaddy. Had I not pushed myself to actively engage in building up my network of contacts and attend that gala, it is unlikely that any of this would have transpired.

Offer to Help

You can't create a relationship with someone who doesn't remember you. And one of the best ways people will remember you is when you offer to help. Being helpful has other benefits for you too. It will move the conversation along more smoothly and boost your self-esteem. People you meet for the first time may naturally be suspicious about your ultimate motives and reluctant to open up. But by removing your self-interest from the consideration set, you pave the path toward a genuine connection, allowing them to put down their self-preserving shields. Further, the person you offer to help will likely remember you and be far more receptive to helping you at some point in the future.

As you build your network, not all connections will remain strong and many will go dormant. And yet, those dormant connections will continue to have tremendous power for you once they are reactivated. And that is where having been helpful previously makes a significant difference. According to professor Adam Grant, this is another benefit of adopting a giver mindset in your networking, "It's easiest to reconnect with dormant ties if you've been generous in the past. If you have a history of self-serving behavior, your old contacts are likely to lock the door to their networks and throw away the key—if they don't use the reconnection as a prime opportunity to punish you. If you've given to them without strings attached, on the other hand, they'll greet you with open arms."[10]

Here is that wonderful paradox about networking again: approaching new connections selflessly will better serve your interests in the long run versus doing so from a self-centered vantage point. Call it what you will (kindness, generosity of spirit, enlightened self-interest, altruism, or simply being a good member of a community), but make sure to consciously adopt a giving posture as a character trait.

Be Authentic

Ultimately, there is no one magic networking style that can work for everybody. Adopting a growth mindset[11] and having confidence in your ability to learn is a perfect starting point. Learn from others by seeking out mentors, coaches, and/or role models. And then practice. You need to summon the courage to experiment and find out what works for you. For the more analytic minded, try out different approaches and measure your success by both how comfortable you were in the approach as well as the number of new connections you were able to establish. For instance, I have experimented with whether attending events by myself or with someone else would make it easier for me to network (test winner: with someone else), whether I meet more people in smaller or larger conferences (test winner: smaller), and whether having a drink in my hand or having both hands free were more conducive to networking (test winner: drink in hand). The more relaxed and confident you feel, the more effective and efficient you will become. Stay curious and positive. Remember that each new connection gets you closer to unlocking tremendous opportunities for your startup.

STEP 3: HARVEST YOUR CONTACTS TO CREATE ALLIANCES

Strategic partners and allies are typically your ideal acquirers as they are the ones with the highest level of familiarity, confidence, and conviction to make a serious offer for your startup. Even outside of any acquisition considerations, developing strategic relationships is a critical business activity as business allies create tailwinds for your success and help combat the headwinds on your path. As your network grows, you will be able to better leverage it to create an ecosystem of alliances with potential strategic partners, that is, those companies that you and team put on the list of key acquirers on your Exit Strategy Canvas. If your network does not already include contacts with potential strategic partners, now is the time to proactively seek them out.

Business alliances are like wildflowers: they come in a variety of shapes and forms and can grow even in the most inhospitable climates given the right resources. Your (hopefully expanding) list of contacts are the seeds from which those alliances can one day germinate.

Some alliances may be loose and as simple as one company sharing market information with another without any larger contractual or commercial entanglement between them. Scott Belsky at Behance, for example, kept Autodesk, Adobe, and LinkedIn informed of the startup's progress for years up until the point of its acquisition by Adobe.[12] At GoDaddy, many startups provided various members of our corporate development team as well as relevant leaders across our business teams with a regular cadence of updates on their activities, making sure they were in our minds and sights for potential strategic opportunities.

Some alliances are formed around a shared specific objective, such as advocacy for a common social or regulatory cause or a shared adoption of a new technical standard. Business partnerships, such as a co-marketing initiatives, technology licensing, or a product distribution partnership constitute the more formal types of alliances. As you start connecting with potential allies, don't get too hung up on the exact form of the future alliance and try to create at least some lasting relationship with each company. Your immediate goal is to establish familiarity and open a communication channel.

Find Warm Introductions

Leverage your growing network of contacts to find ways of obtaining warm introductions to the right individuals at each potential key acquirer on your wish list. Warm introductions, although not absolutely necessary, are an order of magnitude more effective than cold, unsolicited inquiries. Of course, for a warm introduction to be effective, the person you are enlisting as an intermediary must know both you and your intended target fairly well. If you are asking for an introduction from someone with whom you exchanged business cards at a conference, I would not consider that a warm introduction. Further, if your intermediary does not have a solid relationship with your intended target, or worse, is disliked by them, you risk inheriting that negative attribution yourself if you seek an introduction by that intermediary. Make sure to inquire about and understand the strength of the relationship before seeking an introduction. I take no offense when people asking me for an introduction also make it clear that they only want the introduction if I feel I know the other person well enough to do so.

The ideal team members you want to connect with at your potential acquirers are usually the operating leadership members such as product managers, general managers, or senior executives.

If you start with someone in business development or corporate development teams, make sure they eventually loop in someone from the actual business unit. The problem with relying solely on transactional team members is that if there is no immediate deal to be had, you will likely be pushed to the bottom of their priorities and inevitably forgotten.

It is perfectly fine to approach two or three people at a larger company, especially if each of them works at a different business unit and may be interested in different aspects of working with you. Of course, you want to use your judgment and not flood (aka spam) an entire department or organization; word (both good and bad, but especially bad) does travel fast. All it takes to be viewed as a spammer is to annoy one person who would then forward your email to an internal distribution list.

Networking your way to getting that first meeting through a warm contact is the relatively easy part. The hard part is figuring out how to turn that initial meeting into an ongoing interaction. First impressions certainly are important, but only a repeated interaction with some semblance of a pulse has the promise of turning those contacts into true allies and internal champions for you and your startup.

Establish Familiarity

Effective business alliances cannot be forced or rushed; instead, they take time to gradually mature as the parties get to know each other and build mutual goodwill. So, make it your goal to become familiar *with*, and equally important, *to* your potential allies. In my experience with both personal and business relationships, familiarity breeds trust. The more I hear or interact with someone, even if it is a casual interaction such as exchange of pleasantries at an event or local coffee shop or even if it is receiving email updates or annual holiday greetings, the more I feel that I can trust that individual (as long as none of those interactions are negative, of course).

Social psychologists sometimes refer to our tribal tendency to favor those familiar to us as the proximity principle. This tendency is documented in several studies where it has been found that people who encounter each other more frequently (e.g., interact and live closer to each other) tend to develop stronger relationships.[13]

There is also a growing body of psychological research exploring evolutionary and neurologic forces underpinning our preference for anything that is familiar, validating what brand advertisers have been selling for centuries. Known brands sell more and have a lower cost of customer acquisition. In one revealing experiment, researchers placed an ad-like box containing some words from another language on the front page of several student newspapers for a few weeks. The frequency of the appearance of the words varied. When the campaign ended and the students were surveyed about the impression they had of the words, the results showed that the words appearing more frequently were rated much more favorably compared to the rest. This experiment has been confirmed by many subsequent studies containing other words, pictures, and even geometric shapes.[14]

Thus, to be perceived favorably by potential allies, you need to become familiar to them. Otherwise, you will either be ignored or face a high initial burden of proof when you approach them for an actual strategic partnership or acquisition discussion. And as litigators know all too well, whoever bears the burden of proof tends to lose in court. This is why establishing some cadence of repeated interaction with your potential allies is so critical. The sooner you start finding and connecting with the right individuals at those companies, the more chances you will have to build the foundations for a trusted business relationship.

When you approach a prospective ally, it is OK to state that you are looking to build a relationship and that your immediate goal is to let them know who you are, what your mission is, and what you have learned so far. Remain patient and cordial even if at first you don't immediately become the highest priority for the person you contact. Chances are, the person you reach out to would be interested in meeting you, too, but they just have way too much on their plate to make time for you immediately.

It took over a year between my first outreach to Vistaprint at Webs and the commencement of serious strategic discussions with them. Our initial message to them was that we wanted to compare notes and share learnings with regard to the small business space since we were both targeting that market. A simple, cordial, and nonthreatening note is all that you need. Don't create artificial deadlines. If there are real deadlines to highlight, communicate them as far in advance as possible. For instance, you don't want to be sending the following note, variants of which I have received too many times: "We are closing a financing round and have room for one more investor; we thought you would be perfect, but since we are closing next week, we need your answer preferably by this weekend." Or go to the other extreme and make it too vague or nondescript, such as "We are in the same space, so why not meet and see if we could do something"; or be presumptive about the other side's desire to meet immediately, such as "Would love to meet because of x, y, z. Is Monday or Tuesday at 4 p.m. better for you?"

The purpose of your first meeting should be mutual introductions and information sharing. But unless you find a mutually advantageous reason to continue an exchange, you can easily be forgotten. So, in your first meeting, pay particular attention to things that can be grounds for a continuing dialogue. Areas that are ripe for such an exchange are insights about customers (who they are, what they like, how various cohorts perform over time), product development (product launches, milestones achieved, road map), and industry evolution (market size, competitive landscape, regulatory changes).

Once you find such a reason, follow up with periodic check-ins and try to provide any unique insights, information, or data that could be of value. You will have to judge how much of the information is proprietary versus harmless if shared. Note that the more you signal to a potential ally that you don't trust their integrity, the more likely you will find those sentiments reciprocated.

Create Lasting Relationships

Often *how* you do something makes greater impact than *what* you do. This is especially true when you are trying to build a long-term relationship, in which case you have to make sure you embody the character traits of someone worthy of a long-term relationship. And in that regard, business relationships are quite similar to personal relationships where very few people welcome a long-term personal or working relationship with someone who is overconfident, dishonest, or secretive. In particular, I have found the following four character traits to be the hallmarks of great relationship builders: humility, integrity, transparency, and dependability.

Humility

From an acquirer's perspective, humility, or an awareness of one's own limits, is one of the most critical character traits in an entrepreneur because it ultimately determines how well that entrepreneur and his team can get along with, and be integrated into, the acquiring company's organization. Yet humility is a particularly hard trait for many entrepreneurs to exhibit. We are conditioned to believe that good entrepreneurs are supposed to project confidence to signal decisiveness and ability to lead.

While there is some evidence that a healthy dose of optimism and confidence is what leads many to found a startup,[15] economists and behavioral psychologists are increasingly finding that overconfidence (a) leads to psychological biases resulting in poor decision-making with sometimes disastrous consequences (such as the sinking of the *Titanic*, the nuclear accident at Chernobyl, the Deepwater Horizon oil spill, and the Great Recession,[16] to name a few) and (b) alienates potential friends and allies. In place of blind optimism and overconfidence, other character traits such as grit[17] (perseverance in the face of difficulty) and originality[18] (an ability to poke beyond the accepted assumptions) have gained recognition as superior contributors to entrepreneurial success, while humility and vulnerability have gained prominence as the character traits of truly effective relationship builders.[19]

Humility is an extremely powerful relationship building tool as it allays the fears of those with whom you aspire to build new business relationships and facilitates dialogue and information exchange with them. It changes the nature of the conversation in your favor, even though it may make you appear less knowledgeable and certain than you (or your ego) would have originally liked to appear. Always remember that your ultimate goal is not to impress those you meet, but to build a strong relationship with them over time.

Integrity

The role of integrity in the creation and maintenance of relationships cannot be overstated. Since trust is necessary for any strong business relationship, you need to establish that you can be trusted. And the best way to do that is through truthful, honest, and fair interactions with your counterparts. View all your interactions with a potential partner as auditions for your character. And the more you get to meet with your counterparts, the more chances you get to build your reputation. The most effective way to create a strong ally is to ensure that in each interaction, your behavior underscores your trustworthiness as a counterpart. Here are a few areas that will shine a light on your integrity:

1. Truthfulness in portrayal of the facts about your business (how it got started, funding, challenges, resources, etc.)
2. Treating confidential information of others as confidential
3. Fairness in any negotiation you may enter into
4. Willingness to give credit and accept responsibility in interactions
5. Honoring any verbal or written commitments

Integrity is not just about providing truthful answers to questions, but also about filling in the relevant gaps for your counterparts without them having to ask, providing "full disclosure" as lawyers call it. This is not because of a legal obligation, but because you want to abide by a code of conduct that will help you win over allies long before any legal document is ever drafted. Last but not least, integrity is at the core of your reputation as a member of the business community. Your reputation will ultimately determine your success. Take every opportunity to establish and safeguard your reputation as a high-integrity business partner.

Transparency

Master relationship builders have a disarming knack for transparency. I have observed how most experienced negotiators start a meeting by revealing something quite personal or confidential and by doing so turn a potentially hostile situation into a collaborative exchange of information. Just as with humility and integrity, incorporating transparency into your actions creates a congenial atmosphere conducive to better exchange of information and collaboration. Conversely, whenever you act secretively, you signal that you don't trust that your counterpart would act professionally and thus you create roadblocks in the creation of a respectful and trusting relationship.

When you are honest and transparent, you elicit similar behavior from your counterparts. In my experience, transparency is the ultimate truth serum and the most effective way of obtaining the inputs you need about your potential partner's goals, hopes, fears, and constraints. As associate professor Leslie K. John of Harvard Business School puts it, "Humans have a strong inclination to reciprocate disclosure: When someone shares sensitive information with us, our instinct is to match their transparency."[20]

Try to be the first to disclose and set the positive tone for how you expect the relationship to be. What you disclose will most likely also frame and steer the discussion in that direction.

Many new entrepreneurs that I meet tend to be unduly paranoid about confidentiality to the detriment of the relationship. In my first startup, I jeopardized the potential to build a unique relationship with Google because I would not sign their standard NDA. They eventually agreed to our edits to the NDA, but we lost

87

precious time in the back-and-forth discussions. What is worse is that our insistence on the changes signaled to our counterparts at Google that we didn't trust them and thus lost their sponsorship. Not surprisingly, within a year thereafter they decided to acquire one of our competitors without bothering to take a second look at us. If there is something that you absolutely cannot disclose, think of ways to signal that you still trust the other party and are willing to work with them.

Dependability

Business partners depend on one another. A critical obstacle larger companies face when evaluating partnerships with startups is the extent to which they can get comfortable that a given startup can be depended on to handle customer complaints, fix bugs, or reliably maintain a set of products and services. Also, larger companies worry about the dependability of scalability, security, and privacy practices of the startups they consider for partnership as a misstep can have severe negative financial and brand image repercussions on them. Just as you would not hire someone you don't consider dependable, if you are not deemed dependable by a potential strategic ally, you will also not be considered partner material by them.

Startups fortunate enough to have a track record of prior partnerships with other large organizations have an easier time checking the box on dependability. That is why it is so important to win those early reference partnerships and alliances. But if you don't have that track record, you face a classic chicken-and-egg problem: you can't win over a large strategic ally unless you have at least one other large strategic ally as a reference. To break out of that dilemma and get to that first major partnership, you need to ensure that there is absolutely no doubt about the dependability of you as a person and your organization as a whole. Here are some practical tips on how to achieve that.

Follow up. One of the easiest ways to establish dependability is to follow up on every meeting. It is astounding how few people actually take the time after a meeting to send a note of acknowledgment and a summary of what was decided. As I suspect to be the case for other business and corporate development professionals, my email archive is pretty much the repository of the history of every company I meet. Whenever I want to remember where we left things with a company, the first thing I do is search my email records. Knowing that, I usually send myself an email with my notes from a meeting so that I can easily search for and retrieve them later. And when a company that I meet with sends me a follow-up message with the meeting notes and action items, guess what happens? Their message frames the subsequent discussions and next steps for our engagement. This is the easiest way to follow up and keep the communication lines open. On the flip side, if you walk away from a meeting without that follow-up, you put yourself at the mercy of what your counterparts happen to remember or have jotted down during the meeting.

Add value. For extra credit, in each routine follow-up and check-in with a potential partner, make sure to add some incremental insight and value. I find it quite memorable whenever I receive a follow-up email from a potential partner that contains some additional nugget of insight. Such messages truly stand out and get forwarded around. But few folks actually put in the effort to do that. So before you send off that next email shouting, "Hey, have you forgotten about me?," take a few minutes and see what information you can add to that email so that it actually delivers some value to the recipient. Perhaps you have seen a new trend in the market or in usage of your product, or you have been surprised by a recent event. Any opportunity to add a unique insight in your interaction strengthens your credibility with your counterpart.

Follow through. Lastly, when you do agree to an action item in a meeting, make sure you take that action. It is not only common courtesy, but it also reflects poorly on you and the value you assign to a potential partnership when you drop the ball on a commitment, as minor, silly, or irrelevant to the partnership as it may seem. Perhaps it is an introduction to someone you mentioned during the meeting. Or it may be a certain set of metrics that you said you would share. Or perhaps it is to look up the name of a certain restaurant at a location you couldn't recall. No matter what it is, make sure you make good on your commitment. Even if the answer is "Sorry, but I couldn't locate that information," it is orders of magnitude better than not saying or doing anything and inviting your counterparts to doubt your dependability.

STEP 4: CULTIVATE CHAMPIONS AMONG YOUR ALLIES

As any skilled salesperson knows, to make a successful sale, we need a champion pulling for us on the other side.[21] In fact, we need a champion to succeed at pretty much anything important in business, even to get traction within our own organization on a promotion, new strategy, or new product. And as the mother of all sales, this wisdom applies equally well to an acquisition, where having the right champion can make or break a life-changing deal for you. Thus you need to sharpen your skills at identifying and cultivating champions.

"Without a champion you are toast," once reflected a former colleague and seasoned strategy and business development executive, Parthiv Sangani. And in his characteristically sage and measured way, he was being very polite. In my experience, the biggest problem you encounter without a champion is that you can waste months or even years on building a relationship that ultimately stalls for one reason or another. You may find out after many futile interactions that you are not as important to the partner as you were initially led to believe. Or you may discover that you were passed over for another company that did have the benefit of that strong internal advocate.

When a potential good deal doesn't materialize, you can be sure that there was a breakdown in the process somewhere. Most large organizations have more on their plate than they can handle, and it takes an experienced and motivated insider to effectively advocate and prioritize your project over others, convincing multiple stakeholders and overcoming their objections in the process. For instance, when dealing with larger organizations such as Google, Amazon, Microsoft, or Facebook with tens of thousands or even hundreds of thousands of employees, sometimes multiple business units may be interacting with a startup without much coordination or knowledge sharing between those business units. Creating internal alignment and pushing any major initiative through to the finish line with them takes real effort, visibility, and skill.

If you want to maximize your chances of engaging in meaningful acquisition discussions at some point, you need the right champion. You need an insider who is willing to pound the table and advocate for you. Moreover, you need a champion who, like an experienced Sherpa, would competently help you navigate the intricacies of the big company approval processes, rally the requisite resources, and address the myriad of concerns and challenges that will inevitably arise with respect to any significant project. A true champion is someone who is willing to put their job (or at least their bonus and reputational capital) at risk to advocate for your success. In this way, the survival of your company and your ultimate success as an entrepreneur could very well depend on finding and winning over that champion.

The process of finding and winning over a champion requires considerable investment of time and effort, so you need to be very selective. The higher a potential strategic partner is on your wish list of potential acquirers, the more important it is for you to have a champion there should you ever need to pivot the conversation into acquisition discussions. Furthermore, I would not recommend trying to find a champion at a company with which you have not yet established an alliance and actual relationship. You need to have a working familiarity with an organization before you can identify and recruit the right champion there.

Identifying the Right Champion

You need to approach "recruiting" the right champion with the same degree of care and rigor you give to recruiting a senior executive. In fact, just as is the case with your executive recruiting, there is a set of key attributes that would qualify someone as the right champion for you.

As you review the qualifications discussed below, it should become clear why not every insider who is excited about your startup is the right champion for you even though they may very well serve as a great internal advocate. Champions are a special breed of advocates, and putting your faith in the wrong champion carries a high penalty. I would even go as far as saying that you would be better off not having a champion at all than pinning your hopes on someone who is not qualified for the task. What is particularly pernicious about relying on the wrong champion is that an enthusiastic and sometimes overzealous advocate may lead you to chase a mirage, taking you down a path that could end up becoming extremely disruptive and even disastrous for your startup.

Imagine the chaos that could ensue if an excited champion jumps the gun and puts a large acquisition offer on the table without having obtained the requisite internal alignment first. At a minimum, you would have to call an emergency board meeting and discuss the offer with your key senior leadership and major investors. And if the numbers are high enough, many will likely urge you to move fast and not lose the opportunity. You could find yourself in a protracted diligence process, tying up multiple resources for months. You would probably also put other strategic initiatives on hold, losing the motivation to pursue them until the dust settles on the acquisition talks. Now picture the disappointment if at the end of all that distraction and investment of resources and emotions, you find out that there is not enough internal support for the acquisition to be approved by the acquirer or at the price range you were led to believe. You would be left to deal with the fallout, which would include a severely demoralized team (who were likely already making life plans based on the expectation of that life-changing outcome), a stalled road map, and massive organizational inertia at the least. That is what I would call a true nightmare.

I experienced working across the table with an underqualified champion in connection with a startup I was involved with a few years ago. From the early days, this champion showed great enthusiasm for our startup and quickly proved to be a person with tremendous integrity and transparency, so we found ourselves naturally smitten with him. One day he called and told us that he had just come out of a meeting with the CEO and thought that we perfectly met the requirements for a target his company was looking to acquire in our space. He advised that we should immediately put a pitch deck together and present to the senior leadership team if we didn't want to lose this window of opportunity.

We spent the next several months attending meetings with various teams at this potential acquirer and went through a preliminary diligence process. We ultimately did not get anywhere with them, and the deal got shut down by their executive team, saying that it was not on strategy for them at the time. Even though our counterpart was a wonderful advocate, in hindsight we realized that he was not a true champion as he lacked both the influence and the experience to push an M&A transaction through the approval channels. Luckily, our effort was not wasted because in the process, we were able to entice other acquirers to make offers and closed a deal with one of them instead. We were fortunate to have cultivated strong champions elsewhere, who sprang into action once they found out we had another inbound interest.

Don't let the size of a verbal offer or a blurted price range mislead you as it does not necessarily correlate with the level of internal alignment obtained before an offer is made. Even a billion-dollar offer can end up being only as strong as the champion sponsoring it. Serial entrepreneur and author James Altucher once was advisor to a company where he obtained such a billion-dollar offer from GE. But when he relayed the news of the offer to the CEO, the CEO responded "100 percent chance this deal doesn't happen" upon finding out who James had received the offer from. The "champion" making the offer was fairly junior in the organization without real authority. And the CEO's prediction was on the mark: the acquirer ultimately found a much more economic way to achieve their objective. Reflecting on the experience, James wrote in an article for *Business Insider*, "You can only cross the bridge to the other side if someone strong is there holding out their hand to pull you in."[22]

Based on my experience, the right champion is someone with the right combination of authority, influence, drive, and experience to make strategic initiatives actually happen. Let's unpack each of these four essential attributes of a champion with the acronym AIDE, as in your champion is your deal aide. As we dive into each, we'll explore ways in which you can spot them.

Authority

As illustrated by the GE story above, your champion needs to have the organizational authority to push a strategic initiative and have the ability to direct resources toward its successful execution. In other words, the ideal champion is able to make some of the required trade-offs between various items on the corporate road map to facilitate a transaction. Depending on the relative size of your project to the overall size of the acquirer, you will need to find the right level of sponsorship within that organization. Sometimes the CEO is the right champion, but in most situations, you need at least the sponsorship of a GM or a senior VP of a certain business unit behind your project. There are times that others, such as a product manager, may be the right champion for you.

But the key point here is that the right champion should have the right organizational decision-making authority relative to the magnitude of the transaction. This is why I think it is not ideal, for instance, to rely solely on folks in support functions such as business development, corporate development, or finance as your deal champions because they have significantly less decision-making authority than the operating leadership of each business unit.

Influence

Authority does not necessarily come with organizational influence. Without sufficient influence, your champion will not be able to generate organizational support cross functionally (e.g., sales, engineering, product, marketing, finance, accounting, HR, customer support, and legal), which is required to push any major initiative through.

In large organizations, influence tends to come with credibility, responsibility, and likability. Your champion doesn't have to be the ultimate decision maker or approver, but they need to be respected enough by those people to influence their decision. So, the right champion needs to have achieved organizational credibility through a combination of track record and expertise to make things happen. Their opinion should carry weight, even if it is one of many voices to be heard. The farther your champion is from bearing the ultimate responsibility for your project, the less influence they will have in convincing others of its importance. And if you don't find a potential champion likable and a pleasure to work with, chances are those sentiments are also shared internally.

Drive

You should not consider someone a true champion unless you are convinced that they are motivated to go the extra mile and pound the table in internal meetings on your behalf. You want to see in your champion signs of a genuine passion and excitement for the possibilities of joining forces with you and your startup. This is why it is easy to confuse a champion and an advocate as they both exhibit these attributes. Your champion's drive will likely be fueled by a number of factors, including a belief in your shared vision and mission, conviction in the potential for success from your collaboration, and its expected costs and benefits associated with it. Understandably, most champions will not immediately jump on the opportunity to fight for you; you need to gradually discover and tap into what truly drives them. It takes time and a deep level of mutual understanding to win over a champion. Of all the four attributes of a champion, this is the one that you can directly influence as your words and actions will either strengthen or weaken the excitement and motivation your potential champion feels about the relationship.

Experience

Last but not least, experience with sponsoring prior strategic partnerships is another qualification for a true champion. A new GM may not be as effective in sponsoring your cause compared to a seasoned vice president at the same company. This is because there are a lot of organizational processes and politics that need to be navigated (or even fully circumvented) to make a major deal happen. In most organizations, a single department or even influential individual has the power to block or at least delay a transaction. Your champion needs to have insight into the strategic road map, potential problems, and areas of concern for various stakeholders, which can only be learned through repeated interactions and experience with them. I have been involved in failed transactions that resulted from lack of internal back-office bandwidth to execute on a deal (for example, finance or HR being completely swamped) to a board member questioning the strategic rationale for a transaction in light of other priorities. An experienced champion will know how to anticipate, spot, or navigate these issues, has real-time visibility into cross-functional challenges, and will provide you with guidance on how to overcome concerns creatively.

Winning Over and Arming Your Champion

The strength of your relationship with your champion will significantly influence how successful they will be in their internal advocacy for your project and what risks they will be willing to underwrite to close a strategic deal with your startup, especially when it comes to acquisitions. And since their success internally will directly determine your eventual success, you will need to be mindful that in all your interactions you are setting up your champion for success. Here are some of the best practices I have observed in winning over and nurturing one's relationship with a potential champion.

Identify Common Goals

Deepen your mutual understanding with your champion by making your common goals explicit. Find out what success would look like for your champion, his or her business unit, and the overall company. When both parties are aligned around a set of clear goals, for instance defending against a mutual competitor or bringing a specific solution to market, things tend to go much smoother.

Set Realistic Expectations

I firmly believe in the popular refrain that *happiness is life exceeding expectations.* You not only need to set realistic expectations with your champion, but you also need to make sure your champion doesn't get ahead of his or her skis and sets realistic expectations in their organization, too. If your champion, for instance, sets internal expectations on a certain volume of sales coming from a test by a certain date, and you don't meet those expectations, you are the one who will look incompetent. Don't let your ambitions and those of your champion compel you to *over*promise. Of course, you don't want to sandbag or deliberately *under*-promise either, as aiming for mediocre results could sound the death knell for the project before it even gets launched. The key is to be realistic and set expectations accordingly.

Start Small, but Dream Big

As entrepreneurs, we tend to dream big. We shoot for Mars so that we can land on the Moon. It is in our nature. But we need to keep that nature in check when dealing with strategic business partners by setting realistic expectations. Being realistic forces you to start with a smaller engagement. A bite-size project that does not overwhelm a potential partner's resources is much easier for them to say yes to. Then you can build on that success with a bigger project and successively grow the scope and scale of your engagement.

While you set and execute on realistic expectations, don't let yourself and your champion lose sight of the big dream either. Always connect the dots all the way to that big dream and remind your champion how a certain course of action will get both sides closer to the ultimate shared goal. This will help keep the momentum and enthusiasm for the partnership going while you get started with the basics and foundational steps.

Deliver on Your Commitments

Nothing erodes confidence in you and your startup like failure to meet your commitments. As I mentioned in connection with establishing dependability above, no matter how trivial those commitments are, go through hell or high water to deliver on them. Follow through on each commitment, both those that you make to your champion and those that your champion makes to his or her organization. It is much better not to commit at all than to commit and come up short.

Always Stay in Sync

Many projects fail because the parties don't keep each other informed of developments on their respective side. Any change, such as changes in personnel, funding, priorities, road map, or organization structure, can have significant downstream ripple effects. Keep your champion and the team that is working on a given project informed of developments in your company and encourage your champion to share that information with all stakeholders. Ask your champion to keep you informed of changes on their side as well.

Bring Your Champion In

I mean this one literally. Invite your champion to visit your company and attend some of your company events in person. Doing so will not only strengthen the bond with your champion, it will also provide invaluable information to them about your company that they can use to sell you internally. In one particular acquisition for GoDaddy, I recall how our team's perception of a target dramatically changed after we walked through their hallways and noticed how similar our companies were in terms of culture, from how our customer care agents spoke to our customers down to what we chose to hang on our walls and how we named our conference rooms. This target was just as obsessed with small businesses as we were at GoDaddy, and although we had heard that from the founders on several occasions, we didn't really internalize that understanding until all our senses were immersed in it at their offices. This target immediately became our top acquisition target after that tour and was acquired by us six months later.

Increasing your champion's exposure to your company and culture is one of the best ways you can arm them with information critical to your success. Neither you nor your champion may know at the outset what specific information is key to unlocking a strategic relationship, so exposing your champion to as much of your company and culture as possible can help develop a deep level of understanding that they can tap into as specific needs arise. Cultural fit is a critical element in any successful partnership, so make sure your champion understands your startup's culture and can draw on elements from it to properly advocate for you.

Make Your Champion's Life Easier

Each of us has a finite amount of energy and mental capacity for overhead and conflict. Therefore, don't burden or tire out your potential champion with unnecessary tasks or any conflict and friction. If they ask for something and you don't have that information, figure out creative ways to obtain it or find viable proxies without necessarily exposing your champion to all the sausage making that goes into it. Let them save their energy and attention for the many internal negotiations they will have to enter into. For extra credit, go above and beyond and anticipate what your champion may need before they even ask for it. Overdeliver on your commitments so that they can have an easier time delivering on their commitments to you.

Also, keep in mind the human dimension. Understand the ideal hours, days, and location for interacting with your champion and try to accommodate them as much as possible. For instance, if you are on the East Coast and your champion is on the West Coast and has a young family, chances are that any time before 9 a.m. Pacific time (which is noon Eastern time) is not a good time to schedule phone or videoconference calls. Always be sure to act with empathy and understanding of how your interactions can impact or disturb the life and routines of your champion and other counterparts involved in your project.

Create and Build on Your Wins

Lastly, it is very important to make sure you recognize and celebrate each win, no matter how small they may be. Pay close attention to what can constitute a win and seize on the opportunity to highlight it and give credit where due. If your champion or their colleague(s) deserves credit or recognition, make sure that recognition is communicated and they stand out as heroes. You want your counterparts to feel great about their association with you and your startup. They should ideally feel and see evidence that by working with you, they are advancing their careers and have a path toward personal and professional success. Of course, you should always remain genuine and not praise someone or something that does not deserve such praise. False praise will discredit and diminish the value of any real praise you give. The point here is to make sure you don't overlook the opportunity to seize and build on each genuine win.

By all means, don't wait until the final results of the project are tallied to say something positive. A wait-and-see approach will only demoralize the people involved and discourage them from going all-in. Instead, actively look for opportunities to celebrate. For example, you may want to acknowledge the shared vision and values of the teams, the level of openness and candor in communications, the mutual courage and/or agility of the parties in their approach, or any early results in a test or experiment. Even if those results are not what the parties expected, there are likely many learnings worth pointing out and celebrating as those learnings will prevent bigger mistakes and waste of resources in the future. As you seize on these opportunities to celebrate, don't forget to point out the contributions of your champion and other team members involved.

CHAPTER 10

BUILD YOUR EXIT TEAM

If you want to go fast, go alone;
but if you want to go far, go together.
—African proverb[1]

When it comes to mission-critical capabilities for your startup, build them *before* you need them. Readiness for a successful exit is a mission-critical capability for your startup since the ultimate achievement of its mission and seeing the benefit of years of blood, sweat, and tears poured into it depend on it. Putting aside fictionalized portrayals in the media, company sales just don't happen behind closed doors in one-on-one conversations between founders and CEOs. It takes a good-sized village to pull off a decent exit. To have an outcome worth celebrating, you need a motivated and experienced team to keep the trains moving on your side and help you maneuver around many explosive emotional minefields throughout the sale process. You need the guidance of experts with relevant legal, financial, and transactional expertise to help you negotiate and structure the sale, as well as the hands-on involvement of operators who can lead your startup through the ups and downs of the most transformative event in its life cycle. A competent *exit team* is an often-ignored yet vital core capability for your startup.

Very few startups have all the necessary players on that exit team. While some of your executives may have had prior involvement with startups that have exited, that will likely not be enough. For the best outcome, you will need to augment your leadership with both internal and external resources that have substantial M&A-specific expertise. And you need to know how to find, evaluate, and engage such resources, which this chapter is designed to teach you.

Recruiting top talent always takes time and patience as it entails a thoughtful vetting process to find and win over candidates aligned with your mission, culture, and ambitions. To achieve that objective, you will need to start the recruiting engines and network with potential candidates well before you are in M&A discussions. Make it one of your long-term goals to create a world-class exit team. While you should take your time and be deliberate, don't delay too long either, as things that keep getting deprioritized seldom ever get started.

In this chapter, I will help you understand what key positions you will need to fill on your world-class exit team, what role each plays, and when and how to put the right individuals in those positions. We will focus on four key roles: leadership team, legal advisors, strategy advisors, and investment bankers, in that rough order of priority.

LEADERSHIP TEAM

You need a strong leadership team to pull off a successful sale. In fact, you need a strong leadership team whether or not you ever decide to seriously consider a sale, but nothing shines a spotlight on leadership weaknesses quite the way a sale process does. If you have not been through an acquisition before, this assertion may seem odd to you. You may even have assumed that your leadership team would be redundant in an acquisition since an acquirer would already have their executive team in place, making your leadership team more a liability or nuisance to get rid of rather than an asset worth keeping. But in most cases, nothing could be further from the truth.

While most acquirers have their own leadership team, they would still have a need for leaders who would focus on running your business inside their organization. In fact, many acquirers will walk away from your startup, or significantly discount the value they assign to it, if they discover that you don't possess the leadership capability to keep the business going once the transaction has closed. After all, like most other organizations, an acquirer's existing leadership team would hardly have any excess bandwidth to take on new responsibilities. There are two key reasons the strength of your leadership team has a direct impact on the outcome of a potential sale: acquisitions are very distracting, and acquisition process management requires unique expertise.

Creating Leadership Bandwidth

An often-ignored reality is that an acquisition, regardless of the strength of your negotiation position or the size of the deal, will be all-consuming, distracting, and emotionally taxing for you and others involved. Your leadership team needs to keep the wheels on while you and the rest of the exit team are moving fast and riding the roller coaster of the sale process. No matter how hard you may push for a deal to be done and over quickly, given the sheer number of people involved (internal deal teams, board members, major shareholders, advisors, lawyers, accountants, and potentially bankers on each side) and the need to get things done right, chances are that it will take far longer than you expect. Throughout this process, without the adequate level of leadership on the ground who can keep things moving along smoothly for your startup, your chance of a positive outcome will be in serious jeopardy. You certainly wouldn't want your startup to face a major crisis, such as a massive security breach, outage, or product failure, and spook the buyer right when you are about to sign on the dotted line. No acquirer is eager to inherit a liability, and if they do, they will make sure you and your shareholders pay for it accordingly.

Ever since the very-public data breach issues that came to light during due diligence in the Verizon-Yahoo acquisition (for which Yahoo shareholders took a $350 million hit),[2] cybersecurity has become a hot-button topic for acquirers, with one global survey finding that the overwhelming majority of M&A decision makers (81 percent) consider it a top priority in their deal evaluation.[3] But what is even more important to acquirers is the performance of your business during the sale process. Many deals have fallen apart during diligence because a target failed to meet *its own* financial forecast or product milestones before the parties had signed the definitive agreements. Nothing can erode your leverage as a target more than your inability to meet your own plans and forecasts, no matter how many valid reasons or excuses you may have for the shortfall. Declining sales, ballooning customer acquisition costs, a dip in customer satisfaction, shrinking margins, and a myriad of other maladies that may suddenly break out during the diligence process can all become deal killers.

I have been involved in a number of acquisitions on the acquirer side where we encountered an ever-widening gap in some key metrics as we got deeper into diligence and had to pull back up and reassess whether we wanted to do the deal. And without exception, in every such instance where we decided to still proceed with a transaction, we renegotiated the purchase price accordingly.

Only in one instance did the opposite happen: due to unforeseen market changes, the startup's growth suddenly spiked while we were in the diligence process after signing a term sheet, which was an amazingly strong negotiation position for the founder and CEO, who accordingly asked for an improved set of terms. It was very hard to argue against that logic, and we had to concede.

Managing the Acquisition Process

It would be ideal to have at least one executive on your exit team who is experienced with leading transformational changes. This would be an individual with prior leadership roles in shepherding acquisition integrations, major business model changes, or rapid organizational scale. This person will be able to point out the strengths and weaknesses of your startup in executing against the deal hypotheses and help you set realistic execution goals with an acquirer during and after the transaction. As a bonus, having this leader on your team should significantly boost your desirability to acquirers as well due to their own capacity constraint issues I alluded to above.

Acquirers seldom have extra resources to dedicate to ensuring that an acquisition integration proceeds smoothly. And in the rare cases where they do have a dedicated integration person or team, those individuals still wouldn't know all the nuances of your culture and appreciate how best to get your team to go through a radical transformation, which every acquisition ends up being. A successful integration would be one where at the end of the integration process, the employees of both organizations feel that they are part of one entity, wholeheartedly believe in its mission, and are committed to its success. This is much easier said than done. In fact, most acquisition failure stories come from integration challenges that end up resulting in significant rifts in leadership, high-profile executive departures, employee demoralization, and churn—problems that ultimately lead to missed financial or operating goals for the transaction. This is where having experienced leaders on your team will change the outcome for both parties. Such leaders would help you and the acquirer create the integration plans, set baseline and stretch goals that can realistically be attained, and then effectively mobilize the forces to implement them.

For these leaders to be successful in achieving these objectives, they need to have spent sufficient time with your organization to understand its culture and processes and obtained the trust and confidence of your team. Some acquirers, faced with a gap in leadership capabilities of the target, resort to hiring a new leader to fill in that gap right after the acquisition. In my experience, these external hires typically don't work out, causing delays in achievement of goals, dissatisfaction among the employees, and eventually the disillusionment and departure of that leader. Therefore, acquirers place a premium on targets that have a functional and experienced leadership team. And if you want the best shot at the realization of your startup's mission well after an acquisition, so should you.

LEGAL ADVISORS

Here is something you will never find in the history of acquisitions: a successful exit without the involvement of an experienced legal team. Having an experienced corporate counsel on your side during a sale is indispensable. This is the one place you cannot be too cost sensitive. Your counsel will help you determine how to best protect your interests in the terms and structure of the sale transaction while taking into account a number of legal, tax, regulatory, and accounting matters. You will also need an experienced legal team to help you respond to diligence inquiries and ensure that the understanding between the parties is adequately reflected in the documentation. Just to give you a sense of the scale, once the dust settles on the deal activities, a typical M&A transaction will result in hundreds (even thousands) of pages of legal paperwork, including the sale agreement, disclosure schedules, requisite board and shareholder communications, assignment and transfer consents, and regulatory filings.

Qualifications

Just as you wouldn't want a foot doctor to perform brain surgery on you, with all due respect to podiatrists, you wouldn't want a family attorney or a litigator to advise you on the sale of your startup. Like the medical profession, there are many specializations within the legal profession, and doing M&A work is a subcategory within what is considered transactional corporate legal work. Because of the complex legal, tax, regulatory, and accounting issues involved, you need the advice of legal professionals who have significant prior M&A experience, ideally in your industry. These attorneys typically work at larger law firms that have a robust transactional practice, from startup formations to representing companies in their financing, licensing, IPO, and M&A transactions. In Silicon Valley, top-tier law firms usually represent at least one side of any notable transaction. Even large companies that do have an internal legal department use these established law firms when it comes to M&A.

The benefit of working with larger and more prominent law firms with world-class transactional practices is that they have both the depth and breadth of practice to provide an on-demand, one-stop shop for all your needs. They can usually surge resources quickly and meet your timeline whenever you find yourself in the heat of a potential transaction. Such firms are involved with hundreds of transactions per year, so they are well-versed in the latest developments, regulations, and court cases that can have an impact on your sale transaction and know most of the nuances and templates used by other law firms, so they can usually hit the road running very quickly. They have the pulse on market terms and will provide you with guidance on how to negotiate with some of the common serial-acquirers in the industry, whom they may have either represented or been across the table from on numerous deals. Their breadth of practice stems from their ability to have many specializations among their attorneys, from tax to employment matters, from regulatory to IP and securities laws and everything else in between. As you would expect, these benefits come with a price tag. As of the writing of this book, you will generally pay over $500 per hour for their legal services on average, with partners charging over $1,000 per hour, quickly adding up to hundreds of thousands of dollars or more by the time you have closed on a transaction.

For smaller deals, there is an alternative to these large law firms: smaller, boutique firms typically run by former big-law corporate attorneys. You will need to do more homework to find and interview such firms, but there is a growing number of them out there. If you explore this route, make sure to determine whether the attorney(s) you will be working with have had significant experience with startup exits in your industry (that is, having done at least several deals a year for a number of years), and what their track record has been in those deals. Reference checks can help you better understand both their style and level of competence.

Do not put the fate of the most important transaction of your startup in the hands of someone who doesn't have the experience and resources to handle it competently, despite their good intentions or perhaps close social ties to you. Even if they had represented you, your family, or your business in many other legal matters with flying colors, M&A is a specialty of its own. On the acquirer side, some of the most painful M&A experiences for me have been those where the buyer was represented by an inexperienced counsel who would inevitably delay or even threaten to derail the entire transaction. That is why all savvy acquirers will strongly request that you have an experienced legal team representing you.

Engagement Model

The typical engagement model with corporate attorneys is the hourly fee arrangement. Law firms track and charge for the time spent by their staff by the hour (in six-minute increments) and bill you monthly based on the hourly rate of those individuals. You may try to negotiate a cap on your aggregate acquisition-related legal expenses, but be aware that most lawyers shy away from that; even if you do get a cap, it would likely be a very high number, in the hundreds of thousands of dollars. Most lawyers don't do flat-fee arrangements since the amount of time spent on a transaction is hard to predict ahead of time: It will largely depend on the style of negotiation of the parties, number of stakeholders that need to be accommodated, and how reasonable or difficult the opposing counsel is in their approach. Also, there could be all sorts of surprises that come to light during the diligence process. Moreover, flat-fee arrangements may actually not be to your overall advantage anyway as you wouldn't want to create an incentive structure that would encourage your lawyers to skip on important work for you because they are starting to run up against their maximum fee.

Typically, startups working with one of the larger corporate law firms since incorporation or a financing round tend to continue working with those firms all the way through their exit as well. Although that is the most common path, you don't have to hire the same lawyer or law firm that does your day-to-day corporate work for your exit transaction, especially if they are not qualified to do so or if you feel there exists a conflict of interest (for instance, if they do a lot of work for your acquirer). The benefit of going with your existing counsel is that they already are familiar with your startup's corporate history, so you don't need to spend time (and money) bringing a whole new set of attorneys up to speed. If you think you will need to hire a new set of lawyers for your exit, allow sufficient time to search for and do the requisite research before you make a decision.

Cost Management

While good legal advice is not cheap, there are things you can do to keep some of the costs under control. One is to choose a smaller, more boutique law firm as they tend to have lower hourly rates due to less overhead and internal hierarchies. But the most important cost mitigation step you can take is to help your attorneys be more efficient in their work for you. The trick here is to know what work you can do yourself and what work you absolutely need to put in the capable hands of your attorneys.

Based on my experience, some of the work you can do yourself or with the help of nonlegal advisors in an M&A transaction includes:

1. Negotiating the high-level deal structure and business terms
2. Understanding tax and accounting implications of your transaction
3. Preparing cap table and running scenario analysis of deal payout distribution
4. Preparing and responding to business diligence requests
5. Scheduling and coordinating meetings

On the other hand, work only your counsel should do includes:

1. Preparing and responding to legal due diligence requests
2. Review and negotiation of legal terms of your transaction
3. Drafting and negotiating deal documents
4. Preparing deal-related board, shareholder, and third-party disclosure, consent, and approval documentation
5. Making requisite regulatory filings

STRATEGY ADVISORS

When engaged effectively, strategy advisors can significantly impact the outcome of your exit transaction by serving as a sounding board and providing you with critical negotiation guidance. The best strategy advisors are current or former operating executives who have been through a few acquisitions in their past. And they would need to have sufficient bandwidth to have a close working relationship with you throughout your exit strategy creation and sale process. They would become your trusted mentor at every step of your courtship with strategic partners, from building a relationship with potential allies, to navigating around challenges and obstacles that inevitably arise, and ultimately providing you with guidance and feedback on the timing, structure, and terms of a sale transaction. A good strategy advisor is like a coach or a personal trainer that can help you gain perspective, identify weaknesses in your approach, and devise a systematic, custom-tailored plan for you to grow and achieve your goals.

The ability to seek and find the right advisors and mentors is another of those entrepreneurial superpowers. One study of 650 startups found that those that have helpful mentors raise considerably more money and perform better than those who don't.[4] To that point, one of the most successful business leaders of our time, Ray Dalio, founder of top-performing hedge fund Bridgewater, operates by the following guiding principle:

> *Asking others who are strong in areas where you are weak to help you is a great skill that you should develop no matter what, as it will help you develop guardrails that will prevent you from doing what you shouldn't be doing. All successful people are good at it.*[5]

Sometimes board members with a combination of operating and deal experience can fulfill the role of a strategy advisor for you *as long as* they have the bandwidth to spend the required time with you. It is much more common, however, for entrepreneurs to actively seek out and hire one or more external advisors that meet their needs. You may even find out, as I did with one of my startups, that such advisors can eliminate the need to hire an investment banker when you are involved in the actual exit negotiation process. We will take up the subject of hiring investment bankers in the next section. For now, here are my tips on how to round out your team's capabilities with one or more world-class strategy advisors.

Qualifications

For your exit team, a qualified strategy advisor is one who has had significant prior experience with buying and selling companies as an *operator* and not just as an arms-length, third-party advisor or broker. You want such an advisor to not only fill in some of the "known unknowns" for you, but also illuminate areas that are "unknown unknowns" when you are going through an exit process, which require insights typically gained only when someone actually goes through the sale process from the inside. You want your strategy advisor to have experienced all of the steps of selling a company, from the creation of the strategy to courting potential buyers and then going through and negotiating the eventual sale. Moreover, you need your advisor to have been through the post-closing integration process to have a deep appreciation of how certain operating decisions made months before even a term sheet is signed impact the ultimate outcome of the sale. For example, you may not realize why the stated mission of your startup, one or more of your cultural attributes, the metrics you track, or the capabilities within your leadership team would be critical to an acquirer's desire to do a deal with you, but an experienced strategy advisor could bring those factors to your attention and guide you on how to showcase them in your interactions with your counterparts.

To make the responsibilities of your strategy advisor more concrete, these are the core areas where an effective advisor can elevate your process to the next level:

1. Building relationships with potential strategic allies
2. Crafting the right internal and external messaging
3. Structuring and executing on strategic partnerships
4. Negotiating the terms of an acquisition offer

Besides raw experience, be highly attuned to the level of comfort and cultural fit when recruiting and vetting potential advisors. It would be a terrible waste of time to bring an advisor on board and educate him or her on the ins and outs of your startup, only to conclude later on that you do not have a high degree of confidence or conviction in their guidance, or that their communication style or values is not a match for yours.

Get a head start on your evaluation of potential advisors long before an exit transaction is on the horizon. Ask your investors, board, and fellow entrepreneurs for referrals. Network and learn about the background of those whom you meet. Sometimes the person sitting next to you at an event laughing at a comedian onstage could very well change the fate of your startup.

When assessing candidates, augment your background research with reference checks, talking to other startups that have been advised by that candidate. Another way to get to know an advisor is to run a trial project or have a getting-to-know-you period to determine your level of confidence in that advisor.

Engagement Model

Startups typically engage external advisors on an equity basis with grants of options or common stock. If you expect more than one or two hours of an advisor's time per week, though, the advisor may also request milestone payments or a monthly cash compensation to justify the time spent. The equity grants typically vest over one to four years, usually on a monthly basis. As opposed to employee grants, advisor grants do not typically have cliff vesting. The benefit of an equity relationship is that it aligns the incentives of the advisor with those of common shareholders, who are usually the founders and founding employees. In that way, your advisors are better aligned with your ultimate financial success than investors who have liquidation preferences and rights that come before those of common stockholders.

Because advisors are compensated in equity, the further out and the higher the risk of a liquidity event, the larger of an equity stake an advisor would expect. So, you would give substantially more equity (1 to 2 percent) to an advisor who comes in before your Series A and spends several hours a week on your startup, compared with an advisor who comes in later and/or spends less time (0.1 percent to 1 percent). Your ultimate goal is to provide sufficient equity and upside to sustain the interest level and the active engagement of your advisor. Therefore, the numbers vary significantly between advisors and startups. One way to take this out of the purely subjective realm is to actually calculate what the expected return on their efforts would be, taking into account the amount of expected dilution as well as realistic range of exit valuations for your startup. If a risk-adjusted calculation yields something below an hourly rate of compensation for that advisor, then you can see why an advisor would (and logically should) expect more.

INVESTMENT BANKERS

You can think of investment bankers as expert brokers for your company sale. Similar to what a competent real estate broker does when you are selling a house, investment bankers help you "stage" your startup properly, drum up interest for it, and then act as a buffer between you and the buyers in negotiations and throughout the sale process. Whereas lawyers are always indispensable in M&A transactions, you may choose not to engage an investment banker if you have team members who can fill in for the roles that the investment bankers play in a sale process.

In fact, in a majority of M&A transactions, private sellers do not engage an investment banking advisor.[6] For example, as the vice president of strategy and business development at Webs, I served as the de facto in-house "deal guy" throughout the M&A process. Thanks to the business relationships we had built over the years, we were able to bring multiple public and private companies to the table and drum up several acquisition offers on our own. In addition, we were fortunate to benefit from the strategic advice and guidance of experienced board members and advisors, some of whom also did critical back-channel negotiations with our potential buyers.

As the size and complexity of a transaction increases, so does the value that an investment bank can add in your process. They are experts in running the sale process as well as a great buffer for the tough negotiations ahead. Their involvement will not only help you get the most favorable transaction terms possible, but capable bankers do so while preserving your relationship with the acquirer (for whom you and most other team members will likely be working for some time post-acquisition). Competent investment bankers are professional negotiators and will help you understand the best way to structure your transaction, improve your leverage, and avoid costly mistakes. But that comes at a steep cost (usually 1 to 2 percent of transaction amount, with a minimum retainer typically in the hundreds of thousands of dollars range). So, you need to decide whether the size and complexity of your transaction makes it worthwhile to involve an investment banker. Again, if you have the benefit of a strong leadership team, board, and advisors who have relevant prior experience in structuring and negotiating M&A transactions, you may be well positioned to run the process yourself.

It is important to note that you do not hire an investment banker to find your first set of interested suitors. Investment bankers cannot make up for your lack of business relationship with your potential acquirers. That responsibility falls squarely on your and your leadership team's shoulders. You can't outsource relationship building, in the same way you can't effectively outsource approaching potential venture investors to an intermediary. As a VC, I always considered pitch decks prepared and sent to us by bankers to be highly suspect. When I look at the successful M&A and VC deals I have been involved with, they all involved a pre-existing relationship between the parties long before a banker ever got involved. Nonetheless, once you have one or more interested parties actively pursuing you, competent investment bankers are adept at channeling that energy toward a deal and perhaps even finding you some additional suitors.

Where you can and should lean heavily on your bankers is getting an external perspective on your pitch, exploring the right way to position your startup as a target, and developing a valuation framework based on public and private precedents. Good bankers sometimes have insights into who the proper champions and decision makers at a potential acquirer are. Their primary role, however, is to run the sale process, which involves (a) keeping discussions with all potential interested parties in sync with your timing, (b) setting up a data room and coordinating diligence activities, (c) negotiating offers over one or multiple rounds to help you get the best terms for your company, and (d) helping you negotiate the final set of terms.

As such, a banker is not all that helpful if you are too early in your sale process or if you don't have at least two or more parties expressing any serious interest in taking a closer look. In such cases, you would probably be better off working closely with an experienced strategic advisor or board member instead of an investment bank.

Qualifications

There are many investment bankers out there, but only a handful of highly selective ones represent the highest-profile transactions. Top Wall Street banks such as Goldman Sachs and Morgan Stanley and some boutique and specialized technology advisory firms such as Qatalyst lead the pack. Unless your exit valuation is at least in the half-a-unicorn territory, those top-tier banks are unlikely to take you on as a client.

As with other critical players on your exit team, be careful and selective in your choice of an investment banker. Do not consider all bankers the same. As investor and serial entrepreneur Justin Kan (founder of Twitch, which he sold to Amazon for $1 billion) puts it, "like the world of venture capital, investment banking is a field filled with a very small number of extremely well-connected, analytical, and experienced people and a much larger number people pretending to be those things."[7]

Finding a competent, experienced investment banker for a transaction that is relatively small (below $200 million) is not impossible, but it will require patience and diligent investigative work. Ask for referrals from your network and have casual meetings to start building some relationships in that world. As you evaluate and interview potential bankers, it is important to keep in mind the specific purpose for which you want to engage them. Remember that finding your initial set of interested acquirers should not be their job. Give great weight to prior industry experience as well as the cultural fit, temperament, and negotiation style of your banker. In many interactions, a banker acts as your agent and representative, and how he or she comes across could very much color your potential acquirer's impression of you. One of the best ways to assess those attributes is by speaking with founders and CEOs of companies a banker has previously represented.

Engagement Model

You hire an investment banker by negotiating and signing an engagement letter. The engagement letter sets the framework for the relationship, describing the responsibilities of the banker, duration of engagement, how to treat certain important matters such as confidentiality and conflicts of interest, and equally as important, how the banker is compensated. Don't just sign what an investment banker presents to you as their "standard" engagement letter. You would be well advised to carefully review and seek the assistance of an experienced attorney, your board, and strategy advisors in reviewing and negotiating an engagement letter to best protect your interests.

Investment bankers are generally significantly more expensive than lawyers, which is due to the fact that (a) they can impact the upside scenario far more than your attorneys can, and (b) they are also willing to take on more risk in representing you as they don't bill you by the hour and receive the majority of their compensation only after the consummation of a transaction. Thus, their compensation expectation reflects that risk/reward reality. What you need to particularly pay attention to is ensuring that there is as much alignment of incentives as possible for the banker to dedicate significant time and resources toward maximizing the upside for you. As such, the typical compensation structure consists of

(a) an up-front or monthly retainer, and (b) a success fee. You would ideally negotiate away the retainer, but I have found that for many smaller, riskier deals, bankers are reluctant to represent you unless there is some way to compensate them for the time spent if there is no transaction at the end of the day. While you may want to shift all of the risk of a failure to sell onto the bankers, few would accept that risk, especially if they have already more interest from prospective clients than they can handle. And the reality is, you have far more control in determining whether or not a sale would happen than a banker ever would. However, it would be perfectly reasonable for you to ask to get a credit for the amount you pay as retainer against the success fee. As for the success fee, it typically represents 1 to 3 percent of the net proceeds of the sale, but with a minimum (which typically does not exceed half a million dollars) for the smaller deals.

Keep the following points in mind when negotiating the details of that success fee:

1. The percentage of the success fee should vary for deals that you have found as opposed to deals the banker brings to the table; however, the variance should not be so large that the banker loses the incentive to help you close a deal with someone you bring.

2. The success fee calculation should exclude any consideration that is paid by the acquirer for cash on your balance sheet as well as proceeds your team receives to be hired by the acquirer, such as new-hire equity grants and sign-on bonuses.

3. Bankers should get their payment when you are paid, so a success fee applied to any milestone or earnout payment should become due *if and when* those payments are made to you, which is one reason you will find bankers are quite unenthused by earnouts.

Remember that you don't need to officially engage an investment banker until you are seriously considering a sale of your startup; most savvy bankers wouldn't want to waste their time by prematurely rushing you to a sale process either. In fact, many entrepreneurs engage a bank only after they have the first interested party at the table. But start networking and get to know a few sooner rather than later. Note that putting yourself on the radar of prominent investment bankers comes with the added benefit that they may bring you up in their presentations to existing or prospective acquirer clients, which may very well generate inbound acquisition interest for you in the future.

CHAPTER 11

CREATE LEVERAGE

Leverage is influence, and influence is leverage.
—Chris Voss[1]

Why is it that some startups are acquired at seemingly astronomic valuations, while others with similar products in the same industry are not? This question haunted me in May of 2009.

At that time, I was reviewing an acquisition offer for my first startup, Jaxtr. A year prior, our Series B venture round valuation was at $50 million. But when we needed to sell just a few months later, that valuation came crumbling down. The only acquisition offer we were able to muster was an offer for less than $1 million, the value attributed by the buyer to our customers, brand, and intellectual property.

Our nosebleed-inducing drop in value was made worse by the fact that Ribbit, one of our Silicon Valley competitors, had sold to British Telecom for $105 million less than a year earlier, with less VC money raised and no product launched.[2] And the year before that, another competitor named GrandCentral sold to Google for $50 million, again with far less funding and customers than us.[3]

But what truly made us feel like the victims of a cruel cosmic conspiracy was what happened to our competitor Jajah. They had opted to pursue a growth-by-partnership path, which we dismissed as a low-margin, inferior strategy compared with our growth-by-virality approach. Jajah built a business development team and consistently chased ambitious integrations with several global platforms including Yahoo to power their consumer internet calling offerings. As it turned out, they were the ones with the superior strategy. Within just a couple of months of our brutal fire sale, Jajah was acquired by European telecom giant Telefonica for a whopping $207 million in an all-cash deal.[4] With that announcement, any remnants of ego among the Jaxtr team were dealt a swift, fatal blow.

It was clear, in hindsight, that all three of those startups had managed to cultivate relationships with their ultimate suitors long ahead of the acquisitions. But was that strategy pivotal to the incredibly high valuations they received in the process, or were they simply lucky?

As I have come to realize, especially after having done several deals from the acquirer side, that question assumes a false dichotomy. Strategy and luck are closely related. In deal negotiations, what looks like luck is leverage in disguise. And gaining that leverage requires sound execution of a deliberate strategy.

Leverage in its purest form refers to one's ability to influence outcomes. Jajah, Ribbit, and GrandCentral could bend the reality of valuations because they had strong options, connections, and insight into their acquirers. At Jaxtr, we were desperate to sell and didn't have a viable alternative. We were rapidly running out of cash and had not cultivated any meaningful relationships with potential suitors who would be willing to engage in acquisition discussions. GrandCentral and Ribbit sold before the 2008 financial crisis took root, during a period when the default mode for every startup was to raise more money and grow. Jajah sold after the bottom of the economy was clearly established and things were in the upswing. Besides, they had recently raised $5 million from Telus, which not only provided them with additional runway but also signaled their ability to raise money in the worst of times.

Each had built and established trust with their suitors long before the sale, and this gave them the leverage to pick their timing and terms—while we had no choice but to embark on a sale when we had no leverage at all.

In negotiations, those with greater leverage will be the ones who can bend the outcome to their advantage. Unfortunately, when you are a startup, you often find yourself in a low leverage position and at a negotiation disadvantage compared to your potential acquirers, who tend to be larger organizations with significantly more resources, expertise, and sophistication. They tend to be the ones with the most precious commodity on their side: time. That is why many startups are unable to negotiate the terms of an acquisition in a meaningful way and in retrospect wish they could have gone about everything differently. Given that acquisitions for most entrepreneurs are once-in-a-lifetime events, such regrets don't heal quickly, if ever. But this doesn't have to be the case for you.

There is no shortage of forces that are completely out of your control when running a startup—e.g., the economy, competition, and regulations—but, as surprising as it may sound, creating leverage is not one of those. The reality is there are steps you can take to create leverage and improve your negotiation position, especially if you have some time on your side. That is because these steps have less to do with the financial attributes of a transaction and more to do with relationships and psychology.

The techniques used by master negotiators to gain leverage tend be the same tools we all use to build strong relationships: emotional intelligence, deep empathy, and effective communication. According to Chris Voss, former FBI hostage negotiator and renowned negotiation coach, "The language of negotiation is primarily a language of conversation and rapport, a way of quickly establishing relationships and getting people to talk and think together."[5] And who does he consider to be the perfect archetype of a master negotiator? The most successful TV personality of our time, Oprah Winfrey, who on her show would get the world's highest profile individuals to voluntarily open up and reveal personal secrets to a live audience and millions more at home.

As is the case with Oprah controlling and steering the outcome of her interviews, your leverage comes directly from the extent you can understand and influence the feelings of your counterparts. No matter the relative size of your startup to that of your potential acquirers, with enough leverage you can still steer the outcome to your favor and achieve your best possible deal. And you build that leverage over time by working on the following: expanding your options, deepening your insight, and enhancing your appeal. The party with the most leverage in an M&A negotiation is the party who has more alternatives, who understands their counterparts' needs, and who is actively pursued.

It's through these three leverage areas, for example, that an 18-month-old startup with 13 employees and no revenues received an acquisition offer of $1 billion dollars from Facebook. That startup was Instagram. Facebook's offer implied Instagram had created over $50 million in value for each month of existence, or $77 million in value per employee. Facebook needed a mobile strategy on the eve of its IPO, and Instagram checked that box. Furthermore, Mark Zuckerberg considered Instagram an existential threat, admitting in an internal email to his CFO David Ebersman just a couple of months before the acquisition that companies like Instagram, if they "grow to a large scale," could be "very disruptive" to Facebook, and that therefore a $500 million to $1 billion offer might be needed to acquire one of the top players.[6] What made the Instagram acquisition rise to the higher side of Zuckerberg's range was the plain fact that Instagram had options: it had an offer in the $500 million range on the table from Twitter, which Instagram had rejected in favor of a large investment at similar valuation from Sequoia Capital. In fact, Instagram's cofounder and CEO Kevin Systrom initially informed Zuckerberg of his decision to remain independent, on a Wednesday in April of 2012. But Zuckerberg didn't back down and instead invited Systrom to his Palo Alto home for a series of meetings that culminated in a deal finalized by that Sunday, likely setting the world record for fastest M&A transaction.[7] That is how the gods of leverage smile upon mortals. Having leverage doesn't guarantee a billion dollar or more exit as the ultimate valuation and other deal terms also depend on your value to the acquirers and what they can afford, but your leverage goes a long way toward ensuring that you end up with the best possible outcome in your negotiations.

Like anything else worth achieving, leverage doesn't come easy. Improving in any one of the three leverage areas (options, insight, and appeal) requires your attention, focus, and effort. That's another reason you don't want to wait until you are running out of money, or are approached by an acquirer, to start working on your exit strategy. You need to set the wheels in motion early and build momentum that grows your leverage over time. In this chapter, I will unpack each of these three core ingredients to gaining leverage and provide you with practical steps you can take to become a powerful force in any strategic negotiation.

EXPAND YOUR OPTIONS

You have probably heard the tenet that *whoever can walk away from a negotiation has the power to dictate its terms*. While I cannot recommend this particular tactic when you're in acquisition talks with a major suitor, the advice is directionally true. Nothing can boost your negotiation leverage more than having viable alternatives to a potential transaction. Not only will those alternatives render you more confident and resolute in what you demand, the other side's belief that you have the option to walk away will grant you significantly more control in the negotiations.

To gain that leverage, the key is for you to (a) have real, viable alternatives to a deal, and (b) delicately signal that fact to the other side. Your viable alternatives do not spontaneously appear; they take time and effort to create. Furthermore, they won't be of much benefit unless the other side is aware that you have those options. So the process of achieving and framing your options needs to start early.

You may very well wonder: Wouldn't I be able to get the same amount of leverage as long as the other side *believes* that I have viable alternatives? Why go through the arduous process of creating those alternatives when all that matters is that the other side thinks that I have them? Some people do pursue this risky (and less honest) alternative, but their chances of success are quite low. The problem is that unlike in a game of poker, you cannot really bluff about your options in M&A discussions, at least not for long. Most acquirers have far more experience with M&A than you do and can smell idle threats a mile away. Even if they initially believe you, during the due diligence process a lot becomes clearer, and the truth will eventually come out. For instance, you cannot claim you are profitable, or that you have enough cash to sustain the company, if your financials paint a different picture (and no one will buy a company without a thorough examination of its financials). Once the truth is clear, not only will you lose whatever leverage you may have initially gained by bluffing, but you will also permanently damage your credibility.

Trust is a pillar of any meaningful business relationship, and without trust in the target leadership, I have never seen any acquirer be willing to proceed with an acquisition. To create real viable alternatives to the deal at hand as the basis for meaningful leverage, follow these three steps.

Step 1: Understand Your Initial Options

Expert negotiators caution that you should never enter a negotiation without a firm grasp of what you will do if a deal falls apart, a scenario they refer to as the deal's BATNA ("best alternative to a negotiated agreement"). Your BATNA is your negotiating foundation, and determining it helps clarify your bottom line and list of nonnegotiables. But having a BATNA is not the same as having a strong negotiation position or any amount of leverage. For instance, your BATNA may very well be shutting down your startup in a couple of months. That is technically what my BATNA was when I was trying to sell Jaxtr in 2009, and I can fully testify that this BATNA did not add an ounce of leverage or psychological comfort to my negotiation position. If anything, it only made us more desperate to sell Jaxtr at any cost.

Start by objectively assessing your realistic options and their desirability at the point in time that you would be expecting to be in acquisition discussions. Try to anticipate whether by then you will be in the position to have what you would consider a strong BATNA, one that allows you to credibly walk away from a negotiation without shedding a tear, and perhaps even with a smile on your face. This is understandably a very tall order. Unless you are on a solid path to profitability or growth, it is hard to tell what your BATNA would look like in the future. Most of us need to continually work on improving our BATNA. And to start shifting the odds in your favor and gaining a strong BATNA, we will borrow a page from Sales 101 next.

Step 2: Play the Numbers Game

You increase your chances of having a strong BATNA if you have spent the time to nurture and cultivate relationships with several potential acquirers as well as financing sources. As any salesperson knows, sales is a numbers game: not all potential buyers turn into actual buyers, so you have to approach as many prospects as you can. There is a sales funnel, and you lose prospects along the way for various reasons, most of which will be out of your control. However, the more prospects you reach out to, the higher the chances of finding at least a couple of buyers among them. Similarly, to improve your chances of finding several viable suitors, you need to start with a prequalified list of companies for whom an acquisition of your startup could make sense. Chapter 6 provided you with the tools and key questions to create this list following your strategy offsite, and Chapter 9 walked you through the steps to start and nurture relationships within those companies.

Creating several exit options, even if some of them are not all that strong, works wonders for your leverage. In most sales transactions for a common product or service, buyers don't typically compete against one another for a unique, single asset. But that is exactly how startup acquisitions work. In this regard, the M&A market is very much like the real estate market or the art market. As soon as there are multiple bidders involved, everyone's offer size increases and the asset ends up selling above asking price. Some brokers in the red-hot Bay Area real estate market, for instance, even have auction strategies and formulas for how much you should bid in a multiple offer scenario (one agent advised me to bid $5,000 to $10,000 above asking for every offer on the table).

When you are the buyer, the psychological threshold for how much you are willing to pay magically increases as soon as there is competition around. This is because the competition both validates your conviction that the target asset is worth buying, and also pushes you to go beyond your comfort zone to win the auction. If you are buying any asset and there are no other bidders, well, then you are fortunate; you have the leverage to determine whether a deal can happen at all. Conversely, to have leverage as a seller, you need to have viable alternatives to selling to a particular acquirer.

For your startup, those "viable alternatives" include other potential acquirers as well as financing sources (e.g., venture capitalists, lenders, or even large customers willing to make substantial up-front payments). Of course, your strongest BATNA is always your ability to sustain your startup without an existential need to sell, as is the case for instance when you reach cash flow breakeven.

Note that you don't need to have a high-profile offer on the table to get leverage. Your leverage significantly improves with just one viable alternative. And the more of these alternatives you have available at the time of your negotiation, the stronger your leverage will be.

While selling to established public companies is the typical exit path for startups, there are two growing categories of acquirers for startups worth noting: (1) private equity (PE) firms, and (2) other startups.[8] PE firms buy a controlling stake or the entire ownership of your startup from existing shareholders. They typically target startups that have more established financials and a relatively predictable revenue growth profile. Sale of control to private equity firms has grown in popularity, with highest deal volume and values reached in 2021 due to the low-interest environment and trillions of dollars of available capital.[9] PE firms typically take active board seats and install a new management team with the view toward industry consolidation and/or operational efficiency as their core investment thesis. Selling entrepreneurs typically get to take a substantial amount of money off the table while still maintaining some upside potential in their startups. Many M&A processes involve discussions with both PE firms and private acquirers, and therefore, they can provide viable alternatives in a sale that give the entrepreneur negotiation leverage. I have been involved in many transactions where public company acquirers have lost the auction to PE firms or had to significantly improve their offers to stay in the bidding wars.

Step 3: Drop Hints but Not Bombs

Finally, once you've established viable alternatives, how do you ensure that potential acquirers know that you do have those options? While you should ensure that the other side is aware of your alternatives as you near acquisition discussions, you do not want to make an actual threat to walk away, as doing so can cause irreparable damage to the relationship. Acquirers always want to know that they are your first choice. Threatening to walk away can cause the other party to question your level of interest in going through with a deal, or even make them feel rejected, both of which may very well cause them to bow out of the process altogether. In my experience, despite all the spreadsheets and modeling, acquirers tend to be romantics at heart, preferring a passionate relationship to a marriage of convenience.

And there are very practical reasons for this apparent romanticism. Acquisitions are difficult to manage smoothly, and unless the leadership and founding team of the target are fully excited and onboard with a deal, it is extremely difficult to make the combination successful. So, signs of a lack of commitment or outright reluctance to join forces can spoil a deal rapidly.

As mentioned in the previous chapter, acquirers typically lack the capacity and the capability to run the target's business after the purchase. Therefore, acquirers are highly motivated to retain the active engagement of as much of the leadership team members of the target as possible. When that does not happen and the leadership of the target does not fully commit to making the combination a success, many problems arise. They include loss of key talent, inefficient execution, and even negative impact on team morale on the acquirer side, as negativity can be quite contagious. In one transaction, the telltale signs of a lack of commitment by the founders of a startup became apparent during a heated negotiation over earnouts. The executive sponsor of the transaction on the acquirer side kept requesting that there should be some degree of flexibility to adapt to changing business environment during the earnout period and that the founders of the target should manage the business by balancing the needs of both entities. But the founders pushed back and insisted that during the earnout period, their sole focus and highest priority should be on making sure the earnout milestones were met, noting that doing so would be mandatory under their fiduciary obligation to their existing shareholders. Even though the parties eventually managed to figure out a compromise on paper, soon after the deal closed this point of contention resurfaced and caused such a rift that finally the founders decided to resign and forgo some of the earnout. Even worse, while this drama was unfolding, many other valuable team members of the target sought employment elsewhere. Needless to say, because of such incidents acquirers have become particularly sensitive to signals from targets that could indicate a lack of commitment to the success of the combined entity after the deal closes.

Be extremely cognizant of how your words, actions, and subtle hints could be interpreted by the acquirer's team. You will lose all leverage if the acquirer decides to walk away from a deal, so be mindful of how you position and announce your alternatives to an acquirer. At the very least, make it clear to them that they remain your first choice and that you are committed to figuring out a way to work together.

DEVELOP YOUR INSIGHT

In any negotiation, and especially in M&A discussions, insight is a pillar for success. That is why good negotiators aren't the Hollywood cliché of hard-charging, fast-talking, uncompromising bullies; rather they tend to be soft-spoken, inquisitive, and active listeners. Even one single conversation can provide you with invaluable information that could drastically improve your leverage. In particular, your understanding of how the acquirer thinks will help you tilt the outcome in your favor by helping you achieve the following two objectives:

Objective 1: Increase the Acquirer Surplus

Others are only going to be interested in acquiring your startup if the value created by the transaction will exceed the costs incurred. The delta between your startup's value to the acquirer and the cost of the transaction is the "acquirer surplus." And as the acquirer surplus increases, so will their desire and flexibility to do the deal. The problem, though, is that neither the upside nor the costs are fully known to an acquirer before they do a lot of diligence. As a result, acquirers typically apply discounts to their forecast and resort to creative deal structures that account for their uncertainty about future outcomes. This means that, from the start, they are discounting their acquirer surplus, resulting in either a suboptimal offer for your startup or no deal at all.

In many technology startup acquisitions, a great part of the value created—and thus the acquirer surplus—hinges on the retention of the engineering talent. To the extent that the acquirer fears that it will lose some of the talent after the ink dries on the deal, it will implement all sorts of risk mitigation strategies to retain those engineers. One strategy is for acquirers to shift a substantial part of the deal value from the startup's stockholders toward retention bonuses or equity grants to the employees. I have also seen transactions where an acquirer withholds a significant part of the acquisition proceeds as earnouts to be paid out only if a certain percentage of the employees remain employed after a certain period of time, typically a year or two, or sometimes even longer. In other cases, to account for lack of conviction in the financial outcome of an acquisition, buyers make downward adjustments to revenue projections and sometimes significantly increase their cost projections, which ends up knocking down the value they are willing to ascribe to the deal (acquirers typically base their valuation calculations on a multiple of forecasted revenues or profits). All of these risk-based adjustments take away from the economic value you could have captured in a transaction had you been able to address the acquirer concerns.

Your insight into acquirer concerns leads to leverage. When you have insight into what truly matters to the acquirer, you can proactively illuminate the dark spots and put an acquirer's skeptical mind at ease. By increasing the acquirers' level of conviction around the areas that they care most about, you can increase both their interest level and the value they are willing to ascribe to the transaction. That is, you increase the acquirer surplus, which would then make it easier for them to be more flexible and compromising in negotiations.

No two acquirers are the same, and therefore not every acquirer cares about the same things. You may notice in your discussions with potential suitors that while one may be very much focused on your technology and team, another may be focused on the operating financials of your startup. That's why it is critical to listen closely and probe into what truly matters to your counterparts. For instance, I have found customer- and product-centric metrics to be especially important to acquirers in consumer internet and software industries, such as Microsoft, Intuit, Facebook, Adobe, and Salesforce. In acquisition discussions with such companies, startups that have a solid grasp of their customer data and metrics for their products tend to be the ones that rise to the top of the acquirers' pipeline and can obtain a premium valuation. Conversely, those startups that struggle with extracting relevant customer or product metrics leave the acquirers guessing about their quality of products as well as the management's operating capabilities. If an acquirer still decides to move forward, they will apply steep discounts to what they would have otherwise paid.

In strategic negotiations, my advice is to start by demonstrating how combining your organizations would grow the pie before you start dividing the pie and negotiating the size of your slice. The ideal starting point is one where you get to paint a clear and convincing picture of the opportunity ahead. You definitely don't want to start a long-term relationship by haggling over what is in it for you. In company acquisitions, "growing the pie" typically involves creating revenue synergies, cost synergies, or both. Revenue synergies come from a more efficient sale process as a result of the acquisition (for instance, one party is then able to sell its products to the other party's customer base). Cost synergies typically come from elimination of duplicative costs across the two organizations (for instance, the elimination of redundant sales, marketing, or administrative costs).

Those are clear areas of opportunity where you can help your acquirer understand the benefits of joining forces. The more data-driven insight you can provide to support your forecast for both cost synergies and revenue synergies, the more accurately your counterpart will be able to model its acquirer surplus, and the less of a discount it will have to apply to its valuation.

Objective 2: Find the Acquirer's Resonant Frequency

Although a solid financial outcome is necessary to every for-profit company acquisition, it is by no means sufficient. There also has to be a strong strategic rationale for the acquisition. That is why, for instance, you don't see acquisitions across industry boundaries (e.g., car companies buying oil and gas companies or vice versa), or even across customer segments within the same industry (e.g., enterprise focused software companies don't acquire consumer focused software companies and vice versa). Each acquirer has its particular strategic goals and objectives, which may very well change and evolve over time. And in light of their particular strategy, they would have specific needs that an acquisition could meet, such as improving growth and market share, accelerating time to market for a certain product suite, gaining competitive advantage, or obtaining certain operating efficiencies. The initial hook—that a potential transaction will be on strategy for the acquirer—needs to be firmly in place as a foundation for the rest of your negotiation. Which means that in order to further improve your negotiation leverage, you will need to identify your potential acquirers' resonant frequency.

In physics, systems or objects vibrate in accordance with their inherent or resonant frequency. If you tap into that frequency, even the slightest input leads to a result that reverberates. A similar phenomenon is at work when you are communicating with potential strategic partners or acquirers. If you manage to convey your message in a way that is aligned with their strategy and the way they see the world, your message will resonate and take on a life of its own. It will be well-received, shared, and amplified throughout the organization. For instance, in one strategic partnership negotiation we were having a hard time convincing our counterparts to prioritize our product integration requests even though it would result in millions of dollars in annual revenue for that partner. Despite our numerous attempts at finding workarounds and simplifying the integration, we were facing significant resistance by product teams who had other strategic objectives to meet for the year. Everything changed, however, after one of my colleagues pointed out how this integration work would also help this partner's efforts to compete effectively against a sizable competitor. Armed with that framing, our champion there was able to successfully gain the internal green light for the product integration work we had been struggling with for months. To maximize your leverage, then, you need to learn about your acquirer's organizational resonant frequency, working to understand the dynamics at play, what it is that they are really trying to achieve, and what they are missing that you can provide.

Any insight into what a potential acquirer would value (as well as what they would consider a liability) can have a tremendous impact on the outcome of your discussions. When it came time to think about potential acquirers for our startup Webs, we went searching for companies that we suspected would have strategic needs that aligned with our strengths. Vistaprint was among the candidates on the top of our list. We understood that the world was moving toward digital, so companies such as Vistaprint (the leading online printed business card supplier at the time) were going to either be disrupted away or find a way to solve their customers' digital needs. We established a relationship with Vistaprint. Then, throughout our discussions, we validated our hypothesis that they were looking to improve their digital strategy. This was their resonant frequency.

Use every opportunity to learn more about your potential strategic partners. Your champion is a fantastic resource for this purpose. In most cases, if any deal is going to move forward, there will be mutual dependence between you and your strategic partner. Uncover the areas where your strategic partner will need you, and then make sure you put your best foot forward in those areas.

ENHANCE YOUR APPEAL

Effective real estate agents don't just stumble into an above-market sale. They put in the effort to clean up and stage a property, make minor repairs, take professional photos, create virtual tours, and design beautiful collateral before listing a property for sale. It is no different when it comes to the dynamics of selling your startup: sellers who can create appeal create leverage. Not only do these startups draw attractive valuations, but they see much less of that value held back in escrow or tied up in earnouts.

You may believe that your startup is quite appealing as it currently is. But to keep any cognitive dissonance in check, you would do well to step back and make a more objective assessment. Your startup is objectively appealing if you are getting a lot of inbound interest from potential strategic partners and acquirers. If you are not currently being pursued by those kinds of suitors, then you are not *appealing*; at least, not yet. Certainly, you may be tempted to retort: Can't my startup still be appealing even if there are no suitors at the doorsteps yet?

But that's a bit like the age-old philosophical question about the tree falling in the forest. Sure, there may very well be an intrinsic aspect to appeal, but for all practical purposes, it would make no difference to you, your startup, or its stakeholders. At the end of the day, your appeal only matters if it ultimately attracts the right acquirers. Your appeal is truly in the eye of the beholder. And when you do manage to appeal to the right set of acquirers, then you get to flex your leverage.

Just as it is with the other ingredients of leverage, you can't manage to effectively appeal to your potential suitors without taking purposeful action toward achieving that goal. In the M&A market, where your startup is the product, that process tends to take more time and careful planning than in most other markets, such as real estate, where agents can typically stage a property in a few weeks or a month. Your startup, on the other hand, needs to work for months or years to reach a certain level of product/market fit satisfactory to the unique needs of potential acquirers.

Although each appealing startup is unique, there are common attributes shared by all appealing startups in the M&A marketplace. In my experience, a startup can successfully attract suitors if it (1) fulfills a strategic need for them, (2) has alignment in vision and culture with them, and (3) is realistically acquirable by them. As you build on each of these attributes with respect to a set of potential acquirers, you become more appealing to them. You will know you are on the right track if your counterparts start spending more time with you, inviting you to events, introducing you to more of their executive leadership, granting you access to APIs ahead of time, or giving you a heads-up on upcoming releases or changes.

Your goal in enhancing your appeal should always be to establish a true and strong connection with your desired potential acquirers. To ramp up your appeal, start by incorporating the following practices into your interactions.

Practice 1: Broadcast Strategic Fit

Acquisitions are not impulse purchases. At least not the successful ones. There is enough friction built into the whole M&A process to slow things down for some of the initial deal fever to subside and for cooler, more rational heads to prevail. As I will cover in more detail in Part IV, an acquirer will need to justify the rationale for a transaction to various internal and external stakeholders before a deal can be signed. Depending on the size of the transaction, such stakeholders span from the senior leadership team to cross-functional leaders charged with executing the deal and carrying out some of the post-deal integration work, to the board and at times even shareholders and external resources, including accountants and lawyers. They will all have their own questions and doubts about the deal. As a result, those advocating for the acquisition and driving the process will need to articulate the deal rationale clearly and convincingly to everyone involved and be able to defend it against the critics and skeptics.

This is why it is so important to identify the resonant frequency of potential acquirers. Different acquirers have different strategic priorities: Sometimes a strategic need may be to accelerate growth rate, reduce costs, or expand margins. At other times it may be the need to build defenses against competition, solidify their position in an existing market, or enter a whole new market. You can feel the magic in the air when your startup's perceived strengths hit on that resonant frequency of the acquirer's strategic needs. You will then be able to dial in your message to the right frequency and demonstrate exactly how you can meet that potential acquirer's strategic needs.

Listen carefully to any feedback and continue tuning your approach until you find that strategic resonance. And then repeat that message over and over again to the same people as well as others you meet in that organization. It might seem at first blush that you wouldn't want to sound one-note or repetitive, but when dealing with a large organization, that is often the better approach. You need to repeat your core message and reiterate its fit with your target's needs. In any large organization, your counterparts will need to report to others, who will report to others—and having a consistent, resonant message means that it won't get lost in translation. You want to reach the point where all critical decision makers on the acquirer side have a clear understanding and appreciation of the strategic fit and value of your startup to them.

Practice 2: Demonstrate Alignment in Core Values

The more you demonstrate that your startup's core values (vision, mission, and culture) are similar to those of the acquirer, the more appealing you will become to them. That assumes, of course, that you have done your investigative work to understand the core values of the potential acquirers and found a bridge between your startup's values and theirs. Often, especially for companies in the same industry and/or serving the same target customer, there is a tremendous overlap in core values once one peers beneath the surface definition of value statements. For instance, during our preliminary M&A discussion at GoDaddy with Main Street Hub, a startup we acquired in 2018, we were delighted to find that our values of "own outcomes" and "join forces" mapped very well against what they called "take ownership" and "elevate others" respectively.

And to clarify, this is not about performing tricks on the subconscious mind of your unsuspecting counterparts. Beyond our psychologic preference for dealing with those who remind us of ourselves, there is a very tangible practical reality to why acquirers care about value compatibility, which is increasingly a conscious filtering criterion when acquirers consider targets. That is because experience as well as many studies have shown that the primary reason many acquisitions don't perform as expected is due to lack of cultural alignment.[10]

Without a deep alignment in culture and vision, you increase the chances of conflict and tension between the two organizations post acquisition, resulting in decision-making gridlock, wasted efforts, and ultimately loss of valuable talent and expertise. In this sense, acquisitions are very much like hiring decisions, except with a lot more people involved simultaneously. I have known acquisition integrations challenges and loss of significant value resulting from seemingly trivial differences between the two entities involving payroll cycles, benefit plans, sales and support team incentive structure, and cadence of product releases, as well as from more fundamental items like vision or business model differences, such as the high-profile disagreements between Mark Zuckerberg and the founders of both Instagram and WhatsApp over the level of autonomy of those platforms from Facebook and its advertising practices.[11] Savvy acquirers do have their antennas up and are ready to pick up the signals that show existence or lack of a cultural fit. The more signals they pick up that there is a fit, the more appealing you will be to them.

Practice 3: Signal Acquirability

Signaling your acquirability to a potential suitor tends to be challenging for most entrepreneurs. It can be as daunting and potentially as awkward as it is for a middle-school student to ask a classmate out for a date. Signaling your interest and the availability of your startup for a potential acquisition is a balancing act: you don't want to appear too eager, nor do you want to be so aloof that an acquirer wouldn't even put your name down on their potential target list. If an acquirer considers that an acquisition is either completely off the table for you or out of reach for them, they will not consider you "actionable," and therefore, not worth the pursuit.

Don't assume that acquirers consider all targets to be interested in an acquisition. Many entrepreneurs are not interested in selling, and from the acquirer's perspective it is hard to tell who's who. Therefore, your potential acquirers also have their antennas up for signals that indicate whether or not a sale or merger is within the realm of possibility for you. If they ask you point-blank, don't be timid or beat around the bush. Respond by articulating clearly what you would want to accomplish and whether joining forces could be interesting in terms of your longer-term goals and the mission of your startup.

Now, you may ask, wouldn't you lose your negotiation leverage if you let on that you are acquirable? The answer is simply, no. First, you don't have leverage on someone who is not sufficiently interested in pursuing you. Second, you can always preface your discussions by saying "assuming that the terms are fair, we would certainly entertain any serious combination that would do x, y, or z for our company." On the contrary, you improve your negotiation leverage and attract interest when you appear actionable by acquirers.

Beyond your words and presentation, acquirers look for other larger, organizational signals of acquirability. If you have recently raised a large sum of venture funding at a high valuation, for instance, you will be perceived as less actionable by many acquirers; your investors have presumably just invested at your startup's fair market value and will likely want to see how the story plays out, so there is little for an acquirer to gain. Conversely, if you are on the verge of starting to raise a new round of funding, acquirers would consider that to be an opening for strategic discussions, a topic we will turn to in greater detail shortly. The bottom line is that to keep your potential suitors engaged and interested, you need to make sure you don't seem completely out of reach to them.

Improving your options, insight, and appeal are the three core areas at your disposal for attaining leverage. And as such, they will significantly influence the outcome of your negotiations with potential acquirers during the short game of your exit strategy execution.

CHAPTER 12

KEEP GOING BY LEARNING AND TWEAKING

Momentum begets momentum,
and the best way to start is to start.
—**Gil Penchina**[1]

By now you have become quite familiar with the fact that the long game takes time to play out. For many, it can even feel like a frustrating waiting game: you set things in motion for an outcome in the distant future, while nothing seems to happen in the interim. But to have any realistic expectation of success, you need to continue to make progress against your ultimate objective. As such, it will require incredible resolve, commitment, and resilience by you and your team to continue playing the long game and not to take your collective eyes off the ball. There will be plenty of temptations along the way to abandon this *game* altogether. Understandably, whenever we embark on a path toward a seemingly elusive and distant payoff that is fraught with rejections and failed attempts, it is perfectly human to get discouraged and lose our motivation.

Even when you succeed in avoiding demoralization, daily emergencies will give you plenty of reasons to direct your limited time and attention elsewhere. Those emergencies creep up on us in all shapes and forms: one day it is a competitor's new strategic move, another day it is an unhappy customer's complaint on social media, or a major bug threatening to bring down our servers, or the specter of some economic or political calamity looming on the horizon. To top it all off, you will also rightfully feel very frustrated by how long things take with new connections or strategic partners without any major tangible outcome to show your team or your board for all your efforts. While every startup struggles to find the right balance in the allocation of resources between *what is important* and *what is urgent*, what is important usually gets deprioritized until it is forgotten.

As result, your long-term strategy execution can gradually fade into the background. Even when you start the journey with the best intention and strongest resolve, you will eventually start harboring doubts about the relative importance of your exit strategy execution in light of daily fires. After all, we don't have an infinite supply of time and money to tackle everything at once. We have all been there. But there are ways you can make progress despite the hardship and resource constraints—it just takes a bit more mindfulness and advance preparedness.

I consider it a fact of entrepreneurship (and life) that there is no silver bullet solution to our resource constraint and prioritization dilemma. The ambitious among us are fated to perpetually struggle with it on both personal and professional levels. Postponing something important until the day you have more resources to tackle it is in most cases a polite form of self-deception. The successful among us are those who figure out a way to make progress toward what is important *despite* the daily emergencies.

Just as Ulysses figured out a way to carry on with his journey despite the temptation of the enchanting lure of the Sirens' song (he had his crew tie him to the mast of his ship while plugging their ears),[2] there are ways to protect a strategic course of action against premature abandonment. Momentum is a powerful force that can keep you and your team moving forward, but you need to seize every moment to generate and maintain that momentum.

I will conclude my discussion of the long game by sharing some of the tools that I have found extremely helpful in long-term strategy execution. These tools will help you maintain your momentum as you navigate around the inevitable bumps on the road toward creating a viable exit path for your startup.

TOOL 1: RECONNECT WITH YOUR "WHY"

You cannot make progress against a long-term goal without recalling its purpose. Take away the purpose, and any undertaking eventually turns into a chore. To stay the course, you need to deeply connect with *why* you adopted it in the first place. For that reason, it will be important to periodically step back and recall why you decided to take on this strategy. Having put your goals and objectives in writing in a document such as the Exit Strategy Canvas we discussed in Chapter 6 is a great starting place to help you recall that why. Remind yourself and your team why you are doing what you are doing, why it is critically important even though the payoff may seem elusive and many years in the future.

TOOL 2: OBSESS OVER AND CELEBRATE INCREMENTAL PROGRESS

To succeed, you need to play the long game exceptionally well, which necessitates consistent attention and adjustments throughout the process. Like sailing a ship across the ocean, small changes in direction along the way can take you to very different destinations. And the farther you are from your ultimate destination, the bigger the consequences of small actions taken. Thus, you should examine the results of any tweaks you make along the path to ensure that they are getting you closer to your ultimate destination.

And this is where focusing on building momentum really helps. As you orient yourself toward building momentum, you gain the ability to connect the actions you take today with over-all progress toward creating a successful exit strategy. Watch your forward momentum in the areas of creating business relationships, cultivating champions, building capabilities, and creating leverage. Every small improvement in those areas helps build your momentum. Consistent incremental progress rather than achievement of some lofty goal is the key to building forward momentum. Celebrate those moments and improvements. But I know that for many entrepreneurs with outsized ambitions this does not come easy. I am not asking you to celebrate mediocrity. I am asking you not to be oblivious to true success or underestimate the compounding benefit of incremental progress.

Focusing on building forward momentum through incremental progress is the key to winning the long game. The most powerful waves are those that gather their strength over many miles before reaching the shore.

TOOL 3: MAINTAIN A DRUMBEAT

Once you get started, you need to establish a regular pace for this long journey. Your momentum is the driving force behind your strategy execution, but what maintains that momentum? To keep going, you need a drumbeat, a pulse, a heartbeat if you will, for your activities. This beat would serve both as a reminder and as a regulating force to keep the trains synchronized and moving forward. That's why all living organisms abide by the circadian rhythm, a biological clock that is built into their cells.[3] Life could not exist without that rhythm. Neither can your momentum. You breathe life into your strategy when you create a rhythm for your activities.

I have found strategy execution to be very much like keeping a good habit. As we all know too well, *starting* a good habit is relatively easy and fun, be it a new diet or exercise routine, but *keeping* it is a painfully different game. The problem is, once you break a habit and veer off course, getting back on track requires herculean efforts. The same goes for your momentum.

The good news here is that staying on track is not that hard; in terms of difficulty, it's not even close to keeping a diet. A simple recurring calendar invite for a meeting with your leadership team, perhaps at first on a monthly or even quarterly basis, may very well do the trick. The agenda for that meeting should include exchanging learnings and insights, reviewing progress made against incremental goals, setting new goals, and aligning on priorities. Doing so regularly will help you maintain long-term perspective and focus while dealing with near-term emergencies. More important, it ensures that everyone remembers that this initiative remains an important strategic item to execute against.

TOOL 4: BE REALISTIC

In order to sustain your momentum, you need to have realistic expectations. The more you focus on what is truly within your sphere of influence, the more realistic you become. Conversely, you gain absolutely nothing positive from bemoaning, begrudging, or dwelling over events that are beyond your control, such as a deal made between a competitor and a potential strategic ally or when a champion at your largest strategic partner leaves that company. Instead of feeling discouraged or disappointed that a large, multinational company in your space did not want to integrate the product of your 10-person startup and put it in front of their millions of users, celebrate the opportunity to tell your story to one of their executives and get their feedback to learn what you would need to do in order for them to seriously consider distributing your product next time around.

When you are realistic, it also becomes easier to find the upside in the downside and overcome challenges. In business, every downside does have its upside, if and when you look for it. Most often, that upside is the opportunity to learn and deepen your insight. It is the "what doesn't kill me makes me stronger" mindset, put into words by philosopher Friedrich Nietzsche toward the end of nineteenth century.[4] But when our goals are unrealistic, we lose the opportunity to learn from failure. It is like practicing archery with a target that is so far away that it is completely out of reach. Such a target would make it practically impossible to gauge whether you have the right aim, posture, or technique. Only after you bring that target closer within a realistic range can you see the impact of your tweaks and adjustments. As such, missing realistic targets provides great learning opportunities, whereas missing unrealistic goals can just be demoralizing and create friction for your momentum.

Whenever you feel that you are coming up short against things that you realistically could have performed better on, use the opportunity to understand the root cause of the shortcoming so that you don't make the same mistakes again. By having realistic goals and welcoming the reality of any failure to attain them, you open yourself to learning the lessons that those failures bring. Resisting reality with negative emotional reactions or denial of your responsibility only serves to delay, if not permanently postpone, the opportunity to learn. Learn from mistakes and then move on. Don't ruminate on mistakes as that is just wasted time, energy, and emotions. Keep building on that positive momentum until nothing can stop you from achieving those ambitious goals.

PART IV

Mastering the Short Game

CHAPTER 13

FOCUS ON EVERY SHOT

Every shot counts.
—Sir Henry Cotton

n Part III, you learned how to play the long game of M&A during which you build the foundation for mutually advantageous, long-term relationships with potential partners, expanding the horizon of strategic possibilities for your startup. It is now time to turn to the more tactical parts of selling your startup, a process I call the *short game* of M&A. It is at this stage of your startup's life cycle that you get to harvest the fruits of years of effort cultivating your relationships, capabilities, and leverage. You are now ready to drive toward, and negotiate the terms of, the combination of your startup and potential acquirers. The short game is, true to its name, short and fast-paced, at least relative to the long game—lasting anywhere from four months to a year, or sometimes even longer. As a rule of thumb, you are in the short game whenever you anticipate selling your startup in less than a year.

Your skills in playing the short game are as vital to the success of your exit as are your long-game skills. Just as in a game of golf, no matter how well-executed your long drive off the tee or your fairway shots are, much of your success still hinges on those shorter chip, pitch, and putt swings a few steps from the hole. Miss one of those and you could very well lose the game. In both M&A and golf, the short game is where the final score gets tallied. This is not to diminish the importance of what we have discussed so far: doing well in the long game is still necessary for success. In golf, if you hit a bad initial shot, you will end up having to cover a lot of ground on the course, which can render success literally out of reach. A well-executed long game earns you the privilege to play the short game.

Similarly for your startup's exit, if you don't build the right relationships and improve your leverage over time, it will be too late to make up for those deficiencies when you have the urgency to sell your startup. But it is vital not to rest on your laurels and become complacent with your long-game successes; neither a great set of strategic relationships nor strong leverage will by themselves get you a good deal. You still have to ace the short game to get to that successful outcome you deserve. "Every shot counts" as distinguished British golfer Sir Henry Cotton once proclaimed. "The three-foot putt is as important as the 300-yard drive."[1]

Although many startups don't really get into the long game (to their ultimate disadvantage), almost all are ultimately forced to play some version of the short game, both when their business is successful and when it is not. They often do so reactively as a response to an acquisition inquiry, on behest of the board or set of investors who are ready to exit, or compelled by some financial crisis, lack of funding, or other existential threat. Ideally, you enter the short game opportunistically and on your own terms when *you* feel that pursuing a sale is the right next step in executing your mission. And you earn that privilege when you have committed to, and masterfully played, the long game.

As mentioned, playing the long game well does not readily translate into success in the short game. That is because, just as in golf, in M&A the skills and tools required for the short game are quite different from those you utilize in the long game. The short game is actually significantly harder to play because it entails a much narrower margin for error with drastically higher stakes. You're under far more psychological pressure to perform; after all, the survival of your startup may very well be *immediately* at stake during the short game. Uttering the wrong *sentence* in a meeting or even the wrong *word* in a sentence can make or break a deal (more on that shortly).

And even when immediate survival is not at stake, most entrepreneurs still agonize over small missteps in their acquisition negotiations and worry that one wrong move could destroy a once-in-a-lifetime opportunity, which is equally, if not more, stressful for the hottest startups out there. For instance, after Mark Zuckerberg reached out to Instagram's board member and Benchmark investor Matt Cohler to inquire whether Facebook should acquire Instagram, Kevin Systrom's reaction was far more alarmed than celebratory or dismissive, concerned that the wrong response might compel Facebook to go into "destroy mode." This was evident in the text exchange between Cohler and Systrom in February 2012, which came to light during the July 2020 House Judiciary Committee antitrust hearings into the activities of Amazon, Facebook, Google, and Apple:

> **Cohler:** . . . so, not surprisingly, zuck pinged me to say "i'm not sure if this is a good idea yet, but I think maybe facebook should buy instagram, what do you think?" i obviously want to discuss with you before i reply to him
>
> **Systrom:** got it
> You know him better than I do
> a) will he go into destroy mode if I say no
> b) will he understand if we choose to raise instead
> c) will he understand that I don't want to shutter the product and that doesn't align with what FB does with companies
>
> **Cohler:**
> a) probably (and probably also if we just don't engage at all)
> b) no, he'll go harder into destroy mode then
> c) what I think he would most likely want to see is for instagram to turn into a stand-alone mobile facebook photos app, like beluga turned into facebook messenger . . .[2]

As you are aware, Systrom managed to play the short game skill-fully and pull off a record-setting sale. But he had to walk a very fine line to get there, being careful to maintain the positive relationship with Facebook and avoid pushing them into *destroy mode*. As this text exchange illustrates, the predicament is that once an acquirer makes the move, you cannot simply ignore them. Anything you say or do can backfire, so you will need to thread with extreme caution.

Things did not work out so well for serial entrepreneur and venture capitalist Ali Partovi after his first meeting with Steve Jobs back in 2008. Ten years after Ali had sold his first startup LinkExchange to Microsoft for $265 million, Ali got an audience with Steve Jobs in Apple's Cupertino, California, headquarters to pitch his rapidly growing music sharing startup iLike, one of the most popular applications on the Facebook platform at the time. Ali considered Apple with its iTunes platform to be an ideal potential acquirer for iLike (as one would surmise even by the similarity in the names). And the timing for a sale was ripe for him because iLike was under increasing pressure by record labels and the Facebook platform itself that could cut off their lifeline at any time. "Our dream and best hope was for Apple to acquire us," Ali recounted in a series of tweets recently, sharing the lessons and insights learned from that encounter.[3] Toward the end of that pitch session, that dream seemed to have finally become a reality: Steve Jobs was so impressed by Ali and his team's presentation that he said right there and then that Apple wanted to buy the company. But the dream was short-lived. "I wish I could preserve that beautiful moment," Ali tweeted.

What transpired next teaches a masterclass on how the smallest detail, even one word, can separate success from failure in the short game. Instead of taking his time to build a trusted relationship, Ali asked Steve what valuation he had in mind before the meeting adjourned. While this was an error, as he should have waited until much later in the game, it was not a fatal error. Steve, of course, shrewdly replied by inquiring into iLike's revenues and last fundraising round's valuation, using this as data to benchmark and anchor his response. As soon as Steve heard that their last round's valuation was $50 million, he made it his starting number for the purchase price. If that move was meant to put Ali on his back foot, it certainly did its magic. That valuation was from two years prior, before iLike had publicly launched, when iLike had none of its 50 million active users. Moreover, Ali had been floating $150 million as the expected valuation for a new round of financing in informal discussions with potential investors. Ali couldn't hide his disappointment and quickly replied, "Steve, I think we're worth at least three times that. Actually, I *know* we're worth three times as much." Throwing in the word *know* in that last sentence was Ali's fatal mistake. As he recalls, professing to have actual *knowledge* about his valuation was an unnecessary exaggeration that destroyed Steve's trust in him instantly. True to form, Steve called him out on this right away: "Bullsh**. You're lying to me. You're full of sh**. We're done here."

While the teams still tried to salvage a deal after that awkward ending, it was too late. Steve's trust was gone, and without trust, no deal can ever get done. Ali still regrets that mistake and warns entrepreneurs to realize that "trust can be ruined with a single word, and it's not easy to rebuild." As it turned out, iLike never got a chance to recover from that mistake. Soon after that meeting, both Apple's iTunes and Facebook became its competitors, releasing on their own platform some of the key features that had made iLike so popular. Within a year, Ali had to sell his startup for a loss.

Just as with the long game, there are no magic tricks, simple hacks, or handy shortcuts to mastering the short game. To take on its challenges effectively, you need to familiarize yourself with the terrain and learn the frameworks and best practices for success. And you need to understand where others have stumbled and even failed so you don't make the same mistakes. This knowledge and familiarity will put you in pole position to achieve the best possible outcome. Moreover, by providing you with visibility into what lurks around some of the most dangerous corners, they will lessen your stress and anxiety as you navigate these treacherous roads.

This last part of the book is designed to help you master the M&A short game. If you take the time to study the following chapters carefully and follow their guidance, you will be more prepared than most founders when they reach this critical juncture in their startup journey. Some of those founders may even be your competitors vying for an acquisition by the same cohort of acquirers you have on your wish list. We start the process in Chapter 14 by taking a close look at your initial approach to acquirers, examining *when* and *how* you should get into M&A conversations with them. You will learn about ways to test the waters with potential suitors and create urgency without losing leverage or damaging your hard-earned strategic relationships.

Next, in Chapters 15 and 16, I break down the sale transaction into two sequential phases: The first phase, the Term Sheet phase, encompasses the courtship, preliminary due diligence, and term sheet negotiations, which may take several months to half a year or longer. The second phase, the Agreement phase, is typically shorter and spans from a signed term sheet to the signing and closing of the transaction.

I will familiarize you with the key processes, concepts, and tools for each of these phases and provide you with guidance on how to spot and navigate the traps for the unwary along the way. These phases will unfold over several often-trying months. To persevere, you will need to remain stubbornly positive, patient, and focused, as the ultimate success and survival of your startup can hang on just one word.

CHAPTER 14

YOUR OPENING GAMBIT

*The time to eat appetizers is when they
are being passed around.*
—Eugene Kleiner[1]

What do good jokes, startups, and acquisitions have in common? Impeccable timing! Before Facebook, there was SixDegrees, Tribe, Affinity Engines, Friendster, Myspace, and a myriad of other social networking platforms trying to build the social graph and connect friends online. Similarly, before LinkedIn there was Spoke and ZeroDegrees that tried to do the same for professional networks. Yet none of those early entrants managed to succeed on a massive scale. Their failure was not due to lack of foresight or poor execution. They just didn't get the timing right, and in that, they were in very good company. Bill Gross, the founder of MIT Idealab, which launched over 100 startups, studied causes for success and failure among hundreds of startups (including his own portfolio) and shared the results in his popular 2015 TED Talk. His research revealed what many entrepreneurs had long suspected: the single biggest contributor to startups' success or failure is their timing as opposed to team, idea, business model, or funding (in decreasing order of relative impact).[2] In hindsight, I have little doubt that timing had a lot to do with the demise of my first startup (Jaxtr) as well. And getting the timing right is seldom something you can be sure of in advance. You can make educated guesses based on demographic, technological, or economic trends, but until you have a product or service that you put in the hands of the end users, you won't really know. And by the time you find out, you (and likely many others) will have invested a lot of blood, sweat, and tears into the project.

The silver lining here is that although you don't have much control over making sure the timing for the *start* of your startup is right, by following the guidance in this book you can and should do better when it comes to the timing for the *exit* of that startup.

PICKING THE RIGHT TIME TO EXIT

Just as it is with any other critical decision, such as hiring a key employee, raising money, or inking a strategic partnership, you have to take into consideration a number of internal as well as external factors in order to determine the right timing for the sale of your startup. And ultimately, as it is with all such decisions, after taking into consideration all the various factors, you will have to make a judgment call. What makes the judgment call hardest for picking the right time to sell your startup is that this decision is emotionally charged due to the size of the stakes involved. But there are frameworks and processes you can apply to ensure that you arrive at the best possible decision.

The Perfect Storm

Putting emotions aside for a moment, at a fundamental level, the ideal time for you to sell your startup is when the following three conditions come together:

1. You (and the rest of your stakeholders) are willing to sell.
2. You are pursued by multiple interested parties.
3. You have solid leverage in negotiations with those interested parties.

If you can orchestrate things such that these conditions can all be satisfied at a point in time, then you have mastered the art of exit timing. Of course, getting these conditions to converge is not trivial. In particular, the first and last conditions are the hardest to satisfy simultaneously. That is because when we have solid leverage, we feel on top of our game and unstoppable. As a result, many fast-growing startups delay engaging in serious acquisition talks, believing that their leverage will be even better in the future. Thus, ironically, most entrepreneurs and their stakeholders are unwilling to sell until they are desperate to sell, waiting until they have exhausted all viable alternatives to a sale, which is, needless to say, pretty much the lowest leverage position they can find themselves in. That is why it is best to mentally prepare yourself and other stakeholders in advance that if you decide to sell, you will need to strike while the iron is hot and not get too complacent with your own successes. Remember that your critical stakeholders need to be brought along on this journey so that you can move fast when the opportunity presents itself.

Risks of Jumping the Gun

While you don't want to wait too long before you start testing the appetite of potential suitors, you don't want to engage in these discussions prematurely either. Entering these discussions before you are truly ready can spell disaster. You may end up wasting valuable time chasing what will turn out to be a lowball offer, or worse, you could very well taint a strategic relationship by causing your partners to question your long-term viability and commitment to the business. Therefore, if you have the luxury of time on your side, you want to pace your discussions until you are confident you can satisfy all three of the conditions I mentioned above.

It's important to note that it is not always the sellers that get carried away and rush into acquisition talks prematurely. An overly eager strategic partner may also jump the gun and try to make advances at a time that is not ideal for you. As a thought experiment, imagine for a moment that you are faced with that exact situation: a potential strategic ally with whom you have been trying to launch a partnership suddenly turns around in a meeting and says that since they don't typically partner with small start-ups due to potential risks of that startup's long-term viability, they would like to discuss whether you would be interested in selling your startup to them instead.

How would you respond to that overture? Would you reject their advance outright as something that is completely out of the realm of possibilities, or would you tell them that you will think about it and then tell them no?

Actually, neither of those approaches would be conducive to the creation of a strong strategic partnership. While no one cherishes being rejected on the spot, if you seriously entertain an offer and then report back that it is not the right time for you, that could disappoint your counterparts even more. It is very likely that you will destabilize and erode the trust in the relationship with that strategic partner in both scenarios. Even if your counterparts take the rejection with utmost professionalism and emotional maturity, you may very well worry that since this company has shown interest in being acquisitive in your area, they may now be looking at acquiring one of your competitors and become a major threat to you down the road. As Instagram's leadership worried when Facebook approached to acquire them, you may also worry that this rejection may push your counterpart go into *destroy mode*. In light of these doubts, would you be willing to continue to invest time and resources into this partnership and share market or customer insights that could one day be used to destroy you? Probably not. Once trust starts to give way to suspicion, it becomes very hard to continue on the path of a meaningful partnership.

The above predicament underscores why you should open up acquisition discussions with current or potential strategic partners only when you see a clear path to a reasonably successful outcome. It also makes a strong case that whenever you do enter into a partnership or strategic discussions, you should lead with your high-level goals. Laying that groundwork early on enables you to forestall and deflect any premature advances by referring back to your long-term strategy and turning your conversation into a joint inquiry into how best to achieve your ultimate objectives. Once a potential acquirer appreciates your goals and starts to brainstorm ways to jointly achieve those goals, you can then make progress toward building a strong relationship that is the prerequisite for any meaningful outcome.

Since most of us do not have the power to line up suitors for our startups with a checkbook in hand on demand, we need to be quite deliberate in how we cultivate and pace discussions with potential buyers. Ideally, you want each discussion to be as scripted as possible, with clear objectives and messaging points to be conveyed. Thus, the key is far more preplanning than improvisation in these engagements. To get the timing of your acquisition discussions right, make sure that you have those prospective buyers prepared and ready to take the next step when, and only when, you are confident that you are ready to sell and can enter negotiations with solid leverage.

Making the Ultimate Call

While you should not jump the gun on acquisition discussions until you have multiple interested parties and solid leverage, it does not mean that you should prioritize the sale of your startup above other strategic initiatives whenever those conditions are met. Continuing to build your startup as a stand-alone entity may still be your optimum path forward, just as it was the case for Netflix, Google, and Dropbox in their early years. Instead, your decision to pull the trigger on a sale process hinges on how you and your stakeholders evaluate the overall pros and cons of selling your startup at any point in time.

That decision is ultimately an executive judgment, one that should be deeply rooted in your startup's values and goals. Refer back to your definition of success, opportunities, risks, and mitigants that you documented in your Exit Strategy Canvas. Regardless of experience, no one is better situated than you and your team to decide when you should sell your startup.

COMMON CONSIDERATIONS

Familiarizing yourself with what others typically take into account in making this critical, outcome-defining decision will help you come up with a starting framework for deciding whether it is the right time to pursue a sale. To that end, below are the most common motivations and risks I have found entrepreneurs discuss when they start exploring their exit options. Understandably, no such list is exhaustive. There may very well be other considerations that should play a role in how you evaluate a potential sale. Ultimately, you must carefully evaluate the most relevant trade-offs for you to arrive at a decision that is best aligned with your startup's values and goals.

Common Motivations to Start a Sale Process

Let's start with the most common reasons startups enter the short game.

Dilution Avoidance

Back in early 2011 when the founding team started contemplating the sale of Webs, an almost 10-year-old startup where I was leading strategy and business development, we faced a strategic dilemma: we would need to either raise enough funds for a marketing arsenal to compete against our closest competitor Wix.com, which had just announced raising a $40 million Series D round,[3] or sell the company to someone who had that marketing arsenal to capture the tremendous opportunity in online website creation for millions of small and midsize businesses that were just starting to come online. An arms race was afoot. Continuing on our current execution path was no longer a viable, sustainable path to success.

Raising the requisite funding in this arms race would significantly dilute the shareholdings of the team and push out a potential liquidity event by many more years. So, we set out to test the market and see if we could sell the company at a reasonable price. Echoing similar considerations in deciding to sell Behance to Adobe, founder and CEO Scott Belsky recalls that when he was evaluating his alternatives, he was well aware of businesses that were acquired for north of a billion dollars whose founders received a financial outcome of a fraction of businesses that were acquired for $200 million.[4] Getting to that much-envied "unicorn" status usually comes with significant dilution, which may not in the long run be to the financial advantage of the founders and employees compared with an earlier exit. Successive financing rounds come with a hefty price tag to the founders, employees, and early investors.

With every new round of financing, you lose more control over your startup and set a higher threshold for your exit valuation. Venture investors expect voting shares and a healthy multiple on their investment (in the range of 3x to 10x depending on the stage and size of the investing fund), so if you raise your Seed or Series A round at a valuation of $10 million to $20 million, then the exit expectations for those investors would typically be in the $30 million to $200 million range, whereas the expected range is significantly higher if you raise future rounds at a valuation of $50 million or more. Furthermore, typical venture rounds come with some form of liquidation preference, which would at a minimum require you to pay back your investors before you and your team can participate in any of your exit proceeds.

With each successive round at a higher valuation, you raise the bar for what would be considered an acceptable exit for your investors and what it would take to even pay back the amount invested in your startup. Considering that there are very few startups that ever sell for a valuation north of $100 million, you may paradoxically be reducing your chances of a successful financial outcome with each new funding round.

Obtaining Liquidity

As it was the case for Webs, if the founding team or a set of investors have been involved with your startup for many years (typically nearing or exceeding 10 years), it is reasonable to see some of the team members or investors become increasingly interested in an exit as a way to get access to liquidity, especially when you are being acquired for cash or stock of a public company. Typical venture capital firms have a 10-year time horizon. And most early-stage startup founders and employees take significantly lower cash compensation in return for equity, which makes life increasingly harder as the years (and debt levels) pile on. Providing a way for those individuals or investors to see a return on their investment through an exit is why many startups explore a sale.

Leverage Optimization

Leverage is your strongest ally when negotiating a sale. Whenever your startup is in a position of strong leverage, that is a great time to consider starting a sale process, especially when you expect strong market headwinds on the horizon. As discussed in Chapter 11, whenever you have options, superior insights, and are perceived as an attractive target by one or more desirable suitors, you have great leverage. These high-leverage positions take time and effort to get to, but savvy entrepreneurs don't assume they will last forever and make sure to check the market appetite for an acquisition when they feel they have strong leverage.

Almost by definition, all of the high-profile, high-price startup acquisitions of our time resulted from high-leverage negotiation positions. But this does not mean you have to wait until you get to an astronomic valuation for your startup before you explore a sale. Leverage is relative to each startup's unique trajectory, and even a very small acquisition may be the strongest viable option for that startup. If you reach a point where you have a product or service that is growing fast and highly desired by several strategic acquirers in a competitive market, then you may very well want to seize on your high-leverage status even if you don't think the sticker price for your startup would earn you a dedicated article in the *Wall Street Journal* or *TechCrunch* or make anyone involved independently wealthy. Under those circumstances, deciding to sell your startup can still be the most rational and sensible thing to do.

A friend who is a Silicon Valley investment banker representing earlier stage companies once explained that he usually advises companies to start a sale process before a major launch or strategic pivot that has great promise. He was of the opinion that at such junctures, the market values startups on the potential of the opportunity ahead, rather than looking at their track record and poking holes in it. This certainly was the case when British Telecom acquired Ribbit for $105 million in cash in 2008 before they had even launched their offering.[5]

However, be cautious and understand that having the *appearance* of leverage is not the same thing as *attaining* true leverage. While appearance of leverage evaporates under heated negotiations, true leverage strengthens your negotiating position. For instance, it is possible that due to some recent press or early traction with a product launch you may start getting inbound interest from larger companies you would list among your ideal acquirers. You should certainly use those opportunities to learn as much as you can about your suitors and identify and create trusted champions and advocates within those organizations. But don't jump the gun and escalate those overtures into actual acquisition negotiations until the objective performance of your startup can match your champions' enthusiasm.

Be as transparent as you can be and socialize the realistic current state of your startup with your trusted champions and carefully observe whether they remain excited or start expressing reservations. If the latter is the case, then aim to understand what would make you more appealing to your suitors and realistically assess how you can improve in those areas. You would be well advised to tone down the discussions until your objective performance catches up.

Mission Execution

As emphasized throughout the book, selling one's startup to a strategic acquirer may be the best way to ensure the continued execution of its mission. When entrepreneur Subbu Rama entered into acquisition discussions with VMware for his software startup Bitfusion, he was well aware that integrating with VMware's products and distribution channels gave his solution much better chances of wider adoption and market penetration. VMware was already a customer and partner, and they had proven out this thesis together. Moreover, given the "bigger checkbook" of VMware, he felt that by joining forces they could improve the product in ways he could not do in the near term with the limited resources of a stand-alone startup. So, when VMware pivoted from an investment conversation and made an acquisition overture, Subbu seized the opportunity. While Subbu and his team were originally focused on raising their Series B round of financing and building a stand-alone company, they changed course once they were convinced that selling to VMware would accelerate the accomplishment of their ultimate mission.[6]

Survival

While there are some entrepreneurs, like Ali Partovi at iLike, who may foresee existential threats miles away and jump-start acquisition conversations as soon as they notice storm clouds gathering on the horizon, many startups turn to an exit as their last resort when they are on the precipice of a shutdown. Clearly, that would be a very low leverage position and result in an outcome that could become the basis of recurring nightmares. This was the case for me when we decided to sell my first startup, Jaxtr. We had very limited cash runway left in the company and did not have any viable funding sources available. So even though a desperate attempt at survival is the primary reason many startups initiate their sale process, my hope is that with proper advance planning, it does not become the starting point of your exit path.

Market Timing

This one is not in your control, but something to be cognizant of nonetheless. There are periods within each business cycle where valuations in a certain sector are especially attractive for various reasons, be it as a result of pure hype or more rationally, as a result of some optimism about the future or new opportunities presented in that sector. Think of it as the equivalent of a "sellers' market" in real estate for your industry. Should you find yourself in that fortunate situation, it would be reasonable to explore a sale process. Why? Because your negotiation power as well as the outcome you obtain could be drastically different compared with other times.

Team Outcome

Every sale has real consequences for all of the stakeholders in your startup, including customers, shareholders, employees, contractors, lenders, and vendors. Some sales are even primarily motivated to ensure a positive outcome for one specific group more than any other: the employees. Many so-called "acquihires" or "talent acquisitions" have the core objective of continued employment of the team after a sale. This is a variant of the "survival" objective mentioned above and usually a last resort for many startups who are unable to get to either product-market fit or a sustainable path to growth.

Common Risks of Starting a Sale Process

Starting a sale process is not without its downsides, which you will need to carefully weigh against your motivation to do the deal in the first place. If you choose to proceed, you will need to implement safeguards and mitigants against these risks. The following are some of the most common risks entrepreneurs face when they enter into acquisition discussions as well as guidance on ways you can mitigate against those risks.

Team Distraction

A sale process is very time consuming and distracting. Once you enter the short game, it will consume your time as well as a good amount of your leadership team's time for months. You will have numerous meetings with interested parties, advisors, board members, and investors, starting with the courtship phase all the way through deal negotiation and diligence. Now, if at the end of all this activity the deal falls apart, which many deals do, that will be a lot of time wasted that you and team could have spent building your startup.

Investor and serial entrepreneur Justin Kan, who has sold multiple startups ranging in size from the low millions to almost a billion dollars with Twitch's sale to Amazon, describes it this way:

> *Entering the acquisition process is one of the most dangerous things an early-stage startup can do because the process is distracting, demoralizing, and usually involves giving your competition most of your proprietary business data. Founders who have been through the process have said it is ten times as distracting as fundraising. It often cripples your ability to oversee the business operations. Do not enter into an acquisition process lightly.*[7]

Many entrepreneurs misinterpret the signals and intentions of a potential acquirer and end up wasting invaluable time, distracting their team, and ultimately disappointing and demoralizing them. Or worse. A friend who is a general manager at a "unicorn" pre-IPO startup was excited about acquiring a small, 20-person startup. This was the first acquisition for his company and it would significantly accelerate his business unit's product development efforts and time-to-market. This team was perfect for them, and he didn't hide his enthusiasm from the target management. And seeing that level of interest encouraged the target leadership to focus all their efforts on prioritizing their time and efforts on this particular acquirer. After a couple of weeks of negotiation and courtship, they signed a term sheet and proceeded to interview the whole team over several weeks of meetings. There were at least five interviews for each employee, so roughly 100 meetings were scheduled and conducted. Each interview reaffirmed both sides' mutual desire to consummate the transaction. Everyone was excited about joining forces. Everyone, that is, except the CEO of the acquiring company.

When the deal was finally brought to the CEO for his blessing, he vetoed it. Thus, the entire process became a massive waste of time for both teams. This is time that the selling startup could have spent with another potential acquirer who might have been a better suitor. But by then it was too late: they had exhausted all their available funds and had to shut down. The risk for team distraction and transaction failures exists with every deal, but it is particularly more pronounced when dealing with acquirers who have not fully developed the muscles to be serious acquirers, lacking the internal processes and safeguards to efficiently assess and consummate acquisitions. Be particularly cautious if a potential acquirer is doing so for the first time or does not typically do multiple acquisitions a year.

IP and Competitive Risk

As the above quotation from Justin Kan alludes to, opening up your books and allowing the potential suitors a peek under the hood of your proprietary data, technology, and processes comes with a lot of inherent risks. Many of your potential acquirers tend to be competitors in one way or another. The information you provide them may ultimately be used against you if your sale process falls through and you decide to continue to independently compete in the market. Of course, you can have negotiated and signed the most sophisticated nondisclosure agreement (NDA) to protect you, but barring a blatant copying of your code, it will be very hard for you to ascertain what information was used, and by whom, to your disadvantage. Once the cat is out of the bag, it will be hard to put it back in.

But can't you just keep your cards close to the chest until you have signed the sale agreement? Unfortunately, no. Even though you can keep certain trade secrets confidential until at least a term sheet is signed, once you are past that gate, an acquirer will need to confirm their assumptions and know what it is they are buying before they buy it. Even before a term sheet is signed, most acquirers will be unable to provide you with a reasonable offer unless they have done some level of diligence and have had sufficient visibility into your operations to decide whether it is worth their time and effort to pursue the purchase. As a buyer, you most likely wouldn't even buy a house or a car without a tour or test drive, let alone when the stakes are much higher. If you do get an acquirer to make a bid without a lot of diligence and you decide to pursue the sale with that buyer, be ready for the possibility that the deal could materially change or even fall apart once the acquirer gets to learn more about your startup.

The best you can do is to request that the operating business units within an acquirer that compete with your startup not have certain items disclosed to them. But there is always a risk of items getting into the wrong hands over time as roles and responsibilities in larger companies tend to be relatively fluid, and it will be very hard to strictly compartmentalize information for a long time.

News Leak

Acquisition discussions need to be kept highly confidential and private. If the news of your interest in selling your startup or the fact that you are having discussions with a certain potential acquirer leaks, it could not only jeopardize that transaction, but you may even face an avalanche of other undesirable consequences, including the following:

1. **Negative publicity in the press and blogosphere.** Alternative or false narratives may take hold as to why you are embarking on a path to sell the company.
2. **Loss of talent due to aggressive poaching/recruiting by others.** When it comes to one's employment, people generally don't like uncertainty; and since your best employees always have options outside your startup, they may opt to choose one of them to preemptively minimize the risk of a loss of their job

or a demotion that may be associated with an acquisition. That is why savvy recruiters love to approach employees of startups that are rumored to be in acquisition talks

3. **Loss of key partners or customers.** Similar to your employees, partners and customers may also get spooked by the potential uncertainty of the future of your business.

4. **Lawsuits.** Opportunists, such as patent trolls, anticipating you would want to quickly settle rather than deal with a lawsuit in the middle of acquisition discussions, may start threatening legal action against your startup.

Internal Misalignment

If you suspect that some of your key stakeholders, such as major investors, board members, or members of your leadership team, would not be supportive of a sale, that could be a good reason to delay initiating acquisition talks until you have had sufficient time to bring those parties further along on the journey. Although unanimous agreement may not always be possible, you do want to minimize the risk of insiders sabotaging your prospects or halting your momentum when you need it most.

A while ago, a company that I had advised sent me a request to sign off on their sale documentation as a shareholder, which they needed within the next 24 hours. I had not received any updates or news from this startup for years. This sudden rush request caught me and most of their other shareholders by surprise. By the time that CEO was able to schedule one-on-one discussions with numerous confused shareholders to explain the situation and own up to past communication shortcomings, they were weeks past the deadline to respond to their acquisition offer and lost their momentum with the interested acquirer.

BREAKING THE NEWS

As you know by now, an acquisition doesn't spontaneously materialize when you put willing buyers and sellers in the same physical or virtual conference room. The $150 billion US investment banking industry and thousands of brokers and dealmakers would not have existed otherwise. Those intermediaries and market makers serve important and critical roles in bringing buyers and sellers together and ensuring that deals get done. But you don't need or want an intermediary to start the sale process for you. You can, and should, do much of the initial advocacy and break the news yourself as you are the best spokesperson for your startup.

However, to capitalize on your leverage and drive toward a transaction on the best possible terms, you need to have a catalyst for the acquisition discussions. That initial approach and the way you inform your potential acquirers about your interest to sell will set the tone, and can even determine the outcome, of your exit.

Consider Your Message and Its Potential Side Effects

Once you make the decision to sell your startup, carefully consider what you would like to convey to your counterparts. Of course you want to impress upon them that you are open to selling your startup. But, and as importantly, you want to indicate that this window of opportunity is not open forever. The news of this development would, of course, be considered a significant inflection point for your startup by anyone who finds out about it. As such, you want to minimize any collateral damage or unintended consequences that may result from it. You don't want to come across as either desperate or pushy, which could undermine your leverage or put your counterparts on the defensive, respectively. I have been involved in situations when the sudden news of a startup's interest in a sale caused me, on the acquirer side, to suspend any further conversations around a commercial relationship with that startup on the suspicion that the startup could be running out of funds or facing some other trouble. I don't think I am unique in lacking enthusiasm for reaching out and catching what I suspect to be a falling knife.

Mind and Mine the Feelings

There are, as you know, no sidewalk signs, virtual banners, or the startup equivalent of an online dating profile that would announce your willingness to sell your startup to the world. But even if there were such means available to you, I would strongly caution against using them, at least not as your initial move. That's because, in the M&A world, buyers are a sensitive breed and often mirror your feelings about them. So, if you approach them with indifference, which these impersonal methods would convey, don't be at all surprised when you get the same treatment reciprocated.

Despite their sometimes stoic veneer, acquirers are just as governed by their emotions as the rest of us. They would seldom seriously pursue a deal unless on a deep, emotional level they actually felt good about doing so. And how do you get a buyer to feel good about pursuing your startup? By convincing that buyer that there is a genuine interest by you to sell to that particular buyer. Yes, acquirers yearn to feel special too.

But there is more to it: you want to eliminate any suspicion that you may be using an acquirer to get a better deal from someone else or that you are not serious about a sale. Without that basic level of conviction, few buyers would commit the requisite mindshare and resources to pursuing a major strategic transaction with you.

To convey your *genuine interest* to an acquirer, you need to share why you think a sale to *that particular acquirer* makes sense. Do your homework about the acquirer and uncover areas of strategic overlap and operational synergies. Use your potential champions and established contacts within each potential acquirer to validate your assumptions and hypotheses. Although each startup-acquirer pairing can have its unique reasons for being desirable, here are some of the common strategic rationales for a sale that may hold true in your case as well:

1. Gaining broader access to market and customers through the acquirer's marketing channels and customer funnels

2. Building a superior product by combining complementary technical expertise and financial resources of the two organizations

3. Reducing end-customer costs or expanding profit margins through elimination of redundant operating expenses between the two organizations

4. Improving customer experience or the value of an offering by bringing together siloed networks of users or suppliers

5. Providing broader opportunities for professional and personal growth to employees who join the acquirer

Specifics will matter a lot. The more compelling your reason, the more a buyer would feel that you are interested in joining forces with them; which would then encourage them to spend time, attention, and resources on exploring a potential transaction with you and to stretch beyond their comfort zone (be it around valuation metrics, terms, or operational requirements) to make it happen.

Put the "Why" Before the "How"

As mentioned earlier, you should always lead your strategic discussions with high-level goals. The time to have the big-picture conversation with a buyer is long *before* there is any mention of valuation or specific terms of a deal. In fact, you should best postpone the latter until after you receive a term sheet from them. You want to ensure that the buyer fully understands *why* you are interested in selling to them and appreciates the outcome you would like to achieve. The deal terms would then become details of *how* you could get to that ultimate objective. By prioritizing communication of your strategic interest and mission-driven motivation to a buyer, you maximize the chances of that buyer empathizing with you and putting their best foot forward during the negotiations.

176

Don't Play Games

In M&A only interest invites interest, not aloofness or indifference. Since you want your potential acquirers to be very much attracted to your startup, make sure you do your part to convince them of your interest in them. There may come a time to play hard to get, but save that for much later. In the beginning, you want to ensure that a foundational level of mutual interest is firmly established.

Understandably, expressing your genuine interest in selling to a particular acquirer doesn't guarantee that they will immediately turn around and put an offer on the table. It just gives you the best chance of that potential acquirer taking you seriously. Whether it is a priority for them, and if so, whether they are ready and able to pursue a transaction, is a very different story, and something that is beyond your control.

Have the Right Opening

Before I share my preferred approach to starting the acquisition talk in the remainder of this chapter, let's consider some of the most common ways sellers start their acquisition talks with potential acquirers:

1. A phone call or email from the founder or CEO announcing that the startup's board or controlling shareholders want to sell the company, wondering whether the acquirer would like to hear the pitch due to significant strategic alignment between the companies;
2. A variation of the above, except that the stated reason for the call is receipt of an unsolicited offer to buy the startup, inviting the acquirer to participate in what is to become a competitive process; or
3. A variation of either of the above, but this time using an intermediary, such as investment banker, investor, or advisor.

While all such approaches deliver the key messages you would want to communicate to a potential acquirer to start the serious acquisition talks (conveying actionability, urgency, and strategic interest), I would strongly urge you not to adopt them. Here is why.

The Perils of a Direct Approach

None of the successful acquisitions I have been involved in started with the seller directly announcing their intent to sell their startup. Instead, in all those deals the buyers were the ones on the hunt and pleading the case that a sale makes mutual sense. Those startups were *bought*, not *sold*. The problem with the common, direct approaches mentioned above is that each catches most acquirers off guard and puts them in an awkward, reactive posture. Often acquirers on the receiving end of such propositions feel that they are being sold and put on the spot, which causes them to instinctively put up their mental guards. Perhaps it is a result of years of suffering from spammers and telemarketers, or because of some deeper, evolutionary origin, but I have yet to meet anyone who welcomes unsolicited sales pitches with excitement and open arms.

And there is the element of buyer timing that your approach needs to navigate. Clearly it is not just your timing, as the seller, that determines the pace of a transaction. Every buyer has their own universe of fire drills, emergencies, and resource constraints to contend with. So even if an acquirer is or would be genuinely interested in buying your startup, it is unlikely they have spare resources available to immediately jump into action and make a run for your company at the moment you hit them with the news of your desire to sell.

Contrary to the popular saying, a "will" does not lead to a "way" in M&A; even when there is a *will*, you still need to find a *way* to get the deal done. On many occasions, I have had to walk away as an acquirer from transactions that made perfectly good sense on a spreadsheet or slide deck due to a lack of resources to actually do the deal. Those resources span across business enablement functions of HR, IT, accounting, tax, and finance, who would be critical for conducting diligence and handling post-transaction integration tasks. If you convey your interest and urgency to sell at a time when potential acquirers don't have the internal bandwidth and readiness to go through with it, that leaves you and your relationship with those parties in a quite awkward and uncertain state. Those acquirers would either immediately bow out or try to delay and drag out a potential transaction until their resources become available, neither of which would be a particularly favorable outcome for you. And recall that the perceived future uncertainty about the faith of your startup would likely cause many potential acquirers to throttle back or even hit full stop on any existing strategic activities with you until your sale process has concluded. Your lack of perfect timing for announcing your sale process may very well end up destroying the goodwill you had worked so hard to cultivate and nourish with some of those acquirers.

So, what we have here is a perfect dilemma: telling your acquirer directly that you are for sale makes them either defensive or evasive. But they would not lean into trying to buy you unless they thought you would genuinely be interested in selling to them. The good news is that there is actually a way out of this particular predicament. And it has everything to do with how you communicate your willingness to sell. If you do it right, you can manage to convince your potential buyers you are open to a sale and have the truly interested parties pursue you when they are able to consummate a transaction. What you want to accomplish is to have the acquirers realize you are open to a sale without putting them on the spot or exerting timing pressure on them when they may not be ready or able to go through with a transaction. To do this, you have to inject a lot more subtlety into your approach.

The Power of an Indirect Approach

My preferred approach may best be referred to as *inception*, borrowing from Christopher Nolan's science fiction action classic by that name. And don't worry if you have not seen the movie. Most of us, by the time we are toddlers, clue into the magical powers of inception and start using it on our parents, siblings, and peers. Here is a case in point. For years, our young daughters shared a constant stream of cute puppy pictures with my wife and me, with the obvious goal of getting us interested in adopting one. They didn't harass us with incessant requests to adopt a pet. Instead, every now and then they would giggle and come and share a little photo or video of a puppy they found online that they considered super cute or funny. That was inception at work. Our daughters didn't put us on the defensive with this approach and didn't risk losing face if our answer to their request was negative. In fact, they knew our answer was no. Yet, they gently turned up the dial on our interest and left it up to us to decide when the right moment to cave in was. And after years of patience, they finally got the answer they were hoping for when we decided to adopt a puppy at the end of last year.

Inception is all about influencing others' decisions through subtle messages. Our hints and suggestions can plant ideas in others' minds so that they draw the ultimate conclusions we aim for. This eliminates much of the defensiveness and pushback a more direct approach typically results in, while preserving the relationship if the timing or level of interest for a positive response to the request is not quite there yet.

Using inception as your opener for the acquisition talk would mean that instead of surprising a strategic partner with the news that you have started a process to sell your company, you find subtle alternatives that communicate your willingness to entertain strategic alternatives for the future of your startup, which could very well include an acquisition. You can leverage your board or another objective set of circumstances as a conversation opener and a way to raise the possibility of a potential sale. For example, if your investors have been involved with your startup for longer than five years, you could confide in your counterpart that you are starting to get pressure from your investors to think harder about the strategic prospects for the company including exploring alternative paths to accelerate your road map progress. For a more direct approach that also signals your commitment to the partnership you could, for instance, point out that you believe there is tremendous synergy between the two companies and wanted to see whether there are ways to become further integrated and work closer together to capitalize on the opportunity. What you say and to whom will depend on the specific circumstances and particular aspects of your partnership, but what is important is to try to test the waters without applying pressure and escalating the discussions prematurely.

One problem with indirect and subtle hints, though, is that the subtlety may be lost on your counterparts. They may not fully grasp that you are signaling a genuine interest to sell, or even if they get that you are open to a sale, they may not sense your timing or the urgency associated with it. As a result, they may soon forget about what transpired as they move on to more urgent matters.

Although there may very well be others, there is one piece of information that I have found to effectively signal a company's desire for sale while implying in a nonthreatening way that the window of opportunity is time bound. That information is news about the prospect of an upcoming financing round. Sometimes entrepreneurs convey that information to their network of strategic partners as a way to explore their interest in participating in the round or just simply as a courtesy FYI. Regardless of the initial reason, many of the acquisitions I have been involved in heated up soon after a potential acquirer found out that the target was looking to raise a new round of funding.

Announcing the start of your fundraising process is particularly impactful because it suggests both actionability and urgency. It is as close as it comes to a magical wand you can wield to spur an acquirer to action, especially if you combine it with an invitation for the acquirer to participate due to strategic fit. This is, for instance, what entrepreneur Subbu Rama did when he approached his startup BitFusion's strategic partner VMware with an invitation to invest. VMware instead acquired his startup within months thereafter.

If, as a buyer, I am interested and able to pursue a target, there is no better time to do so than before it raises a new round. That is because getting the deal done at that time typically allows the acquirer to buy a target at a more reasonable price than after a new round is raised. New investors would demand a higher price than the valuation they just invested in, rationally expecting a return on their investment and would potentially block any deal in the short term as they may have other strategic aspirations for the company. Moreover, the pressure an acquirer feels to act in connection with a fundraising activity is more forgiving and less threatening compared with the pressure that the news of a sale process entails. Fundraising can take six to nine months, and therefore acquirers generally feel that they have more time to navigate and pull the requisite resources together to make a deal happen, whereas a sale process is usually assumed to be on a much shorter time frame. As a result, upon hearing the funding news, interested acquirers jump into action and try to make a case for the entrepreneur to consider a sale instead, whereas they typically go on the defensive and freeze up when they find out that a potential target is actively pursuing a sale.

The reason acquirers feel particularly emboldened to initiate acquisition discussions when you approach them with your fundraising plans is that they rightfully assume that any company raising money would be genuinely interested in a sale. That logic is simple: whoever is raising a new round is selling somewhere from 10 percent to 50 percent of their startup and therefore should also be open to considering a sale of up to 100 percent of the startup if the price is right. At the very least, fundraising activity gives an acquirer the permission to openly inquire whether an entrepreneur would be willing to entertain an acquisition as an alternative to getting further diluted and thus extending the time to a potential exit by several years.

And for you as the seller, having to go second means that you enjoy the enviable leverage of a company that is being pursued.

This is why breaking the news of an upcoming financing is a fantastic catalyst for acquisition discussions. Use it well by timing it right. As a testament to the inception power of such news, it is remarkable that to this date, I don't really know whether those targets who have approached me on the acquirer side with such news intended for it to precipitate an acquisition discussion or not. All I know is that in cases where we did have the readiness and desire to pursue an acquisition, we did.

So, in the opening gambit of the M&A chess game, you want to neither be white (where you make the first move) nor black (where you react to the other side's first move). You want to be gray! That is, you want the other side to make a move only when you are ready for their move and nudge them to do so.

But what if sharing the news of your upcoming financing doesn't elicit a reaction? That is, what if after sharing the news about your fundraising with your potential acquirers, you don't see any change in their approach or meaningful attempts to persuade you to consider a sale? To me, that would indicate that you either don't have the right set of acquirers at the table or that either the timing is not right for them, or you haven't painted a compelling enough picture for the strategic potential of an acquisition to pique their interest. Of course, you can still try the direct methods mentioned above as a final effort, but know that the chances for a successful outcome at that point would be quite low.

CHAPTER 15

TRANSACTION PHASE 1: TERM SHEET

Everything is negotiable. Whether or not the negotiation is easy is another thing.
—Carrie Fisher[1]

O nce you engage in discussions with one or more potential acquirers about the prospect of selling your startup, you have officially entered the first of the two phases of the short game, which I refer to as the Term Sheet phase. As you would suspect, this phase encompasses all that transpires between those discussions and when you have a signed term sheet. The term sheet, which you sometimes hear referred to as the *letter of intent*, or *LOI* for short, memorializes the general terms and conditions for the sale of your startup. It is not a boilerplate, click-through contract, but a highly negotiated document that sets the expectation of what would be the key financial and nonfinancial terms of the sale. Term sheets are for the most part nonbinding since the parties have not yet had a chance to truly conduct diligence (that is, kick the tires and look under the hood, so to speak) and leave out many details that need to be finalized in the deal documents.

Getting to a term sheet is a significant milestone in your exit process because it generally signals a buyer's serious intent to go through with a transaction. You can think of it as the M&A equivalent of an engagement ring. No reputable acquirer would bother with a term sheet without some amount of internal alignment to proceed with an acquisition. Of course, there may be cases when an acquirer issues a term sheet prematurely and, after going through the full diligence process, decides to walk away. However, experienced acquirers value their reputation and understand that frivolously issuing a term sheet without requisite internal alignment can not only hurt their chances for future deals, but potentially even create legal problems. It is a small world, and the technology M&A community is much smaller.

As happens in fundraising, whenever you get that first term sheet, others seem to suddenly become more interested in your startup. This could be due to FOMO (fear of missing out), an inherent love for competition, the assurance that comes with the fact that someone else has looked at your company and thought it was worth pursuing, or perhaps a combination of all. Once you announce to other interested parties that you have received a term sheet, you force their hand to either participate or drop out of the race. The news of a competitive term sheet allows your champions on the other side to pound the tables louder and advocate for the prioritization of your transaction above others. After all, you are now a perishable opportunity and, as such, quite valuable. This is in line with what psychologists and behavioral economists refer to as "loss aversion," our tendency to value things more when we are about to lose them.[2]

Therefore during the Term Sheet phase your main objective in interactions shall *evolve* from relationship building to receiving one or more term sheets. You will need to turn up the heat on the discussions to determine whether your potential suitors are serious enough to dig in, or whether they are just testing the waters without any real conviction to take the plunge. It is quite possible and likely that some potential acquirers may really want to buy your startup, but the timing is just not right for them. You want to know as soon as possible who among your suitors is willing and able to follow through with a transaction so you can devote your limited time and resources to them.

But while you are in active pursuit of getting a term sheet, don't lose sight of the impact of what you say or do on your relationships. Recall entrepreneur Ali Partovi's hard-earned lesson in his negotiation with Steve Jobs, where a single word sealed the fate of that startup as detailed in Chapter 13. Ensure that your actions or words do not cause your counterpart to doubt your sincerity, integrity, or good-faith intent in building a lasting strategic partnership with them. The four relationship-building pillars of humility, integrity, transparency, and dependability that were discussed in Chapter 9 should continue to guide and constrain your actions throughout the short game. Think of the *strength of your relationship* as the gravitational, *centripetal* force that will keep you and your counterparts within the same orbit around a deal even when everything else about the transaction may at some points seem to be spinning out of control and pulling you apart with their *centrifugal* force. So set your intention to consistently maintain and strengthen the relationship throughout this phase. There will be some difficult times ahead that will test even the strongest relationships.

In this chapter, you will learn about the tactical steps involved in getting to a term sheet. You will learn how to gauge progress and navigate common pitfalls as you invite one or more acquirers to take a closer look at your startup and its operations. Finally, you will become familiar with the common terms and best practices for negotiating that prized term sheet.

PROCESS

While each acquisition is unique, there is a set of common practices that all acquisitions tend to follow. These practices are like footprints on a hill that with the passage of time have created pathways for traveling over that hill. These pathways may not necessarily form the quickest or easiest way over the hill, but they are what everyone instinctively steps on.

When you are in the short game, you will encounter and collaborate with those who are frequent travelers on the M&A pathways. Having gone up and down this hill a few times, they have learned how to utilize these pathways in an effective and efficient way. These frequent travelers include corporate development teams, investment bankers, corporate lawyers, accountants, venture capitalists, and private equity firms, who often find themselves on one side or the other of M&A transactions. Through repetition, they have come up with a set of best practices and playbooks, checklists, agreements, workflow trackers, folder structures, and approval processes that works for them. This is similar to how venture fundraising has a set of best practices and tools among VCs, lawyers, and entrepreneurs. Rather than trying to invent a new path up and over the M&A hill, I recommend that you become familiar with existing paths and use them by default, deviating from them only if absolutely necessary. By doing so you will make the overall process more efficient and save your energy for things that impact your ultimate outcome.

Even though the startup sale process at first blush may seem opaque and arcane, it is basically an auction—or to be specific, a "closed auction." Closed auctions are those where the buyers don't have visibility into the other bidders and their bids. The buyers in the auction for your startup are bidding either against other buyers or against other viable alternatives for your startup, such as your financing options. Although the prospect of getting involved in an auction may seem far more work than you were hoping for, there is a huge benefit to an auction versus a simple one-on-one buyer-seller haggle: auctions are usually the most efficient way to arrive at the fair market value for anything. They have a definite timeline, and the competitive bidding process forces the sellers to put their best offers on the table. That is why unique and valuable assets such as art, classic cars, real estate, and the wireless spectrum are all mostly sold through auctions.

Evaluation complexity and confidentiality considerations make selling a startup far more challenging for you as the seller than with most other items sold in an auction. Since price is just one of many factors that you would take into consideration when evaluating your prospects, comparing your bids against one another is not at all straightforward. Like the venture fundraising process, the decision in favor of an offer is not (and should not be) simply based on valuation. As investor, author, and entrepreneur Chris Yeh puts it, "choosing a VC based on valuation is like hiring the cheapest job candidate."[3] The same applies to your exit. You must take into consideration a number of factors and then decide which set of trade-offs best fit your overall objectives. For instance, would a lower valuation in return for keeping most the team working together in the same geographic location be preferred to a higher valuation requiring that you lay off 20 percent (or more) of the team? Or how would you compare selling to a larger company where your product is at risk of being terminated or retired versus a smaller yet more risky company where your offering would become a critical component of their solution going forward?

Confidentiality plays an oversized role in M&A process and imposes severe constraints on you. While in most auctions sellers tend to prefer a more publicized process that would cast as wide a net as possible, the opposite is true in M&A: you have no choice but to keep the process highly confidential to avoid the myriad of complications arising from leaks that we touched on in the last chapter. In fact, once you set the wheels in motion, you need to proceed as fast as possible because each day opens you up to the increased possibility of leaks and loss of control of the process, the narrative, and ultimately your team, customers, partners, and yes, your whole startup. Once you fire that starting gun, you are in a race against the clock to get the deal done. The news will eventually get out, and your ability to move fast determines whether you or someone else will be the one to break it.

Against this backdrop, the typical company sale process unfolds in five stages: (1) buyer outreach, (2) preliminary diligence, (3) term sheet collection, (4) term sheet negotiation, and (5) deal execution. In the remainder of this chapter, we will walk through the first four stages to get to a negotiated term sheet. In the next chapter, we will discuss the deal execution stage, moving from term sheet to closing the transaction.

Stage 1: Buyer Outreach

In auction terminology, this stage is typically referred to as bid solicitation. As mentioned above, when selling your company, this is a highly confidential process. Depending on your risk tolerance for leaks and the extent you want to keep the information about your startup confidential, you can either cast a wider net that reaches out to a large set of potential buyers or use a highly targeted approach that focuses on a handful of most-likely acquirers. The larger the universe of potential bidders, the more time and resources it will take for you to reach out and engage them. That can slow down the process significantly and will increase the risk of leaks and exposure to your confidential information. The benefit of the broader approach is that it may uncover an eager buyer willing to pay a premium or increase the number of bids you get, so you can theoretically increase your chances for a better set of terms with a broader approach. My preferred approach, however, is not to throw out multiple feelers and hope something sticks but instead go with only a targeted list of potential strategic buyers with whom you have cultivated a strong relationship throughout the long game. The chances of a compelling deal with a new party are quite low, and in my opinion, they are usually not worth the increased risk of leaks.

As detailed in the last chapter, it is more effective when your initial outreach, especially to the parties with whom you have an established relationship, is carried out by yourself and without an intermediary. You want to make sure you convey the right message and paint the overall strategic picture, preferably using the indirect approach as much as possible for reasons shared in the last chapter. Once you gain traction with at least one of those conversations and have managed to drum up some real interest, which you can gauge by the level of engagement of those parties in evaluating your startup, then you should consider a broader outreach to improve your negotiation leverage and create backup options in case your initial discussions stall. That is when you may consider leaning on external resources.

Planning for success is essential here. Once you start the outreach, you want to seize the momentum, especially when you get one or more potential acquirers expressing interest in your startup. You don't want to take weeks or months after you receive an expression of interest to prepare your management presentation or responses to the preliminary diligence questions, a topic we will pick up in detail next. Just as you would have a pitch deck and diligence material prepared for a potential investment round, be at least equally prepared before you do your outreach to potential acquirers. Know exactly who from your side would attend meetings with potential acquirers and the role they would play. Internally, identify who would be the person discussing the strategy and vision for a combination and rehearse that pitch until it is "pitch perfect," so to speak. Take an objective look at your product and financial performance over the past couple of years. Then identify both areas of success and areas of shortfall and draft clear explanations for each and their implication for your path forward, both independently as well as in combination with an acquirer. Also do some housecleaning such as prioritizing any critical report or data tracking projects and chasing down any missing material contracts. Gather and place key agreements, market research, financial statements, corporate records, and anything else you think a buyer would deem important in evaluating your startup in an online data room.

191

The value of a banker and other external strategic advisors increases as you get deeper into this phase. They can help you manage the sale process, including assisting with your presentation material for potential acquirers, collecting the diligence information, and setting up a virtual data room that can disseminate and keep track of information shared. And even more important, they can provide a critical role in your negotiations, as we will discuss shortly.

Stage 2: Preliminary Diligence

Interested acquirers typically start their work by either asking for your teaser presentation or your CIM (short for *confidential information memorandum*, sometimes also referred to as *offering memorandum* (OM) or *information memorandum* (IM)), which is the analog to the Executive Summary or a Pitch Deck during venture capital fundraising. This presentation should provide a high-level overview of your startup, why it would be a desirable target for acquisition, and some of its key metrics. Some acquirers, especially those who already have a working familiarity with you, may choose to skip these formalities and ask to schedule a management presentation to discuss the current state of your startup.

Once you are invited to a management presentation, you are very much at the preliminary diligence stage. To set the right expectations, do not read too much into a request for your CIM or the management meeting as most often they result in a polite rejection, just as how most VC pitches don't yield an investment offer. But they are a required step to move forward, so you need to take these requests seriously and be as prepared for them as possible. Ideally, before you are even asked for a presentation, you will have already gathered the underlying data and prepared the presentation deck for the meeting.

Following the management presentation, if there is continued interest, acquirers will typically send you a preliminary diligence request list. Sometimes these requests can be quite lengthy and intimidating, while at other times they may all fit on one page.

Some acquirers are quite organized and have a spreadsheet that you can mutually update to keep track of what has been provided. Other times, especially when dealing with less-experienced acquirers, you may get piecemeal requests via email, phone calls, and/ or even text messages. The good news is that you should generally interpret any request at this stage as further proof of genuine engagement and interest. The bad news is that you may not have the time, resources, or even ability to address all of those questions, especially if some of the requests entail tracking and pulling data in new ways.

As you evaluate these requests, you will be rightfully concerned about what you should disclose and at what time, worrying whether what you share could become disadvantageous to you and how much to share before you have at least some sense of the valuation the buyer is willing to pay. Let's address these in order.

The Transparency Dilemma

While it can be appropriate or prudent to decline some of the preliminary diligence requests that seem overly burdensome or sensitive at this stage of the process, this is a right you should exercise very sparingly. Before you decide to withhold certain information from disclosure, take a step back and try to examine the situation from an acquirer point of view. For an acquirer, this is the time to build their case and gain conviction around their core deal hypotheses. They need to peek under the hood and see the engine. And they need to do this before going to their leadership team or board for a green light to put an offer on the table. As mentioned previously, most acquirers would rather not make an offer than make an offer and have to retract it after they find out more about your startup. So, in the preliminary diligence phase, acquirers need to be confident that they understand the major upsides and downsides to buying your startup. They need to go beyond gut feelings and intuitions and obtain some evidence that the terms and valuation they are proposing reflect the reality and genuine prospects of your startup.

The preliminary diligence, therefore, is not meant to be a full diligence process that reveals every detail about your startup and its operations and processes. There are trade secrets and other details you may not want to share with an acquirer before a term sheet is signed. That is fine and perfectly understandable by acquirers. However, you need to fully realize that after signing of a term sheet, if anything comes to light that would invalidate any fundamental assumption the acquirer had made about your company, it would be very likely that they would want to either modify or retract their offer.

To sum it up, be as transparent as possible to enable your potential acquirers to build a compelling internal case that will withstand future scrutiny. And that particularly means do not hide any problem areas or put an overly positive spin on a set of facts, developments, or circumstances. You will be in negotiations for a while, and the truth will become evident sooner or later. It's much easier to be honest and transparent from the start than to salvage your reputation after the damage is done. And the best way to damage your reputation and negotiation leverage is to hide the negatives and wait for the other side to discover them.

Note that any liabilities or risks that get uncovered after the term sheet is signed will give the acquirer valid reason to demand a purchase price adjustment or additional dollars to be held back in escrow. You want to know what the acquirer is willing to pay up front rather than painfully discover it later. Be as objective about the facts and data as possible. That does not mean you should not be in sales mode. It just means that your sales pitch should be directed toward the mission and opportunities ahead rather than hiding, misdirecting, or misrepresenting any of your data or financials.

Now that you are about to share confidential information, it is time to get that NDA signed if you haven't already. Of course, even with an NDA in place you are not required to disclose any of your sensitive trade secrets. You can also request for select items to be disclosed only after a term sheet is signed. In the case that an acquirer operates a competing business, you can further require that individuals directly involved in the operation of that competing business be excluded from access to your confidential and competitively sensitive information. However, keep in mind that being overly sensitive about confidentiality may send the wrong message and imply that you either don't trust the other side or are hiding something negative. If you have a very good reason to keep something confidential, share the reason and set the expectation as to when you will be comfortable sharing that information.

The Valuation Dilemma

You may wonder, should you even bother with preliminary diligence before you have a meeting of minds on valuation and basic deal terms with a potential acquirer? What if you spend all this time in management presentations, collecting data, and responding to diligence inquiries only to find out that the terms you were expecting are far off from what the acquirer ends up offering in their term sheet? My answer is a definite yes. Without visibility into valuation, you should still engage in preliminary diligence for at least three reasons:

1. You are unlikely to get any numbers from an acquirer unless they have done some amount of basic diligence to understand your business and its financials.
2. If you do get a number or valuation range, acquirers will have no problem revisiting everything once they have done their homework and found out the actual details about your startup.
3. Most importantly, even having one offer on the table significantly changes the dynamics of your process, forcing other interested parties to accelerate their internal processes and ensuring that they put their best offer forward.

Anyone who has tried to buy or rent a home knows very well how everything changes as soon as you find out that a property you have been eyeing for a while has received an offer. You would assume that the offer is compelling and will try to come up with a better one yourself quickly, lest you miss out on what you will come to view as the opportunity of a lifetime. Offers bring your exit process from the virtual world of slide decks and spreadsheets to the real world of term sheet negotiations.

There are situations where you may want to do some preemptive price discovery, especially if you are not sure whether you should even go down the M&A path with any acquirer at all. Under such circumstances you may want to lob a softball question to an interested potential acquirer and ask about their valuation methodology and how they would come up with an offer. They key would be to focus more on process than on a number.

You will likely get a generic answer that each deal is unique and there is no "standard" method, which would mean the end of that conversation. But occasionally an acquirer may be more specific and provide a thoughtful response. Acquirers, after all, also have an interest in making sure the parties are within the same range on valuation as they wouldn't want to find out after months of investigation that expectations are wildly apart and there is no deal to be had. In that case, you may hear about key metrics that they take into account in their analysis and the multiple ranges they attribute to those metrics (e.g., 2x to 3x multiple on revenue, or 10x to 15x multiple on EBITDA) assuming certain other factors (growth rates, level of competition, potential synergies, etc.) are within some parameters. There have been many cases in which acquirers ask early on for the summary historic and projected financials of a startup to give some preliminary guidance on valuation range before proceeding into diligence. Sometimes, especially when you are working with a banker, your banker may recommend offering your own guidance based on market comparables to provide an anchor and signal. But ultimately, the final valuation is determined based on how competitive the bidding process becomes and how much leverage you have. One problem with guidance ranges is that acquirers typically assume the low end of their guidance, whereas sellers typically only hear the high end. Depending on the spread between the bottom and top of the range, there can still be a wide gap in expectations to bridge.

The Testing Dilemma

One tricky situation that may arise is when an acquirer expresses an interest in running a test to validate certain hypotheses during the preliminary diligence phase. For instance, they may want to run a marketing campaign for their product within your customer acquisition funnel, or vice versa, to validate whether a certain conversion rate would hold true, which would then be an important input into their forecast assumptions and synergy calculations. At Webs, we faced this situation early in our conversations with one potential acquirer. My guidance in such situations is to delay running such tests to the post–term sheet confirmatory diligence stage. Instead, work with the acquirer to find proxies and make educated guesses for the inputs they need for their model, fully understanding and accepting the risk that their proposal may change if a later test invalidates those assumptions. But spending time and resources to run tests and track data for a potential acquirer with whom you don't even have a term sheet–level meeting of minds is more often than not premature and distracting for your startup.

Continue Building Bridges

Take advantage of the interactions during the diligence process as an opportunity to further strengthen your relationship. In particular, leverage these interactions to achieve the following goals:

1. Establish and reinforce mutual trust and respect.
2. Discover areas of strategic alignment in mission, vision, and product offering.
3. Learn about their culture and values and highlight areas of compatibility.
4. Understand how you and your team fit within the acquirer organization.

5. Deepen your knowledge about your champion's motivations and interests.
6. Uncover their internal approval process, timeline, and constraints.
7. Convey your excitement about joining forces drawing on your learnings above.
8. Establish the ground rules and process for upcoming negotiations.

The last point on this list merits some additional explanation. Here your objective is not to issue any ultimatums or create friction. Rather, aim at preparing the other side for what may become points of friction later on so that when the issues are raised, they are not a surprise. You want to psychologically prepare (or prime) the other side for things that could become nonnegotiables for you so that they can respond to them rationally rather than react emotionally.

At a minimum, remind your counterparts that you have responsibilities to all your stakeholders (which include your customers, employees, and shareholders) and that your final decision will be based on pursuing a path that takes into account all of those interests. And be more specific when warranted instead of making vague allusions or passing comments. For instance, if keeping the whole team together is a nonnegotiable, high-priority item for you, make sure to express on more than one occasion that one of the reasons you are excited about this particular acquirer is the opportunity it provides the entire team for career growth and continued collaboration as a team. If valuation is critical, find the opportunity to provide some benchmarks (such as your last round valuation, competitor valuation, or public company metrics) that your investors or board are looking at in evaluating the best path forward.

Stage 3: Term Sheet Collection

Diligence can be all-consuming and exceedingly burdensome, testing the patience of the calmest among us. It expands to fill the time you give it as each diligence request you answer can lead to several follow-up questions to be answered, not unlike the Hydra, the fearsome multiheaded monster in Greek mythology that spawned two more heads for every one that was cut off. But you don't need to be Hercules to defeat this monster; all you need to slay the diligence beast is a simple yet powerful tool: a deadline.

Yield this powerful tool only after consultation with your top potential acquirers to make sure your deadline accommodates constraints they may be facing, such as quarterly or annual financial reports, or other initiatives that could directly impact their ability to do the work required to get you that term sheet. The last thing you want, of course, is to set a deadline that causes your ideal buyers to drop out of the process. I have seen overly eager entrepreneurs or their representatives start a sale process with an artificially narrow window of time allowed for diligence. In response I have witnessed acquirers drop out of the process or simply ignore the seller's timeline altogether. The entrepreneurs are then forced to circle back with a more realistic expectation and plead with the acquirer to stay in the process, which does not bode well for their leverage in future negotiations. So, be thoughtful about your timeline and show your awareness and professionalism by consulting with your suitors before you set that deadline. At the very least, make sure you have seen their preliminary diligence request list and understand your own timeline for delivering that information.

Once you set that well-considered deadline, make sure you clearly and unambiguously communicate it to all of the interested parties. To maintain the integrity of your process, you want to have all the bids arrive by the same deadline and avoid having to make any exception for laggards. You would not want to find yourself in a situation where a bidder is holding up the process because they were unaware of the deadline. Equally important is communicating to your suitors the format of the proposal or term sheet that you expect to receive. This request is usually communicated to participants by a letter that a banker puts together, often referred to as the *process letter*.

Process letters typically require the following information to be submitted by a certain deadline:

- Purchase price
- Methodology and assumptions behind purchase price calculation
- Form of consideration (which is typically cash and/or stock) and its source
- Timing and structure of payment
- Key assumptions, remaining topics and questions for diligence, and nature and extent of diligence
- Timeline to finish diligence, signing, and closing
- Required approvals (internal and external) and other conditions to closing

Usually, when acquirers respond to process letters with their EOI (expression of interest) letters, they also include a term sheet so there is no ambiguity around material terms during the purchase agreement negotiations. Sometimes, in highly competitive processes, the bankers recommend bypassing the term sheet altogether and ask the buyers to submit a markup of the definitive purchase agreement instead.

Depending on how many proposals you expect to receive, you may have one or more rounds of bidding. In a multi-round process, you select the top bidders and allow them to submit another set of bids by a specific deadline. Sooner or later, it will be time to pick just one or two of your preferred bids and either accept or counter their bids. That is, you will be entering term sheet negotiations with them. While your negotiation leverage will have the largest influence in determining the ultimate terms you will be able to obtain, your negotiation skills will play a critical role as I will describe next.

Stage 4: Term Sheet Negotiation

There is a scene in the 1997 movie *Devil's Advocate* where Keanu Reeves (playing Kevin Lomax, an unusually successful trial lawyer who ends up working for the devil's law firm) pointedly asks Al Pacino (his boss, the devil), "Are we negotiating?" To which the devil swiftly responds, "Always!" And that is the simple truth. Whether or not we mean to, we are always negotiating.

This is especially true for the most impactful event in your startup's life. All interactions with your potential acquirers are negotiations, from that initial outreach all the way to today. It has all been a continuous series of negotiations whether or not you were aware of it.

And if you are like most other startup founders and entrepreneurs, you have had little prior training in negotiation skills. The good news is that anyone can become an effective negotiator with guidance and practice. Even a small effort can make a significant difference in the outcome. As a starting point, take advantage of the fantastic books and online resources available to elevate your skill set. One resource I highly recommend is negotiation expert and coach Chris Voss's Masterclass,[4] which expands on the skills he discusses in his accessible negotiation guidebook, *Never Split the Difference*.[5] Make a conscious choice and a priority to improve your negotiation skills; it is a small investment that is likely to change your life.

Much of the content of this book so far has been a series of lessons on effective negotiation. That is because what determines the outcome of your negotiation with your acquirers for the most part happens *before* you sit at the negotiation table. Negotiation favors the prepared.

To ace your term sheet negotiations, you will need to remember to *prioritize the relationship* with your potential acquirers above everything else. Make that your primary negotiation strategy and the main thing you take away from this part of the book. Throughout the short game, seize on every opportunity to continue to connect and strengthen your relationship. The following are some specific tactics on how to apply this relationship-first strategy to your term sheet negotiations.

Assume Good Intent

Term sheet negotiations can get quite heated. To maintain control of the situation and your own reaction, always assume good intent by your counterparts. This is not about giving benefit of the doubt to them, but rather not having doubt in the first place. Relationships don't thrive and flourish when you don't have faith in or respect for the other person. When your actions and reactions show that you have faith in your counterparts and are not judging their character, you set the tone for a mutually respectful exchange in any circumstance.

Avoid Haggling

Instead of posturing, drawing red lines in the sand, or getting into heated exchanges on certain terms, approach the term sheet negotiation as yet another opportunity to deepen mutual understanding and strengthen the relationship with the team on the other side. Always provide your feedback within the context of the ultimate goals of the long-term relationship of the parties and your responsibilities to the larger mission of your startup and its stakeholders. Even in wars, true victories are those that are won without a fight, echoing Sun Tzu's observation in *The Art of War* that "supreme excellence consists in breaking the enemy's resistance without fighting."[6] When you have a strong relationship and behave accordingly, even after you walk out on a set of terms, after a day or two have passed and the parties have cooled off, you will likely get a call to resume discussions with a better set of terms. I have witnessed that course of events on numerous deals. It is only when you don't have a strong relationship as a glue that when a party walks out or pushes back on material terms, that can become the end of the negotiations for good.

Let's take the following scenario, which plays out quite often in acquisition negotiations. Imagine a potential acquirer offers a price for your startup that is much lower than what you expected as the fair market value, for instance as Steve Jobs did in that critical meeting with iLike executives mentioned earlier. How would you, and should you, react if you face that situation? Reacting, as entrepreneur Ali Partovi did, especially with a price of your own, would be haggling. My advice is to try your best not to *react*, but rather *respond* with genuine appreciation for the offer and with humility, providing a clear explanation of why you think this is an unacceptable valuation so that the other side can understand and appreciate your thought process. In fact, you want to bring them to empathize with you, even arriving at the realization that they themselves would have had a similar response were they in your shoes. You may, for instance, voice your disappointment over the valuation within the context of how your shareholders would evaluate offers for your startup in light of the valuation of your last round of financing, or some tangible market benchmarks, or other realistic alternatives that are available to you, such as continuing to run the business or raising a new round of financing. If acquirers ask for a counteroffer, try not to give a number and instead provide the potential buyer an opportunity to improve their offer before you take it to your board or shareholders. Alternatively, you may offer a range you think would be the zone of acceptable offers for your stakeholders. However, at the beginning of your negotiations and especially before you have established a base level of trust and respect, steer the conversation toward the underlying principles and drivers upon which you are basing your expected deal terms rather than just throwing out numbers for the counterparts to react to. Let buyers negotiate against themselves as much as possible.

Stay Positive and Patient

Strengthening a relationship takes proactive steps and hard work. In many cases, that hard work involves taming our negative reactions, disappointments, and hurt feelings. Think about the impact of your words, body language, and actions on the relationship before saying or doing something that could damage the relationship, no matter how gratifying a snippy remark may seem in the heat of an argument.

Never let the constant grind of negotiations cause you to appear less enthusiastic about teaming up with the acquirer. In fact, even if you are disappointed in a set of terms or pace of progress, make sure to emphasize that your disappointment arises from the fact that you were looking forward to combining the companies and achieving the vision and strategy that brought the parties to this point. Make sure you continue to verbalize your excitement and enthusiasm about the joint opportunities ahead even in difficult times. Emotions are infectious, and your continued positivity for the possibilities of the two companies working closer together will translate into their enthusiasm for you.

And always take the time to deliberate before you act. Patience in negotiations is a virtue. "Impatience telegraphs desperation," as Ali Partovi concluded after his rush into the valuation conversation with Steve Jobs.[7] More often than not, we tend to be far less regretful when we take the time to rationally evaluate the pros and cons of a course of action rather than emotionally react to the situation at hand. This is a skill that does not always come naturally especially since as entrepreneurs we constantly face so many situations that demand our immediate reaction. Negotiation, however, is not one of them.

Lean on Intermediaries

It is not easy to maintain a positive relationship with someone when every time you interact with them, you are having a difficult conversation. There was one founder with whom I was negotiating a small acquisition, and every time he would call me, he wanted to discuss one more "outrageous" term that he had found in our proposal. After the fourth or fifth such discussions, I felt anxiety every time I saw a call, text, or email come from him. I started dreading having been an advocate for the acquisition and began to wonder whether he was the right cultural fit for our company, which had *joining forces* as one of our core cultural attributes. While I did have some empathy for him because he had the difficult task of looking out for the best interests of the various stakeholders of his startup, my negative emotional response was quite real and was echoed by multiple individuals on our side. As Sophocles wrote almost 2,500 years ago in *Antigone*, "No man delights in the bearer of bad news."[8] And the people you are negotiating with, in most cases, will be your future bosses and colleagues after the deal closes, so it is important to preserve your relationship with them.

This is where intermediaries such as bankers and lawyers really earn their keep. Let them do the hard work of taking the first crack at pushing back on various terms. Let them especially fight the smaller fights for you while, of course, you monitor things from behind the battle lines. Only get involved if they hit an impasse and you are brought in to save the day and strike a grand bargain. By leaning on intermediaries to do the bulk of the negotiations, you become the *problem solver* as opposed to the *problem creator*!

Furthermore, there is a tactical negotiation advantage to having others do the negotiation rather than yourself: it is much easier for the negotiator to push back on terms when the negotiator is not the decision maker. Savvy negotiators usually don't want the ultimate decision maker to be in the trenches as they would be susceptible to pressure and could make rash compromises on the spot. The old adage that "if you want to get things right, you ought to do it yourself" definitely does not apply to high-stake negotiations.

Explain Yourself

Prioritizing relationship means making the effort to communicate clearly and explain your position. When we were in the process for the sale of Webs, for instance, we made it clear to interested buyers that given that our business was growing at a healthy pace and was cash flow positive, our investors were not in a rush to sell and therefore we would only seriously consider an offer that would "stop us in our tracks." Barring such an offer, we informed our suitors, we would double down on growing the business by raising a new round, which was a very credible outcome as our competitors Wix and Weebly had recently raised growth funding. This explanation made it clear to our potential buyers what the stakes were and how we were going to evaluate offers, which made pushing back on offers that didn't fit those guidelines much more credible and less contentious. We stuck to our guns on terms without appearing unreasonable or causing any damage to our relationship with any of the parties.

Keep in Touch

One relatively easy way to maintain and elevate your relationship with your champions and key stakeholders on the other side is to increase the frequency of your interactions. To the extent you can, make those interactions as real-time and in-person as possible, such as through in-office meetings (when feasible) or video calling. While prior to entering into M&A negotiations asynchronous communications, such as email updates, are a great way to stay in touch and top of mind, during negotiations it is best to pivot to a regular cadence of live interactions. You gather (and convey) a substantial amount of critical information when you interact in real time. You are staying in touch not to negotiate specific terms in every meeting, as that work is best done through the intermediaries as described above, but to connect on the big-picture strategy. You want to ensure that both sides remain connected to the *why*, the shared goals and objectives underpinning the two companies coming together. In M&A, with distance the heart does not grow fonder. In fact, in the busy dealmaking world, *out of sight* will very likely keep you *out of mind* and widen the gap in objectives.

The above guidelines are most effective when you mold them to fit your personal style. The best negotiations are grounded in interactions that come across as genuine and authentic. In fact, the best negotiations feel less like negotiation and more like collaborative interactions between two parties who are committed to a mutually advantageous outcome.

TERMS

The term sheet is a written summary of the key terms for the purchase of your startup. For all intents and purposes, term sheets are nonbinding, except for specific provisions around confidentiality and exclusivity discussed below. Term sheets are intended to capture the high-level understanding between the parties so that each side enters the detailed diligence and documentation phase with clear expectations on key financial and structural aspects of the transaction. A lot of details are left out of the term sheet to be worked through and addressed in the definitive agreements. That is a critical reason term sheets are nonbinding. Another reason is that the buyers have not yet conducted their full diligence and have a lot of open questions that will impact how they perceive the trade-off of risks and benefits associated with buying your startup. Depending on what gets uncovered in diligence and what transpires in the world in the meantime (say a global pandemic, war, or market correction) between the time of your term sheet signing and the definitive agreements (a situation in which many targets found themselves throughout 2020 to 2022), the buyers may very well still back out of the deal or ask to change some of the key terms of the deal. Nevertheless, the term sheet does set a common reference frame for what the deal should look like if the transaction continues on the happy path with no major surprises.

In that light, a term sheet is just an interim step and does not guarantee that a deal will get done. Nevertheless, receiving a term sheet is a milestone and significant achievement. Take a moment to recognize and celebrate this milestone, no matter what the actual terms written on the term sheet are. I realize the actual terms will inevitably color your excitement about the term sheet, but even if the terms are absolutely horrendous, the term sheet indicates there is at least one other company that values what you have created and is trying to figure out a way to merge your story lines together.

Also, from a more tactical perspective, recall that getting that first term sheet usually makes it a lot easier to get other, competing, and often better term sheets. Now you have a perfectly valid reason to reach back out to all other interested parties and exert urgency on their process. That first term sheet does wonders for your leverage as well in what can now be perceived as a potentially competitive bidding process for your startup. That is why you should separate the *terms* written on the term sheet from the *receipt* of a term sheet and congratulate yourself and the working team that has helped you arrive at this opportune juncture.

Devil in the Details

Unless you are in the business of negotiating M&A term sheets, they can be quite complex to understand and negotiate. Don't be deceived by any apparent brevity or simplicity. Even seemingly simple terms such as the "purchase price" can hide an arsenal of dangerous assumptions behind their innocuous appearance. Details will matter, and they usually matter *a lot*. So, you will need to enlist the help of competent deal advisors and corporate lawyers whose day job involves reviewing M&A term sheets. It is best to have at least one business advisor and one legal advisor as each will view the transaction from a different point of view. Business advisors will tend to help you maximize the upside, while legal advisors will be more focused on potential risks and liabilities, including nuanced compliance and tax matters. This is not a do-it-yourself project by any stretch of imagination, even if you single-handedly negotiated the term sheet for your last venture round very successfully. Don't have a false sense of confidence just because this document is also called a term sheet.

Nonetheless, you still want to be familiar with the general terms to efficiently manage the negotiations while guided by the advice of deal experts. After all, you will ultimately have to make the call on trade-offs between various terms and negotiate the final agreement. To that end, below I have listed the most common terms contained in an acquisition term sheet, what they mean, and common pitfalls you will need to watch out for. It is fully understandable and expected that not all of these terms will be equally important to you. What terms you consider of material importance or even as deal-breakers compared to others will depend on your ultimate objective and what will satisfy your stakeholders, especially those whose approval you require to get the deal done.

Purchase Price

Each acquirer can have its own unique way of calculating purchase price and what they mean by it. Therefore, you need to make sure you understand what the nominal value that they put as "purchase price" on the term sheet stands for and, even more important, what *adjustments* the acquirer anticipates making to this purchase price in determining the amount they owe you after the closing. Some of the most important assumptions you want to understand are (a) how they have accounted for cash that you currently have in the bank as well as any additional cash you will receive from sales before the definitive agreements are signed, (b) how they have accounted for the liabilities and debt that you now owe or may incur until the deal is signed, and (c) treatment of any major customer contract with a large up-front multiyear payment or commitment before the deal is signed.

Ideally, you want the purchase price to be stated as "enterprise value" at the time of signing of the definitive agreements, which is the value of your startup without taking into account the amount of debt and liquid assets (such as cash) on your balance sheet. Then, any debt on your books at time of signing will reduce the amount they pay you, and any cash or other liquid assets would increase that amount. Treatment of customer prepayments, known as deferred revenue, is often heavily negotiated. The amount of "working capital" an acquirer expects you to have at time of signing or closing will also play into what the actual final payment to you and your shareholders will be.

Depending on the unique aspects of your startup, there may be further adjustments that would impact the purchase price. Note that earnout payments and any holdback or escrow amounts, as discussed separately below, will also have an impact on how much you get paid and when. You need to develop a full grasp of the interplay between the various components of the term sheet and how they impact what you and your shareholders receive, so don't hesitate to ask for as much clarity as possible before you react to any number on the term sheet.

Form of Consideration

In M&A, not all dollar figures are equal, especially if they are not paid out in cash. Make sure you understand whether the purchase price is paid out in cash or equity or a combination thereof. If the payment involves any amount of equity, then you need to have a clear definition and understanding as to how that equity is valued and what vesting and other trading restrictions may be attached to it. Ascribing the correct valuation to the acquirer's equity will be challenging if the acquirer is a private company and relatively easier for reputable public companies whose stock is traded on national stock exchanges. Also, note that in hybrid cash and equity transactions, there are further tax implications that you need to carefully evaluate under guidance of your financial, tax, and legal advisors.

Structure

A company sale can be structured either as an *asset* sale or a *stock* sale. Acquirers usually prefer asset sales since they exclude the liabilities of the target. In asset sales, acquirers get to choose what assets they want to purchase. Asset purchases also have certain tax advantages for acquirers. However, the opposite is usually the case for the seller, whose shareholders would continue to be on the hook for the liabilities and will be subject to double taxation in an asset sale. That is because typically the selling entity would pay taxes on any income generated from the sale of the assets, and then its shareholders pay taxes on any proceeds distributed to them as dividends or share buybacks. Consequently, sellers tend to prefer stock sales. Although theoretically acquirers should be willing to pay more for asset sales and targets should ask to be made whole for any tax burden imposed on them, I have not seen that play out in practice. What happens instead is that the party with higher leverage dictates the structure of the transaction.

Earnouts

In cases where there is a gap between the seller's expectations of the future and those of the buyer, establishing certain future milestone events at which time additional deal consideration would be paid may seem like a decent compromise and a rational path forward. Many entrepreneurs face the following situation: once a potential acquirer has obtained their forecasted financials and projections, the acquirer then attempts to hoist the entrepreneurs with their own petard by proposing that although they are skeptical about the projections, they are willing to take the entrepreneurs' forecast at face value and pay a certain percentage of deal consideration once they achieve those targets. This effectively shifts the risk of missing those targets back to you as the entrepreneur. After all, the acquirer would argue, you are the expert about your own business and have all the insights on how to make it successful, so you should be able to stand behind your own projections. And if you push back against this request, you may worry, wouldn't you signal a lack of conviction in your own forecast?

While that is a valid concern, you can and should push back to the extent that your leverage affords you. Everyone who has ever been involved in a deal with earnouts strongly cautions against them. One fundamental problem with earnouts is that it is hard to predict the future and set in stone goals that are supposed to be valid 12, 18, or 24 months in the future. The world changes, sometimes in quite dramatic ways, as we all know quite well.

A more fundamental problem is that earnouts create a divergence in incentives between the target leadership and that of the acquirer. The larger the earnout, the bigger the problem. This is because after the acquisition, you and your leadership will typically not have the ultimate control over all the resources needed to ensure that those milestones are met. You will be part of a larger, dynamic organization that will have its own evolving set of priorities and resource allocation requirements that can change on a quarterly basis. In fact, from a typical acquirer's perspective, once the deal closes, your team becomes a part of the larger team and they want everyone, including you and your team, to pull in the same direction to make the combined company successful. But with earnouts in place, you and your leadership will have to both help the acquirer as a company meet its goals and fight for resources and priorities that would ensure you meet your earnout milestones—two goals that will often be at odds. Many bitter disagreements and even lawsuits between entrepreneurs and their acquirers find their origin in well-intentioned earnout provisions. So, proceed with extreme caution.

Escrow and Holdback

The concept of escrow in M&A is quite different from the one you may be familiar with in real estate. When you are buying a property, you typically make some amount of good faith deposit before the closing of the transaction, which is held in escrow until the transaction is closed. At a typical closing for a property transaction, the funds held in escrow are released to the seller. However, when you are selling your company, at closing some amount of the purchase price is held back by the buyer or put into an official escrow account at a bank for a certain period of time to provide some comfort to the buyer against unknown liabilities and risks, details of which will be heavily negotiated in the definitive agreements as part of your indemnification obligations. You may see anywhere from 5 percent to 25 percent or more of the purchase price placed in escrow for a period often ranging from six months to two years after closing, depending on the specific facts and circumstances of your deal. As a seller, you would certainly prefer the smallest amount withheld for the shortest duration of time as possible so that you can get your sales proceeds and move on with your life. But the acquirer would prefer the opposite.

While escrows are uncommon in acquisitions of public companies, almost all acquisitions of private company targets include some escrow or holdback amount. And they are often there for very valid reasons. Escrows are an effective way to help you get to closing faster and not be stuck in an infinite diligence cycle. There will be certain items that it would not be efficient or even possible for a buyer to conduct a full investigation on. Allowing the buyer to withhold some of the consideration signals to them that you, as the seller with most knowledge about your business, feel comfortable that the risk with those assumptions is not material and you are willing to put skin in the game behind your convictions. The details of what risks you are willing to underwrite for your acquirer and the way they are calculated and deducted from the escrow are negotiated painstakingly by the legal teams and memorialized in the definitive agreements.

Stock Options and Equity Awards

If you or anyone else from your startup is joining the acquirer as part of the sale, then the acquirer will want to provide the joining employees some financial incentive to stay and be motivated to help the combined entity execute its mission. As with new hires, this is usually achieved through equity awards, which could be in the form of restricted stock, stock options, or a combination of both, subject to certain vesting requirements typically spanning two to five years. When acquirers look at the overall deal consideration, they typically include equity as part of the total cost of consummating the transaction. While the term sheet often sets out the overall size of the equity component, it usually does not get into the details of the allocation of the equity among the various team members or vesting provisions unless you ask for guidance and further specificity.

The more a transaction's core value and success is dependent upon the team that joins the acquirer, the more an acquirer would want to shift the deal consideration toward equity for the team versus what gets distributed to the shareholders. As a result, your cap table and liquidation preferences become subject to negotiation, and an acquirer may very well ask that the transaction proceeds be distributed in a way that is quite different from what your cap table would otherwise mandate.

Parachute Payments

In M&A, payments to you and certain key employees could be considered "excess parachute payment" and trigger the excise tax provisions of Internal Revenue Code Section 280G (the so-called "golden parachute" tax), which would impose additional tax liability on those payments and disqualify that excess compensation from tax deduction by the employer. The most notable exception under current law is that with a vote by 75 percent of disinterested shareholders, you could avoid application of this tax liability. Sellers will often require receipt of such approval as a condition to closing. You need competent tax and legal advisors to help you with the so-called "280G analysis" and navigate the risks and potential financial exposure.

Representations and Warranties; Survival Period

Like the stock purchase agreement in venture financing transactions, the M&A definitive agreements contain detailed representations and warranties that sellers make to the buyer, with specific exceptions listed out on a disclosure schedule. These representations (reps) are intended to memorialize what facts about your business the acquirer relied upon when they made the final decision to buy your startup. These reps and warranties "survive" for a negotiated period after closing, during which the buyer may make claims of breach of representations if after closing they discover anything that is at odds with what was disclosed. Sellers want this survival period to be as short as possible, such as a year or

214

shorter, whereas a typical buyer would ask for two years or more. For certain reps, such as those related to IP, security, cap table, and incorporation documents, buyers ask for longer or even indefinite survival periods. These details are seldom addressed at term sheet stage and typically relegated to definitive agreements.

Indemnification

Breaches of reps and warranties can be grounds for financial recompense to the acquirer by the seller and its shareholders after closing. The extent and manner of such indemnification is detailed in the definitive agreements, including whether there is a cap on the potential liability. Sellers will push to get as much of the purchase price as possible back from you and your shareholders for such breaches, whereas you and your shareholders will negotiate to minimize your exposure as much as possible, and preferably even limit most of it to the amount held back or put in escrow.

Due Diligence and Timing

As a seller, you want the acquirer to spell out in their term sheet the key diligence items remaining. You also want as much clarity as possible on their process expectations (such as in-person meetings in certain geographic locations, access to certain team members and data, etc.). Even if the acquirer resists providing an exhaustive list, you should at the very least ask about and memorialize what they consider to be the critical outstanding items and their expected diligence timeline.

As mentioned previously, diligence will take all the time you give it, so it is good to have a preestablished timeline that everyone can march toward. It is an accepted wisdom in the M&A community that *time kills deals*, and the cause for delays is usually unfinished diligence. The more you can control and rein in the diligence process, the more certainty you will bring to the completion of the transaction itself, and the less distraction the transaction will cause to you and your team. We all know that a lot can happen in the span of even a few weeks, so pay close attention to every single day on the calendar. Although I have never seen a deal that goes from signing of the term sheet to signing of the definitive agreements in less than four weeks, I have seen many deals for which it takes two months or more, with some of them getting derailed, deprioritized, and canceled because of that delay.

Governance and Required Approvals

Although the deal team members on the acquirer side *drive* the transaction by coordinating the various workstreams and stakeholders who need to be involved, they do not typically have the authority to *approve* the transaction. They will need to go up the chain of command for final approval, all the way to the board or even the shareholders depending on the size and strategic implications of the transaction. Any approval obtained at term sheet stage is more or less a "hunting license" and not final, just as the term sheet itself is not final and is subject to modifications; only after reviewing the completed diligence report and negotiated deal documentation will the approvers on the acquirer side be able to provide their fully informed consent to the deal. Your term sheet is the perfect place to ask for and gain visibility into those internal processes and understand their implications for the timeline of the transaction and its approval risks ahead.

Closing Conditions

In M&A, the "signing" of the definitive agreements and the "closing" of the transaction are two separate and distinct events, even though some deals are structured to sign and close simultaneously. As a seller, you want the closing to happen as fast as possible, but it may not be possible. Many deals contain closing conditions that cannot be satisfied immediately at signing, such as obtaining antitrust regulatory approvals if your transaction size falls above certain thresholds. Sometimes, also, an acquirer may require that you obtain specific waivers, consents, or assignments from key contractual parties between signing and closing.

Exclusivity / Lockup Period

Buyers typically demand a period of time during which you will be exclusively negotiating with them. This is to give them assurance that while they devote significant time and resources to conduct diligence and negotiate the legal documents, you are not shopping the deal. This exclusivity will be binding on you, your board, and controlling shareholders and can range from weeks to two or three months. Buyers, of course, would want as long an exclusivity period as possible, and sellers the opposite. You may be able to negotiate certain specific exemptions to this exclusivity, such as discussions with other parties you have already been negotiating with or for fundraising activities, but understandably, buyers will be very reluctant to grant any exemptions. Every exemption chips away at the buyer's leverage against you. The best argument you can have for these exemptions is that since you don't have any concrete assurance from the buyer that they will consummate the transaction, you will need to keep some alternative options open in case things fall apart.

Breakup Fee

A breakup fee is hardly seen in public-private mergers, but I mention it here in case you are considering whether or not you should ask for it. As a target, it is understandable that you would want to hold the feet of an acquirer to the fire and have them give you some financial reparation if they change their minds and back out of the transaction. After all, you will have spent countless valuable hours indulging the acquirer with their numerous diligence requests. You may have even decided to forgo a financing offer or some other kind of strategic alternative due to the acquisition offer. So, a buyer that backs out after signing a term sheet may cause irreparable damage to your startup. Those are all valid arguments. However, acquirers seldom agree to a financial penalty for their decision to withdraw from a deal because they too will have incurred both direct and indirect costs by spending time and resources pursuing a transaction with you.

Expiration Date

As mentioned above, once a buyer puts an offer on the table, they want to eliminate the possibility of someone else swooping down and snatching the deal away from them. So, they put an expiration date on the term sheet to exert pressure and urgency for you to sign. This is called an *exploding offer* because once the deadline is reached, the offer is theoretically off the table. In the hundreds of deals I have been a part of, however, I have never seen this clause become an issue or the reason a deal falls apart. An interested buyer would seldom walk away from a deal because you didn't keep to a timeline they set, unless in rare situations when they are looking at purchasing or investing in more than one target at the same time and face resource or regulatory constraints on how many they can pursue simultaneously. Acquirers will not be happy if you are taking too long to decide on their term sheet, but these deadlines are there as guideposts and are almost always extended with each markup of the term sheet, especially if they see good faith effort on your part to move forward. Don't let a deadline on a draft term sheet be the reason you make a rash decision or agree to a term before you fully understand and evaluate it with your advisors.

The Big Picture

Once you take a step back and look at the term sheet in its entirety, you will note that much of it addresses risk allocation between the parties. Aggressive buyers push to put all of the risk of the transaction on the shoulders of the sellers and their shareholders.

Aggressive sellers do the reverse. When you negotiate and eventually compromise, have that full picture in mind and look at the interplay between various terms. Take on those risks that you believe you are in the best position to mitigate (such as those associated with incomplete or inaccurate disclosure during diligence or the obtaining of certain approvals from your own stakeholders) and push back and create as much buffer as you can on other risks (such as reaching earnout milestone targets after closing). Also, if something is important to you, make sure it is addressed in the term sheet. Whatever is left out can, and often will, come back to haunt you in the definitive agreements. You can be sure that if you leave anything important out of the term sheet, the acquirers will complain that if it was so important, the time to bring it up was at the term sheet stage so the deal as a whole and the valuation attributed to the transaction could have reflected it.

Psychologically, you may also find that you have less appetite to negotiate later as deal fatigue and the number of issues subject to resolution pile up. Many experienced entrepreneurs even feel that they have less leverage in negotiation once the term sheet is signed as they become beholden to that specific acquirer, feel the pressure from their stakeholders to get the deal done, and face mounting costs if the deal falls apart.

It warrants repeating that before you respond to a term sheet in any substantive way, make sure you fully understand it and uncover the assumptions underlying various terms. Don't be shy to question everything and ask for explanations. And don't worry that if you take the offer seriously and ask questions about it, somehow it would signal that you have agreed to their terms, especially if you make it clear to your counterparts that before responding, you want to make sure you understand their offer and present it as accurately as possible to your board and other stakeholders.

CHAPTER 16

TRANSACTION PHASE 2: AGREEMENT

It ain't over till it's over.
—Yogi Berra[1]

Once the term sheet is signed (another milestone on your exit path you should not forget to celebrate), you will be in a race against time to negotiate, sign, and close the transaction. The deal is still far from being done, and it can fall apart, especially if you don't have the bandwidth in your leadership team to run both the deal and the business at the same time. And deals do fall apart quite often. Recall that term sheets are for the most part nonbinding; that means both you and the acquirer can decide to walk away from the deal, setting aside the impact on the reputation of, and the relationship between, the parties. And it is usually the acquirers who are the ones to back out from a deal and leave the sellers at the M&A altar.

Since the longer it takes to get to a signed agreement, the more likely it is for things to unravel, speed is your strongest ally throughout this phase. Of course, you wouldn't want to rush through carelessly and either miss important terms on the deal documents or fail to do your own proper vetting of the acquirer and its strategy.

This phase is all about parallel processing. Map out the various workstreams and work backward from your desired signing and closing date to arrive at a realistic timeline for each workstream. As you go through this exercise, pay attention to major holidays, events, or previously scheduled engagements that your timeline and the gating approvals along the way need to accommodate. For instance, public acquirers typically don't want to close a deal in the last month of a quarter. Furthermore, if a board vote or shareholder vote is required, aligning that vote with the timing of a previously scheduled board or shareholder meeting may make good sense.

As you work backward, note that your closing follows the signing, which follows obtaining the requisite approvals on each side, which follows having completed diligence and negotiated and drafted all the legal documentation, which follows having answered all diligence requests (including, but not limited to, those from finance, accounting, tax, legal, product, technology, security, facilities, HR, PR, IT, and support) and the requisite meetings between the various teams. In parallel and concurrent with legal and diligence activities, you will also be working on Day One, announcement, and integration planning with the relevant team members on the acquirer side. Laying out the timeline in its entirety should give you a good sense as to whether your expectations are realistic and what needs to happen to keep to your desired timeline.

As you will undoubtedly note, the sheer volume of tasks can and will be overwhelming for any mortal. But take solace in the fact that tens of thousands of other startups and entrepreneurs go through some version of this process every year. And in my experience, the most successful ones are those that are able to get through this phase as efficiently as possible.

During the agreement phase, your outside legal team will work on drafting the definitive transaction documents while you and the rest of your deal team will focus on diligence and operational aspects of the two companies coming together. It is fair to expect that this phase will take the majority, if not all, of the available time for those involved. Serial entrepreneur Jason Nazar, who sold his startup Docstoc to Intuit for $50 million in 2013, captures the intensity of this phase by recounting how he managed to get from term sheet to closing in a month:

> *So many things can go wrong from the LOI to closing, and I've seen countless deals fall through due to market conditions, cold feet, or just poor communication or taking too long. . . . My executive team and I worked around the clock for 30 straight days working nights and weekends to get out all the diligence requests. I think we turned those around in record time.*[2]

PROCESS MANAGEMENT STRATEGIES POST TERM SHEET EXECUTION

To keep things manageable after the term sheet is signed, you need to get as much ahead of the process as you can. Below are three strategies I have found significantly helpful in managing this process efficiently.

Strategy 1: Anticipate and Plan for What Can Slow Down Progress

Determine what can remove potential roadblocks. For many deals, what will take the most time to complete, causing weeks or months of delay, is the acquirer's due diligence process. So start gathering and organizing your diligence material soon. Some deals are delayed because a certain stakeholder, be it a founder, investor, or board member, cannot be made comfortable with the terms. Make sure you identify who the potential troublemakers are and make sure you give them extra time and attention to be brought along the journey. I have also been involved in deals where closing was delayed while the parties waited for the blessing of a regulatory agency to transfer an important license or for the waiver by a strategic partner of their right to terminate a material contract upon change of control. Identify potential champions and build or repair existing bridges with those parties. Evaluate all potential roadblocks with your team and create an action plan and timeline on how to best mitigate and address them as soon as possible.

Strategy 2: Create Bandwidth

Keeping in mind the time demands and distraction entailed by the activities in this phase on you and your deal team, make sure that inside your startup you have other team members who can competently fill the gaps and keep the wheels of your business moving along smoothly. You need reliable lieutenants who can effectively step up and take as much of the daily operational burden off of the deal team as possible. You certainly don't want to see your metrics nosedive; have a PR fiasco with one or more employees, customers, or partners; or have some avoidable security breach while you are in diligence with an acquirer. A lot of acquirers get buyers' remorse, and nothing can spook them more than such mishaps. Also, like it or not, despite the high fives and social niceties, you and your team are all still being carefully watched and scrutinized by the acquirer. Don't squander your hard-earned first impression that got you to a negotiated term sheet by making a poor second, third, or fourth impression. The more time and attention you and your deal team can devote to this phase, the faster and smoother it will go.

Strategy 3: Keep the Deal Team Small

Involving more people will not necessarily speed up your process. It is actually better to have a handful of people who are focused on the transaction and can carve out significant time to dedicate to it as opposed to a dozen or more employees, advisors, and consultants parachuting in and out with diluted or vague responsibilities. The key is to be agile and focused, which favors smaller team sizes. Of course, you will need the involvement of subject matter experts, which typically include your leaders in product, HR, engineering, finance, and accounting. Involve others only if absolutely necessary. As an added bonus, having fewer people involved also reduces the risk of accidental leaks. Who among us hasn't had a misplaced file, left a document on the printer unattended, or sent an email to the wrong recipient? Slipups happen, but the fewer people involved, the less likely they are to happen before you publicly announce the deal. So, carefully pick the members of the deal team and get them spun up as soon as you have a line of sight to the signing of the term sheet.

In the remainder of this chapter, I will share with you additional guidance and best practices specifically related to the three core areas of activity of this final phase: confirmatory diligence, integration planning, and the announcement and Day One planning. My overarching guiding principles for all three of these areas, which should be a familiar mantra by now, are to:

plan ahead,

build on your momentum,

and keep strengthening the relationship.

CONFIRMATORY DILIGENCE

Most entrepreneurs are more eager to get a root canal than to go through detailed diligence. But as mind-numbing and frustrating as chasing down and preparing responses to hundreds of diligence requests can be, an acquirer's confirmatory diligence serves a very important purpose: it enables the acquirer to fully evaluate what they are buying, confirming their deal hypotheses and assumptions.

The acquirer deal team typically kicks off their confirmatory diligence process right after the term sheet is signed, enlisting the help of cross-functional deal leads who will be responsible to assess your startup from their respective areas of expertise, most often including legal, finance, accounting, tax, HR, product, engineering, marketing, PR, facilities, IT, and security. That is right, get ready to be introduced to the equivalent of an army on the acquirer side, which is great for you because it (a) provides you with ample opportunity to get a panoramic view on the culture, values, and organizational style of the acquirer, and (b) allows you to further deepen and strengthen your relationship with the acquirer. Moreover, the acquirer diligence itself provides you with a legal and financial safe harbor: it reduces your potential future liability associated with lack of proper disclosure or withholding of material information, which in extreme cases would be considered fraud and ground for various financial and legal repercussions.

That is why when it comes to disclosure in diligence, my general advice to entrepreneurs is that more is better. You will never hear an acquirer complain that you are providing them *too much* information. Of course, I can fully appreciate the hesitation and reluctance to provide certain sensitive information, such as data related to identity of customers, key partners, and the "secret sauce" of your offering. To start with, all the information you disclose in diligence should be under the protection of a strong NDA agreement with the acquirer in case the transaction falls apart. Make sure your legal counsel has fully reviewed and negotiated that NDA and explained the nuances to you. Some information you may also be able to anonymize or redact due to its sensitive nature or your confidentiality obligations to others.

But if the acquirer insists on obtaining certain information that is of such sensitive nature that you cannot get comfortable sharing it, have an open and honest conversation with the acquirer about your concerns and try to understand why they need that information. You may then find creative ways to achieve their goals while addressing your concerns. Sometimes that is accomplished by restricting access to that information to a specific person or team on the acquirer side. For instance, on many occasions a target rightfully requests that only a "clean team" should have access to material contracts between that target and direct competitors of the acquirer. This "clean team" would consist of individuals who are operationally separate from employees that would have a conflict of interest in accessing that information and will be under contractual obligation not to share that information with the rest of the organization on the acquirer side. I have also been involved in transactions where certain information, such as pending patent applications, could only be disclosed by the target to the acquirer's outside legal firm. But those would be the rare exceptions here. Under most circumstances, your default response to a diligence request should be to do your best to provide it.

To shift the diligence process into gear and not lose the momentum of the transaction, get started as early as you can on gathering all documentation and data you think someone buying your startup might be interested in. Organize and upload that information to a virtual data room to be ready to share with the acquirer when the time comes. Don't wait until the term sheet is signed to start gathering and organizing the material, as that would result in weeks of delay for the acquirer's team to get started.

Ideally, ask for the diligence request list during term sheet negotiations so that you can structure the data room in a way that is efficiently accessible to the acquirer and maps onto the way they are conducting their diligence. Let the acquirer know that you are preparing the data room, and ask that they be ready to kick off their diligence team immediately after the term sheet is signed. One helpful tactic is to use a folder structure and file naming system that can easily be cross-referenced from the acquirer's request list. Ask your deal advisors for recommendations on the pros and cons of different file sharing platforms for your virtual data room. Being thoughtful and considerate in the way you organize, package, and disseminate the information to the acquirer not only increases their appreciation and respect for your efforts and your organizational skills, but it also helps shorten the time it takes them to review and complete their diligence. Remember that if they can't be efficient in their review, that would simply come back to haunt you in the form of undesirable, and sometimes fatal, delays.

While you try to stay afloat in the tsunami of diligence questions and requests, it would be perfectly reasonable for you to ask the acquirer to prioritize their requests so that you can get them what is most important first. Legal and financial documentation usually ranks high on diligence request lists, followed by product metrics and technical architecture information. Sometimes security issues necessitate a security deep dive, conducting penetration tests or code reviews, which can also be extremely time-consuming and thus require long lead times. Identify those issues as soon as you can and get ahead of them. Perhaps rather than think of diligence requests as a tsunami, a better analogy here would be to think of yourself as a skilled surfer and those requests as waves coming onshore: your job is to be able to spot the strongest waves so well in advance that you can swim toward and catch them at the right time and location to successfully ride them rather than be crushed by them.

INTEGRATION PLANNING

The time to start planning for what happens after the deal closes is before you sign the definitive agreements. Experienced acquirers know and appreciate that you should never shortchange integration planning. Ironically, the less time there is between signing and closing of the transaction, the more detailed and thorough you and the acquirer need to be in the integration plans you create to make sure nothing important slips through the cracks.

The good news is that from the acquirer perspective, the same workstream leaders who are involved in doing diligence are most often the individuals who will be leading the integration efforts for their respective domains. So the right folks should already be involved once the acquirer kicks off their confirmatory diligence efforts. This ensures continuity of engagement throughout the acquisition phases and beyond the closing, avoiding any abrupt handoffs or lack of ownership and accountability for the success of the acquisition between those who decided to do the deal and those who are responsible for operation and execution post-closing.

As the seller, pay close attention to how the acquirer approaches integration planning. Find out who on their side will be leading integration efforts during your term sheet negotiations. Is that person already involved at the term sheet stage? How much do they already know about the company, and has their input been incorporated into the buyer's offer? Will that person stay on and continue to be involved after the deal closes? Does that person have a team? What has been the track record and prior experience of that person on other deals? What are the integration team's guiding principles and objectives? The answers to these questions will reveal a lot about the maturity and sophistication of your potential acquirers' organization as well as potential surprises that may arise during diligence.

If the integration leader is not involved at the term sheet stage, be concerned as that does not bode well for how things will unfold during the agreement phase. Without an integration leader involved, the acquirer may later stumble upon areas that will cast a doubt on whether the deal is desirable, as well as uncover potential costs and delays that will necessitate adjustments to the offer and purchase price that was in the term sheet.

Thus, experienced acquirers seek input from their integration teams as they draft the term sheet and definitive agreements. Integration planning should start with (a) the *value drivers* of the transaction from the acquirer perspective (such as certain financial and operating goals during the 18 to 36 months post-closing), (b) the formulation of a set of *hypotheses* around how the two companies will come together, and (c) what the *end state* should look like.

Integration hypotheses and end-state goals usually address each of the following critical areas to best achieve the value drivers for the transaction:

1. **Team and organizational structure** (roles, titles, and responsibilities after the closing; who will report to whom across various functional areas within the acquirer organization; plans for any reduction in force, as well as recruiting and team growth plans)

2. **Locations** (which offices will be kept, phased out, or immediately eliminated)

3. **Products** (which products and services will continue to be sold, phased out, or cancelled; how they will be integrated into other offerings by the acquirer)

4. **Technology and platforms** (how the technology and IT infrastructure of the two companies will come together)

5. **Sales and support** (what will be the goals for sales, marketing, and support teams and how will they stay coordinated with the acquirer teams)

6. **Business enablement functions** (how accounting, finance, tax, legal, PR, and HR teams will work together and get access to the data they need)

For each of these critical areas, an acquirer will need to devise integration hypotheses and end-state goals. Be sure to understand them. Moreover, inquiring about integration plans provides you with the perfect opportunity to learn about the culture and inner workings of the acquirer itself, giving you much-needed visibility into how the future will unfold before you sign on that dotted line and hand over the keys.

Be forewarned that on the acquirer side, deal and integration teams can be multiple times larger than your team. That is because there are typically a lot more business units and stakeholders on the acquirer side that need to stay informed and in sync with an acquisition for it to go smoothly. As a result, your strategy and deal rationale need to be clearly articulated and communicated in these meetings so that everyone pulls in the same direction and has the same end goal in mind. Such communication of strategy is typically the responsibility of the corporate development team of the acquirer, but I recommend that you attend all integration planning meetings to make sure you understand and reinforce both the big-picture strategic rationale and its implications on the day-to-day activities of the team after the acquisition. Similarly, make sure the right folks on your side are involved and present at integration planning meetings, especially your HR leader if you have one.

ANNOUNCEMENT AND DAY ONE READINESS

For both target and acquirer teams, the announcement day and Day One of the acquisition tend to be the two most exciting events of the entire acquisition process. While some acquisitions may forgo a major announcement event, all acquisitions will have a Day One, which is the day after you close on the transaction and the two teams officially join forces under the same organizational umbrella. Public announcement of a transaction may occur weeks or even months before Day One because most parties choose to announce the acquisition upon signing of definitive agreements due to regulatory requirements or out of a fear that the information could leak to the press, opting to better control the public narrative and story line.

Announcement

There is much to consider, both in terms of the content of the announcement and the logistics of how to convey it. For instance, what aspects and deal terms do you share with the world about the acquisition? How do you best position and clarify the strategic rationale and expectations for the transaction? How, where, when, who, and in what sequence will the announcement be made to your employees, customers, partners, and others who may be impacted? Will there be a major signing event, an in-person townhall, or a virtual meeting? How about personal outreach to key customers, partners, and other stakeholders who may have been in the dark about the acquisition?

Announcement planning typically involves leadership from PR, internal communications, and investor relations on the acquirer side. Messaging needs to be consistent across various channels, although there would be nuances and specifics that would be relevant to certain audiences only. For instance, your employees will be very eager to know how the acquisition impacts their job, responsibilities, benefits, and compensation. Any change is hard, and there will be a lot of anxiety and nervousness among your employees. Strategic partners will want to know how this impacts their partnership with you. And customers will be eager to know whether they will continue to be cared for or whether they should start looking for substitute services or products. Be aware that as soon as news of the acquisition makes its rounds, headhunters will be trying to recruit away your key talent and competitors will get started on poaching away your customers and key partners. There may even be political blowback that could translate into regulatory obstacles. So, you have to anticipate those eventualities and plan your next several moves carefully and well in advance.

Day One

Pulling off a successful Day One requires planning and coordination between the teams. You need to consider what you want the experience of your team to be like on the first day after the acquisition. For instance, who from the acquirer side will welcome the employees to their new family? How will access to your back-office systems (HR, payroll, banking, accounting, finance, etc.), communication and collaboration tools, and the like be managed? How will your team access and connect with the acquirer's employee portals, collaboration platforms, and messaging channels? Will they get a new email address? What will happen to their old email?

These are just the tip of the iceberg in the universe of questions that will inform a smooth Day One transition.

You will pursue and align on a well-considered Day One plan in parallel with your diligence and integration activities. On the acquirer side, the same business enablement functional leaders who are involved in diligence and integration planning should be the ones making recommendations regarding Day One readiness. In fact, Day One readiness for many acquirers is part of their integration planning workstream. Make sure you are involved in the formulation of those plans and provide guidance and feedback on them so that those plans remain consistent with your startup's values and reflect your aspirations for the acquisition.

Developing the right messaging and communicating it consistently is the key to success. Ideally, the way the transaction is announced and how you and the acquirer orchestrate the beginning of your combined story lines builds momentum and enthusiasm not only for the merger, but also for your founding vision and mission of your startup. After all, the key impetus to sell for many founders is the hope of accelerated realization of their strategy and achievement of their mission. That is why you should not abdicate responsibility here but stay closely involved. Even if you have no financial interest in the transaction after closing, you have both a reputational and personal vested interest in ensuring that your "baby" continues to grow and thrive under the new roof.

CHAPTER 17

FINAL THOUGHTS

The best way to predict the future is to create it.
—Abraham Lincoln[1]

The most common regret of the dying is not having maintained meaningful relationships amidst the busyness of daily life. One can say the same about dying startups, many of which (including my first startup) could have received a new lease on life through strong strategic relationships. Unfortunately, it is all too human to ignore our own mortality and all too entrepreneurial to be overly optimistic about our chances of success. The antidote, of course, is not to be morbid or pessimistic. It is to be realistic; to adopt a long-term perspective and have an objective view of what the future has in store for us. To accept our startups' realistic chances of success and failure. To appreciate that it is more than likely that our startups will not be able to succeed and survive as stand-alone entities.

Awareness of mortality tends to bring clarity of purpose and urgency to one's actions. "Keep death in mind at all times," advised the Samurai warrior code.[2] And that guidance is not just to win a battle, but to live a good life. Philosophers, dating back to the Greek Stoics, have often argued that in order to live a meaningful and authentic existence, we should not lose sight of our own

235

mortality. We need to adopt the same stance toward the future of our startups to give them the best chance at success and survival. While we cannot control all the external forces that lead to the demise of a majority of startups, there is much we can do to change the destiny of our startups. If we actually take the time to plan in advance and take purposeful steps throughout our entrepreneurial journey, we can create viable strategic options and relationships that would not only prolong the survival of our startups, but also tilt the odds of a successful outcome in our favor. While success is never guaranteed, we deserve our best shot at it.

The key is to create a thoughtful long-term strategy early and maintain our momentum in executing it over the years. As former world heavyweight champion Mike Tyson once famously said, "Everyone has a plan until they get punched in the mouth."[3] That is why momentum is essential. With momentum, we will be able to keep our balance, maneuver around the obstacles gracefully, and survive the numerous punches that fate will inevitably throw our way.

If you haven't started this journey yet, now is the time. You can start by socializing some of the ideas of this book with your key stakeholders or simply attempting an initial draft of your own Exit Strategy Canvas. An old Persian proverb says, "Whenever you catch the fish, it is fresh." Getting started today is much better than tomorrow. If you have the luxury of a long runway and no urgency to sell your startup, then you can start from the beginning, with a strategy offsite to kick off the formulation of your long-term exit strategy, document it, and gradually execute it by building your relationships, capabilities, and leverage. However, if you are considering the sale of your startup in the near term, then tailor the guidance of this book to your specific situation. I have specifically made every chapter accessible and relatively independent from other chapters so that you can jump in wherever is most appropriate to your present situation or refer back to it as your circumstances necessitate. If, for instance, you need some guidance on how to announce your willingness to sell your startup to potential strategic partners and suitors, consult Chapter 14. Or if you are at the term sheet negotiation phase with one or more acquirers, refer to Chapter 15 for recommended guiding principles throughout the negotiation as well as an orientation to the key terms and the steps involved. No matter the stage of the process you are in, you can always improve your negotiating position and chances. The proper preparation enables you to strategically *respond* to the challenges when and where you face them, rather than emotionally *react* to them, which makes it possible for you to steer the process toward an outcome best aligned to your values and ambitions.

While the process and steps I have recommended in this book take time and effort to properly implement, they are designed to tap into and unlock your startup's hidden strategic potential and options. Thus, they will optimize your chances of success and survival in the startup game, much of which hinges on the strength of your relationships with other players in the industry. Remember that strong strategic relationships come to fruition only after the people involved come to like and trust each other. It is never too early to get started on building and nurturing those relationships.

Also remember that being committed to creating a profitable, lasting company is not at odds with having a viable exit strategy. Just as jumping off a cliff without a parachute would be ill-advised, so is toiling away at a startup without an exit path to mitigate against existential risks and maximize your upside potential.

Best wishes on your entrepreneurial journey ahead. The future is yours to create.

Acknowledgments

This book was inspired by the sacrifices, hard work, and achievements of all the founders and innovators whose entrepreneurial journeys I have had the privilege to be a small part of, be it as a lawyer, entrepreneur, VC, angel investor, mentor, or friend.

The outline of this book took shape after I had the privilege to spend a few years on the M&A team at GoDaddy, where I had the opportunity to closely observe some of the best strategic thinkers and dealmakers of our time in action. Among them, I owe a special debt of gratitude to David Popowitz, head of corporate development at GoDaddy during my tenure, who by his own example demonstrated how savvy dealmakers blend humanity, humor, and integrity into their craft with superior results. I am deeply grateful to my former colleagues Steven Aldrich and Parthiv Sangani, not only for recruiting me to GoDaddy, but also for their mentorship and strategic guidance as my earliest mentors in the world of M&A long before we became colleagues at GoDaddy.

I learned the art of networking, humility, and selfless giving from my longtime friend and colleague Pejman Nozad, who has been a constant source of inspiration and positivity in my life from the first day I met him almost 20 years ago. I could never thank Pejman enough for the doors he has opened and the lifetime friendships he has made possible for me, including my initial introduction to Haroon Mokhtarzada at Webs and to hundreds of world-class entrepreneurs through our collaborations at Amidzad and Pear VC, the powerhouse seed-stage venture capital firm he cofounded with serial entrepreneur Mar Hershenson. Indeed, the entire Pear VC community with whom I have had the privilege of interacting since its inception has been an unparalleled fountain of support and inspiration for the creation and launch of this book.

As I started my first draft of this book's manuscript, many friends and colleagues generously contributed their time and attention and served as a constant source of energy and motivation. Leading the pack was my dear friend and entrepreneur extraordinaire Lily Sarafan, who took an entire weekend out of her incredibly busy life to read my draft manuscript in its entirety, providing comprehensive feedback and validation of core concepts. I am also grateful to my dear friend and co-traveler on many entrepreneurial paths, Ali Kashani, as well as my cousin Ario Jafarzadeh, who spent countless hours reading early chapters and discussing foundational ideas of the book with me. Their input along with conversations with several other friends, colleagues, and entrepreneurs who had recently successfully navigated the sale of their own startups including Jeff Seibert, Steve Loughlin, Subbu Rama, Ajay Kamat, Josh May, Benjamin Ross, Nicolai Bezsonoff, and Eric Thomas helped me strengthen my arguments and enrich the narratives in the book.

As a first-time author, I was lucky to learn about the book publishing process from my friend and author Chris Yeh, who graciously introduced me to his agent, the incomparable Lisa DiMona of Writers House. Lisa's belief in the potential for this book and thoughtful advice since our first encounter helped me develop a more confident voice, overcome personal inhibitions, and broaden my target audience. She patiently coached me on creating a book proposal and provided detailed feedback on the key chapters. Without her guidance and hard work, I also would not have been able to find and sign with the most encouraging editor an author could wish for, Cheryl Segura of McGraw Hill. Cheryl's keen editorial insights has helped me focus the arguments in the book and deliver them in a much shorter format. I also owe special thanks to Lisa Stone and Ali Tamaseb, who graciously gave me a masterclass on what running an effective marketing campaign for launching a book involves.

Every entrepreneur needs a strong support network to overcome challenges throughout their journey, and I am no exception. I wouldn't have made the transition from law to business so early in my career were it not for the late Vera Kallmeyer and Roland Manger at Earlybird who took the chance on a newly minted law firm associate to try his hand at playing venture capitalist. And I would not have realized my dream of becoming an entrepreneur had it not been for my cofounders and early employees at Jaxtr, Farzad Mobin, Eugene Mandel, Darwin Ling, and Paul Baclace who took that initial leap of faith along with Konstantin Guericke, Norberto Guimaraes, Stephanie Katcher, Bahman Koohestani, Jason Meresman, Taneli Otala, Chung Meng Cheong, Jeff Seibert, and Megan Zoback, as well as the rest of the Jaxtr alumni network and family. I am also grateful to the unconditional support and faith of my first seed investors including my friend and law school classmate Peter Kellner, friend and Stanford dormmate Dale Edmondson, mentor and friend Steve Ciesinski, friend and advisor Mike Fazeli, angel investors Steve Anderson, Ron Conway, Reid Hoffman, David Lee, Asha Motwani, the late Rajeev Motwani, as well as my first institutional venture capital investors Bill Draper, Tim Draper, Howard Hartenbaum (who generously took the time to teach us how to create a compelling one-page executive summary in our initial meeting), David Hornik, Chamath Palihapitiya, the late David Ladd, Ken Howery, Luke Nosek, and Warren Packard, each generously sharing their wisdom and bringing their energy and enthusiasm to every interaction.

I feel blessed to have had the opportunity to work with the founders of Webs, brothers Haroon, Zeki, and Idris Mokhtarzada as well as our investors Bobby Yazdani, Shervin Pishevar, Arun Gupta, Phil Bronner, and Nigel Morris, who gave me the operating freedom to devise our exit strategy and supported its execution wholeheartedly.

Experienced advisors can be an unfair advantage for every entrepreneur, and I have had the privilege of the benefit of the strategic advice and guidance of Michael Jackson, Greg Tseng, Fay Kallel, and David Weekly on the Jaxtr journey and Steven Aldrich, Sean Ellis, Hiten Shah, Aimee Irwin, and Marcy Simon at Webs and beyond.

I have been incredibly lucky to have had the privilege to work with and learn from many visionary, mission-driven, and inspiring entrepreneurs, investors, and executives who have forever shaped my perspective of what it means to be an effective leader, including Faraj Aalaei, Samuel Adeyemo, Arash Afrakhteh, Susan Akbarpour, Alex Algard, Kayvan Alikhani, Rahim Amidi, Saeed Amidi, Lauren Antonoff, Nima Asgharbeygi, Alex Austin, Cameron Bahar, Monica Bailey, Svanika Balasubramanian, Narges Baniasadi, Kayvan Baroumand, David Benjamin, Chris Bennett, Aman Bhutani, Judy Blegen, Arnold Blinn, Michael Boswell, Ben Boyer, Julie Bryant, Christopher Carfi, James Carroll, Scott Daggert, Danis Dayanov, Alexander Debelov, Nick Dellis, Akshaya Dinesh, Kevin Doerr, Arash Fasihi, Ramin Farjad, Adam Foroughi, Greg Goldfarb, Auguste Goldman, Babak Hamadani, Noosheen Hashemi, Arash Hassibi, Sam Hodges, Christopher Hopper, Joe Hurd, Blake Irving, Tapan Kamdar, Chris Kelly, Ahmad Kiarostami, Jeff King, David Kirven, Mareza Larizadeh, Eric Lax, Nissim Lehyani, Brandon Leonardo, Andrew Low Ah Kee, Jakob Lykkegaard Pedersen, Bilal Mahmoud, Farhad Massoudi, Mike McLaughlin, Alex Mehr, Tony Miranz, Mohsen Moazami, Mike Molinet, Lou Montulli, Jeff Mosler, Bob Mountain, Eric Moyer, Raj Mukherjee, Lawrence Murata, Ullas Naik, Farzad Naimi, Sam Nasserian, Adrian Nazari, Zod Nazem, Marta Nichols, Paul Nicks, Charlie Olson, Marek Olszewski, Kim Orumchian, Maria Pacella, Babak Pahlavan, Brian Park, Ali Partovi, Tony Perez, Marc Piette, Patrick Pulvermueller, Hooman Radfar, Mahesh Ram, Adeel Raza, Barb Rechterman, Rene Reinsberg, Charlie Robbins, Mostafa Ronaghi, Arad Rostampour, Poorya Sabounchi, Itai Sadan, Mada Saghete, Sunil Saha, Mehdi

Samadi, Pouria Sanae, Cameron Scott, Sharon Segev, Shahram Seyedin-Noor, Darian Shirazi, Antonio Silveira, Aditya Siroya, Sohale Sizar, Bryan Solar, Colin Tai, Andrew Tan, Karen Tillman, Scott Wagner, Borui Wang, Irana Wasti, Donna Wells, Derek Yan, Shayan Zadeh, Oren Zeev, and Amin Zoufonoun.

This book would have never seen the light of the day had it not been for the feedback and uncompromising positivity of my family and friends, most of all my wife Shabnam, who for years patiently supported my taking nights, weekends, and even weeks away from our family to focus on writing even when that meant shouldering the burdens of parenting two very young daughters by herself. Shabnam was the first person to encourage me to seriously consider writing this book, and her love of writing and relative ease with creating beautiful narratives inspired me to muster the courage. While Shabnam has been my muse, our young daughters Sophia and Cece have been my guiding lights. Their enthusiasm for my writing and graceful patience with my lack of availability sustained my motivation through the years to see this project through to completion. I hope one day they find the advice in this book of benefit to them on their own entrepreneurial journeys.

Notes

INTRODUCTION

1. See "RIP Good Times," Sequoia Capital, last accessed March 19, 2022, https://articles.sequoiacap.com/rip-good-times.
2. See "Smartphone Penetration in the United States from 2008 to 2014," Statista, released January 2012, https://www.statista.com/statistics /218529/us-martphone-penetration-since-2008/.
3. See Tirthankar Roy, *The East India Company: The World's Most Powerful Corporation* (India: Penguin Books Limited, 2016).
4. See "Number & Value of M&A Worldwide," Institute of Mergers, Acquisitions & Alliances (IMAA), last accessed March 19, 2022, https://imaa-institute.org/mergers-and-acquisitions-statistics/.
5. See "The State of the Deal: M&A Trends 2020, " Deloitte, last accessed March 19, 2022, https://www2.deloitte.com/content/dam/Deloitte/us /Documents/mergers-acqisitions/us-mna-trends-2020-report.pdf, 2.
6. See "2022 M&A Outlook: Continued Strength After a Record Year," Morgan Stanley, January 14, 2022, https://www.morganstanley.com /ideas/mergers-and-acquisitions-outlook-2022-continued-strength -after-record.
7. See, e.g., "2020 Global Startup Outlook," Silicon Valley Bank, https:// www.svb.com/globalassets/library/uploadedfiles/content/trends_and _insights/reports/startup_outlook_report/suo_global_report_2020 -final.pdf, 7.
8. See Baker McKenzie, "Historic Year Sees Highest Global IPO Activity in a Decade with Surge in Domestic Listings and Continued Growth Predicted for 2021," December 16, 2020, https://www.bakermckenzie .com/en/newsroom/2020/12/ipo-report-2020.
9. See "Number & Value of M&A Worldwide," Institute of Mergers, Acquisitions & Alliances (IMAA), last accessed March 19, 2022, https://imaa-institute.org/mergers-and-acquisitions-statistics/.
10. See Brian McCullough, "The Real Reason Excite Turned Down Buying Google for $750,000 in 1999," *Internet History Podcast* (blog), November

17, 2014, http://www.internethistorypodcast.com/2014/11/the-real
-reason-excite-turned-down-buying-google-for-750000-in-1999/.

11. See Jade Scipioni, "Why Netflix Co-Founders Turned Down Jeff
Bezos' Offer to Buy the Company," *CNBC Make It*, updated September 23, 2019, https://www.cnbc.com/amp/2019/09/21/why-netflix-co
-founders-turned-down-jeff-bezos-to-buy-it.html.

12. See "Dropbox Said No to a "Nine-Digit" Acquisition Offer from Apple,
Steve Jobs," *TechCrunch*, October 18, 2011, https://techcrunch.com
/2011/10/18/dropbox-said-no-to-nine-digits-acquisition-offer-from
-apple-steve-jobs/.

13. See "Mark Zuckerberg On Yahoo's Billion Dollar Offer," excerpt of
Mark Zuckerberg's *How to Build the Future* interview with Y Combinator's Sam Altman, August 16, 2016, video, October 30, 2017, https://
www.youtube.com/watch?v=mH11ImPJeDc.

14. *Merriam-Webster.com Dictionary*, s.v. "unforced error," accessed March
19, 2022, https://www.merriam-webster.com/dictionary/unforced
%20error.

CHAPTER 1

1. Wayne Dyer Quotes, BrainyQuote.com, accessed September 30, 2021,
https://www.brainyquote.com/quotes/wayne_dyer_384143.

2. See "Frequently Asked Questions," U.S. Small Business Administration
Office of Advocacy, October 2020, https://cdn.advocacy.sba.gov/wp
-content/uploads/2020/11/05122043/Small-Business-FAQ-2020.pdf.

3. According to a study at Harvard Business School that examined data
from more than 2,000 startups with at least $1 million in funding from
2000 through 2010; see Deborah Gage, "The Venture Capital Secret:
3 Out of 4 Start-Ups Fail," *Wall Street Journal*, September 20, 2012,
https://www.wsj.com/articles/SB10000872396390443720204578004
980476429190.

4. See Steve LeVine, "U.S. Startups Are in a Surprising 13-Year Slump,"
Axios, May 27, 2018, https://www.axios.com/startups-slump-13-years
-artificial-intelligence-us-ef914164-78f7-4783-b912-2ea50a06968d
.html.

5. Wikipedia, s.v. "Present Bias," last modified October 11, 2021, https://
en.wikipedia.org/wiki/Present_bias.

6. See, e.g., Drake Baer, "How LinkedIn's Reid Hoffman Jumped off a
Cliff and Built an Airplane," *Fast Company*, May 17, 2013, https://www
.fastcompany.com/3009831/how-linkedins-reid-hoffman-jumped-off
-a-cliff-and-built-an-airplane.

7. Fortunately this important mental health issue is starting to get
recognition. See, e.g., Jessica Bruder, "The Psychological Price of Entrepreneurship," *Inc.*, September 2013, https://www.inc.com/magazine
/201309/jessica-bruder/psychological-price-of-entrepreneurship.html;

Caroline Castrillon, "Why It's Time for Entrepreneurs to Eliminate the Stigma Around Mental Health," *Forbes*, May 14, 2019, https://www.forbes.com/sites/carolinecastrillon/2019/05/14/why-its-time-for-entrepreneurs-to-eliminate-the-stigma-around-mental-health/#11177ff9221c; and C. David Shepherd, Gaia Marchisio, Sussie C. Morrish, Jonathan H. Deacon, and Morgan P. Miles, "Entrepreneurial Burnout: Exploring Antecedents, Dimensions and Outcomes," *Journal of Research in Marketing and Entrepreneurship* 12, no. 1 (April 2010): 71–79, https://doi.org/10.1108/14715201011060894.

8. See Roy F. Baumeister and Brad J. Bushman, *Social Psychology and Human Nature, Comprehensive Edition* (United States: Cengage Learning, 2016): 107.

9. See Adam Grant, *Originals: How Non-Conformists Move the World* (United States: Penguin Publishing Group, 2016), 19–22.

10. See "Keynote by Aaron Levie CEO & Co-founder of Box," fireside chat at ICON 5th Annual Conference, Palo Alto, California, October 10, 2018, video, October 17, 2018, minutes 33:51–35:14, https://www.youtube.com/watch?v=8tU3d-SDC78.

CHAPTER 2

1. "Risk Guru Nicholas Taleb Explains How Warren Buffett Made Billions by Avoiding Stocks," *Financial Express*, August 28, 2017, https://www.financialexpress.com/market/risk-guru-nicholas-taleb-explains-how-warren-buffett-made-billions-by-avoiding-stocks/829032/.

2. See "We're Acquiring Zoox to Help Bring Their Vision of Autonomous Ride-Hailing to Reality," Amazon, June 26, 2020, https://blog.aboutamazon.com/company-news/were-acquiring-zoox-to-help-bring-their-vision-of-autonomous-ride-hailing-to-reality.

3. See Tim Higgins and Matt Grossman, "Amazon to Acquire Self-Driving Startup Zoox," *Wall Street Journal*, updated June 26, 2020, https://www.wsj.com/articles/amazon-to-acquire-self-driving-startup-zoox-11593183986.

CHAPTER 3

1. Rich Leigh, *Myths of PR: All Publicity Is Good Publicity and Other Popular Misconceptions* (United Kingdom: Kogan Page, 2017), 50.

2. For some more data and stories of major M&A fails, see also "Fools Rush In: 37 of the Worst Corporate M&A Flops," CB Insights, Research Briefs, October 30, 2018, https://www.cbinsights.com/research/merger-acquisition-corporate-fails/.

3. See, e.g., Victoria Pei-Zhuang Yeow, "Post-M&A Performance in Mobile App Developing Startups," May 2017, https://pdfs.semanticscholar.org/c623/47ee87801b3adc73a2ca4cfab336558bba40.pdf, 8.

4. See Roy F. Baumeister and John Tierney, *The Power of Bad: How the Negativity Effect Rules Us and How We Can Rule It* (United States: Penguin Publishing Group, 2021).

5. See "The State of the Deal: M&A Trends 2020, " Deloitte, last accessed March 19, 2022, https://www2.deloitte.com/content/dam/Deloitte/us /Documents/mergers-acqisitions/us-mna-trends-2020-report.pdf, 13.

CHAPTER 4

1. See Renée Dye and Olivier Sibony, "How to Improve Strategic Planning," *McKinsey Quarterly*, McKinsey & Company, August 1, 2007, https://www.mckinsey.com/business-functions/strategy-and-corporate -finance/our-insights/how-to-improve-strategic-planning.

CHAPTER 5

1. "Clarifying Three Widespread Quotes," *The Pauling Blog* (blog), October 28, 2008, https://paulingblog.wordpress.com/2008/10/28 /clarifying-three-widespread-quotes/.

2. See Wikipedia, s.v. "Know Thyself," last modified March 17, 2022, https://en.wikipedia.org/wiki/Know_thyself.

3. "Keynote by Aaron Levie CEO & Co-founder of Box," fireside chat at ICON 5th Annual Conference, Palo Alto, California, October 10, 2018, video, October 17, 2018, minutes 37:21–37:53, https://www .youtube.com/watch?v=8tU3d-SDC78.

4. See Vivian Hunt, Lareina Yee, Sara Prince, and Sundiatu Dixon-Fyle, "Delivering Through Diversity," McKinsey & Company, Report, January 18, 2018, https://www.mckinsey.com/business-functions /organization/our-insights/delivering-through-diversity.

5. See Erik Larson, "New Research: Diversity + Inclusion = Better Decision Making At Work," *Forbes*, September 21, 2017, https://www.forbes .com/sites/eriklarson/2017/09/21/new-research-diversity-inclusion -better-decision-making-at-work/#2f1daed4cbfa.

6. See David Rock and Heidi Grant, "Why Diverse Teams Are Smarter," *Harvard Business Review*, November 4, 2016, https://hbr.org/2016/11 /why-diverse-teams-are-smarter.

7. See Tim Brown, "Design Thinking," *Harvard Business Review*, June 2008, https://hbr.org/2008/06/design-thinking.

8. Tina Seelig, "Brainstorming—Why It Doesn't (Always) Work," *Medium* (blog), January 8, 2017, https://tseelig.medium.com/brainstorming -why-it-doesnt-always-work-6a4546e8c4a8.

9. See Alexander Faickney Osborn, *Applied Imagination: Principles and Procedures of Creative Problem-Solving* (United States: Scribner, 1963).

10. See, e.g., Tomas Chamorro-Premuzic, "Why Group Brainstorming Is a Waste of Time," *Harvard Business Review*, March 25, 2015, https://hbr .org/2015/03/why-group-brainstorming-is-a-waste-of-time.

11. Peter F. Drucker, *The Effective Executive: The Definitive Guide to Getting the Right Things Done* (United States: Harper Business, 2006), 136.

CHAPTER 6

1. Rick Kazman, Paul Clements, and Len Bass, *Software Architecture in Practice*, 3rd ed. (United Kingdom: Pearson Education, 2012), chap. 18.
2. See Wikipedia, s.v. "Business Model Canvas," last edited February 13, 2022, https://en.wikipedia.org/wiki/Business_Model_Canvas.
3. Alexander Osterwalder and Yves Pigneur, *Business Model Generation: A Handbook for Visionaries, Game Changers, and Challengers* (United States: Wiley, 2010).
4. Osterwalder and Pigneur, *Business Model Generation*, 12.

CHAPTER 7

1. Drucker, *The Effective Executive*, 142.
2. See Teppo Felin, "The Fallacy of Obviousness," *Aeon*, July 5, 2018, https://aeon.co/essays/are-humans-really-blind-to-the-gorilla-on-the -basketball-court.

CHAPTER 8

1. Wikipedia, s.v. "Vision," last edited November 27, 2021, https://en .wikiquote.org/wiki/Vision.
2. See Drucker, *The Effective Executive*, 136.

CHAPTER 9

1. Porter Gale, "Why Your Network Is Your Net Worth," *The Huffington Post* (blog), updated August 3, 2013, https://www.huffingtonpost.com /porter-gale/why-your-network-is-your-_b_3375954.html.
2. See Tim Ferriss and Doug McMillon, "Doug McMillon—CEO of Walmart," November 8, 2018, in *The Tim Ferriss Show*, podcast, episode 345, minutes 27–29, https://tim.blog/2018/11/08/doug-mcmillon-ceo -of-walmart/.
3. See, e.g., Gaurav Mathur, "5 Insider Tips on Selling Your Startup to Google," *Entrepreneur*, December 12, 2017, https://www.entrepreneur .com/article/305862.
4. See Ben Gilbert, David Rosenthal, and Scott Belsky, "Behance (with Scott Belsky)," October 1, 2018, in *Acquired*, podcast, season 3, episode 6, minute 36, http://www.acquired.fm/episodes/2018/10/1/season -3-episode-6nbspbehance-with-scott-belsky.
5. Houman Haghighi, "Today's announcement of Scout RFP acquisition by Workday is a great example of how important it is for founders to get to know corporates and work towards partnerships and customer engagements that lead to . . . ," LinkedIn post, November 4, 2019, https:// www.linkedin.com/feed/update/urn:li:activity:6597265273848496128/.

6. See Cari Romm, "This Is How Many Hours It Takes to Make a Friend," *The Cut*, April 6, 2018, https://www.thecut.com/2018/04/this-is-how-many-hours-it-takes-to-make-a-friend.html.

7. See, e.g., Mark S. Granovetter, "The Strength of Weak Ties," *American Journal of Sociology* (1973): 1360–1380; Hans-Georg Wolff and Klaus Moser, "Effects of Networking on Career Success: A Longitudinal Study," University of Erlangen-Nuremburg, Labor and Socio-Economic Research Center (LASER), 2008; Maggie Fox, "Happiness Is Contagious: Study," *Reuters*, December 4, 2008, https://www.reuters.com/article/us-happiness/happiness-is-contagious-study-idUSTRE4B400H20081205; Nicholas A. Christakis and James H. Fowler, "The Collective Dynamics of Smoking in a Large Social Network," *New England Journal of Medicine*, 2008; 358:2249–2258, https://www.nejm.org/doi/full/10.1056/NEJMsa0706154.

8. Adam Grant, *Give and Take: Why Helping Others Drives Our Success* (United States: Penguin Publishing Group, 2014).

9. Jocelyn K. Glei, "Why Entrepreneurial Thinking Is for Everyone Now," 99U by Adobe, April 3, 2012, https://99u.adobe.com/articles/7161/why-entrepreneurial-thinking-is-for-everyone-now.

10. Adam Grant, "Finding the Hidden Value in Your Network," *The Huffington Post* (blog), updated August 18, 2013, https://www.huffingtonpost.com/adam-grant/finding-the-hidden-value-_1_b_3458536.html.

11. See Carol S. Dweck, *Mindset: The New Psychology of Success* (United States: Random House, 2006).

12. See Behance (with Scott Belsky), minutes 36–37.

13. See Wikipedia, s.v. "Proximity Principle," last updated November 15, 2020, https://en.wikipedia.org/wiki/The_Proximity_Principle.

14. See Daniel Kahneman, *Thinking, Fast and Slow* (United States: Farrar, Straus and Giroux, 2011), 66.

15. See, e.g., Mathew L. A. Hayward, Dean A. Shepherd, and Dale Griffin, "A Hubris Theory of Entrepreneurship," *Management Science*, Vol. 52, No. 2, Entrepreneurship (February 2006), 160–172.

16. See, e.g., Don A. Moore Ph.D., "Overconfidence: The Mother of All Biases," *Psychology Today*, January 22, 2018, https://www.psychologytoday.com/us/blog/perfectly-confident/201801/overconfidence.

17. See, e.g., Angela Duckworth, *Grit: The Power of Passion and Perseverance* (United States: Scribner, 2016).

18. See, e.g., Grant, *Originals*.

19. See, e.g., Dan Schawbel, "Brene Brown: How Vulnerability Can Make Our Lives Better," *Forbes*, Apr 21, 2013, https://www.forbes.com/sites/danschawbel/2013/04/21/brene-brown-how-vulnerability-can-make-our-lives-better/#4b91800b36c7.

20. Leslie K. John, "How to Negotiate with a Liar," *Harvard Business Review*, July-August 2016, https://hbr.org/2016/07/how-to-negotiate -with-a-liar.

21. See, e.g., Paul V. Weinstein, "To Close a Deal, Find a Champion," *Harvard Business Review*, September 12, 2014, https://hbr.org/2014/09 /to-close-a-deal-find-a-champion; Mark Suster, "Finding Your Sales Champion," *Inc.*, July 1, 2013, https://www.inc.com/mark-suster /finding-your-sales-champion.html.

22. See James Altucher, "The 10 Worst Things You Can Do in a Negotiation," *Insider* (blog), *Business Insider*, https://www.businessinsider.com /the-worst-things-you-can-do-in-a-negotiation-2015-3.

CHAPTER 10

1. Joel Goldberg, "It Takes a Village to Determine the Origins of an African Proverb," KQED, NPR, July 30, 2016, https://www.npr.org /sections/goatsandsoda/2016/07/30/487925796/it-takes-a-village-to -determine-the-origins-of-an-african-proverb.

2. See Ingrid Lunden, "After Data Breaches, Verizon Knocks $350M off Yahoo Sale, Now Valued at $4.48B," *TechCrunch*, February 21, 2017, https://techcrunch.com/2017/02/21/verizon-knocks-350m-off-yahoo -sale-after-data-breaches-now-valued-at-4-48b/.

3. See "Forescout Study Reveals Cybersecurity Concerns on the Rise Amid M&A Activity," Forescout, June 24, 2019, https://www.forescout .com/press-releases/forescout-study-reveals-cybersecurity-concerns-on -merger-and-acquisition-activity/.

4. See "Discover the Patterns of Successful Internet Startups in the Startup Genome Report," Startup Genome, May 28, 2011, https:// startupgenome.com/articles/discover-the-patterns-of-successful -internet-startups-in-the-startup-genome-report.

5. Ray Dalio, *Principles* (United States: Simon & Schuster, 2018), 161.

6. See Anup Agrawal, Tommy Cooper, Qin Lian, and Qiming Wang, "Does Hiring M&A Advisers Matter for Private Sellers?," December 21, 2021, draft 2, http://dx.doi.org/10.2139/ssrn.2400531.

7. Justin Kan, "The Founder's Guide to Selling Your Company," *Newsletter* (blog), Justin Kan website, November 11, 2016, https://justinkan.com /feed/the-founders-guide-to-selling-your-company.

CHAPTER 11

1. Chris Voss, "The 3 Laws of Leverage," *Negotiation Tactics* (blog), The Black Swan Group website, April 8, 2019, https://blog.blackswanltd .com/the-edge/the-3-laws-of-leverage.

2. See Erick Schonfeld, "BT Acquires Ribbit For $105 Million," *TechCrunch*, July 29, 2008, https://techcrunch.com/2008/07/29/bt -acquires-ribbit-for-105-million/.

3. See Contributor, "Deal is Confirmed: Google Acquires GrandCentral," *TechCrunch*, July 2, 2007, https://techcrunch.com/2007/07/02/deal-is -confirmed-google-acquired-grandcentral/.
4. See Sam Diaz, "Telefonica Acquires Jajah VoIP Service For $207 Million," *ZDNet*, December 23, 2009, https://www.zdnet.com/article /telefonica-acquires-jajah-voip-service-for-207-million/.
5. Chris Voss and Tahl Raz, *Never Split the Difference: Negotiating as If Your Life Depended on It* (United Kingdom: Random House, 2016), 46.
6. See House Committee on the Judiciary, file FB-HJC-ACAL-00063220, https://judiciary.house.gov/uploadedfiles/0006322000063223.pdf.
7. See Kara Swisher, "The Money Shot," *Vanity Fair*, May 6, 2013, https://www.vanityfair.com/news/business/2013/06/kara-swisher -instagram; see also text log between the two CEOs chronicling the fast pace of developments in March and April 2012 at House Committee on the Judiciary, files FB-HJC-ACAL-00091648 to FB-HJC-ACAL-00091654, https://judiciary.house.gov/uploadedfiles /0009164800091654.pdf.
8. See, e.g., Sophia Kunthara, "Startups Are Acquiring Other Startups At An Unprecedented Pace," *Crunchbase News*, July 20, 2021, https:// news.crunchbase.com/news/startups-are-acquiring-other-startups-at-an -unprecedented-pace/.
9. See "New Heights: US M&A H1 2021," White & Case, July 30, 2021, https://www.whitecase.com/publications/insight/us-ma-2021/private -equity-deal.
10. See, e.g., Michele Gelfand, Sarah Gordon, Chengguang Li, Virginia Choi, and Piotr Prokopowicz, "One Reason Mergers Fail: The Two Cultures Aren't Compatible," *Harvard Business Review*, October 2, 2018, https://hbr.org/2018/10/one-reason-mergers-fail-the-two-cultures -arent-compatible.
11. See Minda Zetlin, "Instagram Founders Are Latest to Depart Facebook Amid Rumors of Conflict With Mark Zuckerberg," Inc., September 25, 2018, https://www.inc.com/minda-zetlin/instagram-founders-kevin -systrom-mike-krieger-leaving-facebook.html.

CHAPTER 12

1. Gil Penchina Quotes, BrainyQuote.com, https://www.brainyquote.com /quotes/gil_penchina_851248, accessed September 30, 2021.
2. See Homer, *Odyssey*, book 12.
3. See University of Cambridge. "Ancient body clock discovered that helps keep all living things on time." *ScienceDaily*, accessed March 22, 2022, www.sciencedaily.com/releases/2011/01/110126131540.htm.
4. Friedrich Nietzsche, *Twilight of the Idols*, trans. Richard Polt (United States: Hackett, 1997), 6.

CHAPTER 13

1. Matt Castonguay, "75 Greatest Quotes About Golf," Southern California Golf Association, accessed March 24, 2022, https://www.scga.org/blog/8620/75-greatest-quotes-about-golf/.

2. House Committee on the Judiciary, file FB-HJC-ACAL-00101438, https://judiciary.house.gov/uploadedfiles/0010143800101441.pdf; see also Tyler Sonnemaker, "New text messages show Kevin Systrom worried about Mark Zuckerberg going into 'destroy mode' if he didn't sell to Facebook," *Business Insider*, July 29, 2020, https://www.businessinsider.com/instagram-cofounder-feared-zuckerberg-destroy-mode-facebook-acquisition-texts-2020-7

3. Ali Partovi (@apartovi). 2021. "As the world celebrated Steve Jobs's life last week, I recalled a lesson he taught me. My one meeting with Steve didn't end well. It's one of my most painful memories, and a warning to startup CEOs about the danger of taking hype too far. Here's the story. (1/n)." Twitter, October 10, 2021, 10:23 a.m. https://twitter.com/apartovi/status/1447251334814523392.

CHAPTER 14

1. "Kleiner's Laws," *Venture Capital Journal*, January 1, 2004, https://www.venturecapitaljournal.com/kleiners-laws/.

2. See Bill Gross, "The single biggest reason why start-ups succeed," TED Conference, video, March 2015, 3:30, https://www.ted.com/talks/bill_gross_the_single_biggest_reason_why_startups_succeed.

3. See Leena Rao, "Exclusive: Flashy Website Creator Wix Raises $40 Million," *TechCrunch*, March 28, 2011, https://techcrunch.com/2011/03/28/exclusive-flashy-website-creator-wix-raises-40-million/.

4. See Ben Gilbert and David Rosenthal, "Behance (with Scott Belsky)," October 1, 2018, in *Acquired*, podcast, 25:13–25:26, https://www.acquired.fm/episodes/season-3-episode-6nbspbehance-with-scott-belsky.

5. See Erick Schonfeld, "BT Acquires Ribbit For $105 Million," *TechCrunch*, July 29, 2008, https://techcrunch.com/2008/07/29/bt-acquires-ribbit-for-105-million/.

6. See "Subbu Rama—sold software company to VMware," interview by Everyday M&A, November 20, 2019, video, 10:05–13:17, https://www.youtube.com/watch?v=RRYXt_BcBVI.

7. Justin Kan, "The Founder's Guide to Selling Your Company," *Newsletter* (blog), Justin Kan website, November 11, 2016, https://justinkan.com/feed/the-founders-guide-to-selling-your-company.

CHAPTER 15

1. Carrie Fisher Quotes, BrainyQuote.com, accessed September 30, 2021, https://www.brainyquote.com/quotes/carrie_fisher_466615.

2. Daniel Kahneman and Amos Tversky, "Prospect Theory: An Analysis of Decision Under Risk," *Econometrica* 47, no. 4 (1979): 263–291. CiteSeerX 10.1.1.407.1910. doi:10.2307/1914185. JSTOR 1914185.
3. Chris Yeh, "Choosing a VC based on valuation is like hiring the cheapest job candidate," Chris Yeh website (blog), January 24, 2022, https://chrisyeh.com/2022/01/choosing-a-vc-based-on-valuation-is-like-hiring-the-cheapest-job-candidate.html.
4. See https://www.masterclass.com/classes/chris-voss-teaches-the-art-of-negotiation.
5. See Voss and Raz, *Never Split the Difference*.
6. Sun Tzu, "Attack by Stratagem," chap. 3 in *The Art of War* (United States: Dover Publications, 2012).
7. https://twitter.com/apartovi/status/1447324896904638467.
8. Sophocles, *The Plays and Fragments. Part III: The Antigone* (United Kingdom: University Press, 1891), 61.

CHAPTER 16

1. Yogi Berra Quotes, BrainyQuote.com, accessed September 30, 2021, https://www.brainyquote.com/quotes/yogi_berra_110034.
2. Wil Shroter, "Startup Acquisition Process: The Magic Behind the Merge—Interview with Jason Nazar, Founder of Docstoc," startups.com, November 14, 2016, https://www.startups.com/library/expert-advice/startup-acquisition-process-the-magic-behind-the-merge.

CHAPTER 17

1. Paul B. Brown, "The Best Way to Predict the Future," *Inc.*, February 3, 2022, https://www.inc.com/paul-b-brown/the-best-way-to-predict-the-future.html.
2. Thomas Louis and Tommy Ito, *Samurai: The Code of the Warrior* (United States: Sterling, 2008), 71.
3. Francis J. Greene and Christian Hopp, "Research: Writing a Business Plan Makes Your Startup More Likely to Succeed," *Harvard Business Review*, July 14, 2017, https://hbr.org/2017/07/research-writing-a-business-plan-makes-your-startup-more-likely-to-succeed.

Index

To come after 2nd pass pages.

About the Author

Dianne Sullivan Morton

Touraj Parang is a veteran Silicon Valley insider. He is a seasoned entrepreneur, investor, adviser, and M&A expert who has sat in almost every seat around the table structuring and negotiating strategic transactions in Silicon Valley since the late 1990s, including as a corporate attorney at legal powerhouses Wilson Sonsini Goodrich & Rosati and O'Melveny & Myers. Touraj has been a founder, executive, and trusted adviser to several fast-growing technology startups with exits to LinkedIn, Instacart, Vistaprint, Postmates, and Amplify among others. He has also spent nearly a decade on the acquirer side of M&A deals as a corporate development executive at Webs and GoDaddy. *Exit Path* draws on Touraj's decades long unique experience involving hundreds of M&A transactions, strategic partnerships, and venture capital investments totaling billions of dollars in aggregate value. He is currently the chief operating officer at Serve Robotics, which he helped spin out of Uber, and an operating advisor at Pear VC, an early-stage venture capital firm, where he enjoys collaborating with and providing strategic guidance to mission-driven entrepreneurs. He earned his JD from the Yale Law School where he served on the editorial boards of *Yale Law Journal* and *Yale Journal of International Law* and his AB in Philosophy and

Economics from Stanford University where he was the founding editor-in-chief of the *Dualist Journal of Philosophy* and won the Ethics in Society Honors Program award. Visit www.exitpath.net for supplementary material and tools to help create your exit path.